Random Recollections
of an
Anachronism

KEYES DeWITT METCALF
At a Library Consultation in 1976

RANDOM RECOLLECTIONS
OF AN ANACHRONISM

or
Seventy-Five Years
of Library Work

By

Keyes DeWitt Metcalf

Published by
READEX BOOKS
Division of Readex Microprint Corp.
101 Fifth Ave.   New York, NY 10003

To E.E.W. and E.G.M.

Preface

It never occurred to me until nearly three years after my retirement in 1955 that I or anyone else would have any interest in recording my library recollections. The matter was first brought up in the Spring of 1958 when I was in charge of a thirteen-week intensive seminar on library administration at Rutgers University, financed by the Carnegie Corporation. During most of nine of these weeks we spent the evenings having informal talks on library problems and I often regaled (if that is the proper word for it) the eight members of the group with some of my library experiences which differed from those to which they were accustomed. As a result, it was suggested that these experiences should be put into print on the basis that they might be of interest to future generations of librarians and library school students and others who are interested in library history. I paid little attention to these suggestions until some ten years later when I happened to be reading within a month three different autobiographies—Dwight Eisenhower's *At Ease,* George Kennan's *Memoirs,* and Wilmarth (Lefty) Lewis's *One Man's Education.* These reminded me of the suggestions made by my former students. I was still convinced that I had nothing worthwhile to write and I doubted my capacity to do it. But in the years that followed, perhaps because of a failing that is too frequent among octogenarians, I have told stories to librarians with whom I have been dealing, and they have seemed to be interested and have often suggested and sometimes urged me to make them available to others. I have also had two requests from well-known librarians who have had experience in such matters for permission to write my biography, and quite a number have suggested that I put my story on tape for use later and have offered to make arrangements for the tapes. All of this I have put off, but in the summer of 1974 Albert Boni, whom I have known and had dealings with in connection with microreproductions for forty years, asked me to prepare for publication by him a volume made up of chapters relating to various librarians whom I had known and dealt with in my more than seventy years of library experience. After considerable hesitation, I said that I was unwilling to do this because it would require more time and research to make sure of my facts than I was ready to undertake at 85. I then made a counter proposal that I prepare something called *Random Recollections* which might include among other things some chapters on individual librarians whom I had known well. He agreed to the change and asked me to go ahead. I said I would try it.

As the oldest surviving member of my father's 185 descendants (including spouses) I have inherited the family archives which go back long before father's graduation from Bowdoin in 1847. The Oberlin College archives and those at the New York Public Library and the Harvard University Library have been made available to me. I have at my house in Belmont the letters that I wrote to my future wife, Martha Gerrish Metcalf, between July 1911 and June 1914 when we were married, during the time when I was going to library school and working in Oberlin and in the New York Public Library. In addition, I have my personal archival material relating to my activities in connection with the American Library Association and the Association of Research Libraries during my New York Public Library and Harvard years and copies of most of my outgoing and incoming correspondence dealing with my different consultation assignments since my retirement in August, 1955.

This volume is not an autobiography but is what the title indicates—*Random Recollections of an Anachronism, or 75 Years in Library Work*. The addition of the word "anachronism" is explained in Chapter I and is obvious throughout the volume.

My decision to prepare the volume was reached for three reasons: (1) to please the persons who have suggested it; (2) because I decided that my library life had been so different from that of librarians today that a record of some of it might give present-day and prospective librarians a little historical background and (3) because it includes among other things a record of various events that have not yet appeared in library literature and which I believe can properly be made available and perhaps should be. I hope that it will be useful and not hurt unduly any living librarians or friends of those who are no longer living. I have no desire to record scandal although I do report some unfortunate as well as pleasant events which have taken place in libraries since early in the century, some of which few, if any, persons now living are in a position to relate.

I have not attempted to document the stories recorded and

realize that as I approach 90 there may be minor errors but I hope no egregious ones.

President Richard Couper and James Henderson of the New York Public Library have made available to me documentation relating to that library. The same situation holds for Oberlin and for the Harvard archives. I hope that the quotations lifted from correspondence with my library friends will not disturb them or those spoken of.

My life has been divided into four parts, unequal in length as far as my life and the recollections are concerned, and I leave it to my readers as to which of the four has been the most important. I hope that the division will make the whole easier to understand.

Part I includes my family background and formal education, 1889 to 1913 (I hope and believe that my education still continues).

Part II deals with twenty-four years as a fulltime employee of the New York Public Library, where I had expected up to the last few months of that period to remain until retirement.

Part III covers my eighteen years as director of Harvard's library.

Part IV tells of my years of "retirement" from September 1955 until 1980.

The first two parts are published as Volume One and in spite of my 90 years I hope that the third and fourth can be published later.

My part-time secretary, Mrs. Florence Pacl, and my earlier secretary, Mrs. Esther MacSwan, have exhibited remarkable patience in recopying my dictation and scribbles almost endlessly. Edwin E. Williams of the Harvard Library, without whose help I would have made a record as an illiterate librarian, has in the past warned my readers that my prose style cannot honestly be described as exceptionally deserving of admiration. Now he has been good enough to say that the style is *not* the man. He has, as he has done countless times in the past, done wonders in making this volume readable. Much to my pleasure John McDonald, a close friend ever since he was a member of my Rutgers seminar in the spring of 1958, has prepared the Foreword.

My wife, Elinor Gregory Metcalf, has put up with five more years of neglect without complaint while I have struggled with this task, and this volume, which deals with the 48 years of my life before I met her, is dedicated to her.

Keyes D. Metcalf

FOREWORD

In his preface to this book Keyes Metcalf mentions the thirteen-week seminar in library administration he directed at the Rutgers Library School in 1958. He writes, ". . . I often regaled (if that is the proper word for it) the eight members of the group with some of my library experiences which differed from those to which they were accustomed." As one of the eight members of that seminar I can assure Mr. Metcalf and the reader of these *Random Recollections* that "regaled" is indeed the proper word. Among other things, regaled means "entertained by providing a splendid feast," and this is surely what Mr. Metcalf did in sharing with us the fruits of his long and remarkable career.

That his experiences differed from those to which we were accustomed is also as accurate as it is understated. Although the eight of us were not exactly babes—our youngest member was 33 and our oldest was 51—and although we were not without experience, none of us had begun library work at 13, supervised the moving of a college library at 19, held key positions in both the largest public library and the largest academic library in the United States, nor been President of the American Library Association. All of these things and many, many more Keyes Metcalf had done, and it is not surprising that we stood in awe of his achievements and marvelled at the detail with which he recalled and described them. Now, more than twenty years later, that feeling returns as I see those achievements recorded in print in the same detail and with the same modest and unassuming quality that was so characteristic of Keyes Metcalf in 1958.

It is also worth noting that Mr. Metcalf refers to the eight of us as "members of the group" rather than students. Indeed we did not refer to ourselves as students—we called ourselves "The Knuckleheads," a term that was both richly deserved and keenly felt when we were in the presence of our mentor, which was usually about sixteen hours a day. Our education began at breakfast and continued through a post-dinner session in the room of one of the group. Sometimes we recapitulated the day's work, but more often Keyes, as we eventually learned to call him, would introduce a new topic. He might describe a particularly successful or unsuccessful library building; he might talk about Oberlin College Librarian, Azariah Smith Root, as he does in the third chapter of this volume; he might mention how it felt to be the only male in a class of 40 admitted in 1911 to the brand-new Library School of the New York Public Library; he might tell of his two stints as acting librarian at Oberlin College; he might speak of the great figures associated with the New York Public Library—of John Shaw Billings, Edwin Hatfield Anderson, Harry Miller Lydenberg, C. C. Williamson, Paul North Rice, and many others; he might talk about the politics of the American Library Association, his work on its committees, or his admiration for Carl Milam, ALA's long-time Executive Secretary; he might recall the formation of the Association of Research Libraries; or he might describe the factors leading up to the development of the Farmington Plan.

All of these events he could and did discuss from first-hand knowledge, so great was his professional commitment and so deep was his personal involvement in the most important library activities of the time. This first volume of *Random Recollections of an Anachronism* treats many of the topics mentioned above, in fact all that occurred before 1938. Those not covered here (the Harvard years and after) will be covered in a later volume, but for the moment this volume offers richness enough.

Keyes Metcalf's recollections of his first forty-eight years leave several abiding impressions of the man: first, of cheerfulness, optimism and a sort of gentle innocence; second, of astonishing energy, great will-power and healthy ambition; and last, of intellectual curiosity, immense capacity for work, and most characteristic of all, unfailing enthusiasm for his chosen profession. It is a pleasure to note that this enthusiasm continues undiminished into his ninety-first year. Mr. Metcalf regularly attends meetings of the American Library Association and other professional groups, and he is still active as a consultant, adding to his world-record total of more than 600 consultations on five continents and in forty-six of the United States. Two months ago he visited the new library building here at the University of Connecticut where he was in the forefront of a touring group and as ready as ever with knowing comment and accurate observation.

If I were allowed just one word to describe Keyes Metcalf it would be the one that David Weber, a Metcalf protege and a sort of adjunct "Knucklehead," once used in referring to him. The word is "admirable."

Read this book and see for yourself.

John P. McDonald

The University of Connecticut
Storrs, Connecticut
July, 1979

CONTENTS

Part I

Background and Education

xv

Random Recollections
of an
Anachronism

Part I

Chapter I
Family Background
and
Formal Education

If some of those reading this volume believe there is need to explain the final word of the title, this 13-point summary might be useful and should be kept in mind as they read further.

1) My paternal grandfather, with the good Biblical forename of Isaac, was born during the American Revolution.

2) My father, Isaac Stevens Metcalf, was born several months before Ulysses Simpson Grant.

3) My middle name, DeWitt, was the last name of an uncle, Elijah DeWitt, who was born in the 18th century and who lived long enough to give me a coin-silver dessert spoon marked with my name, which I use regularly with my breakfast food.

4) My father married first when he was 30 years old in 1852 and as a natural result I received what might be called an 1850 upbringing. This, I can assure you, was quite different from the 1950 one that my grandchildren received, to say nothing of the present-day upbringing of my great-grandchildren.

5) My father had read Malthus, but apparently was not worried about the population explosion and had eighteen children. I was the seventeenth. There are now 130 of his descendants living, of whom I am the oldest.

6) We had family prayers after breakfast every morning at which each of us read a verse from the Bible in turn until the chapter was finished. By the time I was 8, I suppose I had heard the Bible through from the first Chapter of Genesis to the last one of Revelations. By the time I left home for college, when I was 20, I had heard or read it several times and, as we used both the King James and the Revised editions and often as many as six different languages—English, French, German, Latin, Greek, and Hebrew—I had picked up at least one side of a liberal education.

7) Christmas was a Church day, not a holiday, and family gifts were distributed on New Year's Day, following the old New England Congregational Church custom.

8) My father retired from his profession in 1855, when he was 33, and spent the remaining 43 years of his life bringing up his large family, chiefly by what might be called subsistence farming, carried on by himself and his children.

9) I became an orphan at 8 when my father died three years after my mother, his second wife and the mother of five other boys, died of pneumonia. This left 13 surviving children, ranging from 7 to 42. The five youngest boys were brought up by my oldest sister, who had previously been a

college professor for 14 years, nine of them at Wellesley, where she was one of the early women science instructors, and who had planned a very different career from her childhood on.

10) My father had six strong opinions which formed the basis of my bringing up:

(a) Hard physical work for everyone was essential. To make the work go around for his growing family, we were trained to do everything possible by hand instead of with energy-saving devices and machines.

(b) We must always be on time for any appointment, particularly the three meals a day and family prayers, at each of which the family was all together. In this punctuality we were aided and abetted by the fact that we lived across the street from the town school clock and the added fact that for nearly 30 years at least eight of my older brothers were, each in turn, responsible for ringing the school bell at exactly the right time. I might add that as a result my children complain that they have spent large parts of their lives waiting for other people.

(c) Money was always at a premium because a "rainy day" with hard times might come. Therefore you did not spend it for candy, chewing gum, or even for fireworks on the 4th of July, to say nothing of other luxuries.

(d) It was foolish and unnecessarily expensive to have a telephone in the house because the only real need for one was to call the doctor in an emergency and the doctor was only a half mile away and there was always a boy available who could easily run to get him in a few minutes.

(e) Since we had gotten along reasonably well with no running water or bathroom in the house, except for the kitchen pump which brought water up from the cistern, and a well near the side door, why should we go to the expense of making a change?

(f) An education, at least through a liberal arts college, was essential. As a result, 13 of his 14 children who grew up graduated with at least a college degree, and 12 of those

13 went on for graduate work in law, the ministry, medicine, engineering, library work, teaching, or social work. Most of us grew up before the time of the Ph.D. degree, but six of us had three to six years of graduate work and four of the first five boys of the next generation, as well as some of the later ones, acquired Ph.Ds.

11) When my daughter applied for entrance to Oberlin College and was asked to include some biographical information in her application, she wrote, without consultation with her parents, that "she was born of Mid-Victorian parents."

12) I did my first library work in September, 1902, and definitely decided on this field as my life work three years later in the summer of 1905. As far as I can learn, I have been actively in library work as long as any other living person, if not longer, and am still at it.

13) Daily newspapers were not received in our house because they contained so much material not fit for young people's consumption and we could wait until the weekly news magazines were received.

With this background in mind, it seems only fair to assume that I am and probably always have been an "old fogy" and an anachronism, which thus makes the last word in this book's title appropriate.

I shall add some further details of my background and childhood, not because I have any particular interest in remote ancestry, but simply to indicate some things in my genes that may have affected my library career.

My great-grandfather, Peletiah Metcalf, was named (if I figure it correctly) from one of the sixth generation after David of the Old Testament. At any rate, he was one of the sixth generation in the Metcalf line in what is now the United States. He was born in Wrentham, Mass., but settled before the American Revolution as a farmer in West Royalston, Mass., near the New Hampshire border, where he built a house which is still standing at the foot of a steep hill road called Jacob's Ladder. His mother was Hepzibah Mann, a great-aunt of Horace Mann. As was not unusual in Colonial days, Peletiah had twelve children, but only four of these survived to adulthood, something which again was not unusual in those days, particularly in rural areas, where epidemics and children's diseases were prevalent. In spite of this, I might add that Peletiah's father had nine children, eight of whom were married, and his grandfather had 13, all of whom survived at least until after marriage. Of the combined 22, 16 were male, a percentage which seems to have held in the family down to the 10th generation in this country. So it is not surprising that Metcalf is a reasonably common name in New England and in other parts of the United States. Indeed, most persons of New England ancestry probably have many thousands of relatives now living somewhere in the country.

My grandfather Metcalf was his father's sixth child and fourth son (another Isaac and two Peletiahs preceded him). His parents' first three children died within 17 days of each other in August, 1777, and were buried in one grave in the family cemetery in West Royalston under a single tombstone, with three half circles at the top. My grandfather was born 106 years before my birth and several months before the Treaty of Paris brought the American Revolution to a close. I remember talking about this one day with Archibald MacLeish and Wilmarth S. Lewis, each of whom is several years younger than I, and finding that their grandfathers were born a number of years earlier than mine, so it is less unusual than might be supposed.

Grandfather Isaac acquired some education and was known as a successful country schoolteacher in Royalston and adjacent towns. He ended his career in Boston, to which he moved when his health broke in the late 1820's. I might note that in addition to teaching school (his account books are now in the library of the Harvard Graduate School of Business Administration) he and his younger brother, Jacob, would make you a suit of clothes for $3.00 or a pair of shoes for $3.50 and in addition would plow your field for whatever was deemed a reasonable amount. One of Isaac's early teach-

ing assignments was in Warwick, Mass., the next town west of
Royalston, in a red one-room schoolhouse which still stood
150 years later. Here one of his students was Anna Mayo
Stevens, the daughter of Wilder and Elizabeth Mayo Stevens
of Warwick, who lived half a mile northeast of Warwick
Center in a house which is still occupied by the Stevens
branch of the family. Grandfather fell in love with Anna
when he was in his early twenties and she was still in her
teens, but she turned him down and instead married Charles
Rich of Warwick, sometimes called at that time the "rich Mr.
Rich," in May, 1807, when she was just twenty. Some four
years later he died, leaving her with three children practically
penniless, as he had "fallen upon evil days." Meanwhile
Grandfather Isaac, a year before Charles Rich's death, had
built a fine eight-room Colonial house on a hill, a mile north
of Royalston, with a wonderful view of Mount Monadnock,
and had married Lucy Heywood, who was apparently in
poor health and died childless ten years later. As far as I am
personally concerned, she left little but a large coin-silver
serving spoon which came down in the family through four
hands and which is now in use in my house.

By her second marriage my grandmother became Anna
Mayo Stevens Rich Metcalf. She married my grandfather,
Isaac Metcalf, a year after Lucy Heywood Metcalf died and
ten years after she herself had been widowed. It seems appropriate to add that my stubbornness and slowness to adapt
to present-day conditions can be explained at least partly by
her picture, which appears in this volume.

As noted, Grandmother had become a widow with three
children at 24 and her second marriage took place when she
was 34. In the nine years that followed she had four more
children and then lost her second husband in 1830 when he
was 47 and she was 43. Her strong jaw must have been
particularly useful after this. Her three children by her first
marriage already were teaching school but with her son,
Charles, she moved to Milo in central Maine to a farm which
is still at the "end of civilization." You can go out into the back

yard and walk north for 150 miles without running into anything except forest, lakes, and lumber camps. To Maine with Uncle Charles and Grandmother went the four younger children, three boys and one girl, all four of whom taught school before they were 20. The girl, named Lucy Heywood after her father's first wife, married while she was still comparatively young and died early, leaving the man whom I was brought up to think of as Uncle Sam Furber, but whom I never saw because he died soon after I came into the world.

Father was the oldest of the Isaac Metcalf children. His next younger brother, Joseph Mayo Metcalf, was named after his great-grandfather, Joseph Mayo, his mother's maternal grandfather. He died as a young man as a result of a fall on the ice which resulted in a gradually increasing paralysis. My special interest in him stems from the fact that he was ambidextrous and kept the left page of his account book with his left hand and the right page with his right hand, with no difference between the two pages that anyone could detect. He died nearly 40 years before I was born, but one of my own brothers of whom I am particularly fond was named Joseph Mayo Metcalf after this uncle.

Father had another brother, Eliab Wight Metcalf, named after his father's first cousin, who was the printer for Harvard University in the first two decades of the 19th century and was in some ways the predecessor of the present-day Harvard University Press, Little Brown, and Houghton Mifflin. This cousin had already lost two sons by death while they were still very young, both named Eliab Wight Metcalf. When Grandfather's son was born just a few weeks after the second death, my grandfather must have felt that he should keep his cousin's name in the family in this way. As a result, one of my older brothers also was named Eliab Wight Metcalf. But the name has not gone on among my father's descendants or those of his brothers or sisters.

My uncle, Eliab Wight Metcalf, was one of the stubbornest men I have known or learned about. As a young man he taught school at seventeen years of age (as each of his older

brothers and sisters had done before him), this in spite of the
fact that his formal education had ceased after one term at
the Foxcroft (Maine) Academy. When just eighteen, he
walked 33 miles to Bangor and worked there for five years as
a clerk and accountant before going into business for himself
in lumber, as a ship chandler, and in ship building. During
the Civil War one of his ships was burned by the British-built
privateer, Shenandoah. After the Geneva Award that settled
the "Alabama claims," my uncle spent twelve winters in
Washington advocating the theory (which he originated) that
the 49 marine insurance companies which had claimed the
millions of the Geneva Award were entitled to nothing unless
they could show actual loss above war premiums received.
This theory finally was adopted by Congress, thus making it
possible to pay from the Geneva Award for the losses caused
by the Confederate cruisers for which the losers had received
no indemnity and also for about a third of the proven losses
from the payment of war premiums. As attorney in fact,
Uncle Eliab collected claims for others in addition to that for
his own ship. He gathered an extensive collection of books
and documents referring to the Treaty of Washington and
the Geneva Award, but they were lost when his house in
Elyria, Ohio, was destroyed by fire shortly after his death in
1899. He was also actively interested, both in Maine and later
in Ohio, in temperance legislation. He drafted the local op-
tion bill which under different names and forms was before
the Ohio legislature and had much to do with the establishment and support of the Anti-Saloon League. I bring this up
primarily to call attention to the family stubbornness which
most of us possess to a greater or lesser degree and which
influenced my own career.

My grandmother needed that strong jaw which the picture
shows. Her mother died when she was six, leaving her father
with seven children. He married again and Anna did not get
along with her stepmother and in her early teens lived with
relatives for a year or more in the backwoods of Maine, to
which she returned after her second husband died. She

remained there with her oldest son until persuaded by Father and one of the older daughters to join them in Elyria, Ohio, in the middle sixties. She died there in 1866 at 79. Some sixteen years earlier her second daugher, Anna Rich DeWitt, had written, as if it were her mother's autobiography up to the time of her second marriage, a volume entitled *Home,* which was published in hard covers but on poor paper in 1855, under the name of Anna Leland. It was published by J. C. Derby, Nassau Street, New York, and Phillips Simpson & Company of Boston, and is based on the stories that Grandmother told her children in their youth. (The American Antiquarian Society has four different editions of it.) The names were changed purposely as Grandmother did not always speak pleasantly about her neighbors. I am fortunate enough to have acquired a pencilled table showing the real names of all the 81 persons mentioned. They were chiefly residents of Warwick, except for the persons she met in Bangor and central Maine in the early 1800's. Now, 170 years later, I would not be afraid to show it to the descendants of those included in the volume. Several members of the Metcalf family have copies of the book.

My copy is one that you might say I bought three times. In the middle 1930's a second-hand book seller, who lived in a cold water flat over a saloon in downtown Jersey City and who specialized in American literature (particularly books by and about women) and who was more interested in acquiring books than selling them, reached the stage where his eight-room apartment was so full of books that his wife decided that she or the books would have to leave. The book seller finally decided that he cared more for his wife than the books and sold the whole lot to the Reference Department of the New York Public Library. They filled three five-ton trucks. The New York Public Library catalogued and kept all that it did not have and placed the rest in an exchange collection. Not long after this, I shifted my base to Harvard University and one of my early actions there was to buy the duplicates of the collection from the New York Public Library at 5¢ or 10¢

a volume. Harvard naturally lacked many of them, but among the duplicates a copy of *Home* was found, which I then acquired at something like ten times what Harvard had paid for it. Thus I finally owned a copy of a volume I had been looking for for some 30 years. Full of statements that are pious almost beyond belief, it gives a picture of the first 34 years of my grandmother's life, which was probably quite typical for the time that it covered in rural areas in central Massachusetts and central Maine 175 years ago. It gives at least a hint of why my grandmother required a strong jaw and why Keyes Metcalf is an anachronism.

My father (my grandmother Metcalf's oldest child by her second marriage) was born on January 29, 1822. At five he was taken into Boston as his father's health was failing. After his father's death in 1830, when he was eight, he and three younger brothers and sisters and his oldest brother, Charles Rich, and his mother moved to Maine to a farm just outside of Milo. They lived there in a small house with an adjacent barn under primitive conditions and in the "snow belt" through the severe central Maine winters. After going to the local schools, my father managed to get to Bangor for three years to prepare for college. He worked his way by teaching country school during the winter and working the farm in Milo during the next two summers. He was then able to enter Bowdoin in Brunswick, Maine, as a sophomore in 1844. There, in addition to full-time college work, he taught at large schools in various neighboring towns from three to six months in the year and graduated with his class in 1847. I might properly add at this point that I received a Bowdoin degree 118 years after my father got his, thus, as far as I can tell, breaking a record, and that my oldest grandson lived for one of his Bowdoin years in the same dormitory in which his great grandfather had lived.

Directly out of college Father joined a surveying party on the Vermont and Massachusetts railroad. He was promoted at once when it was found that, in spite of being a college boy, he was the ablest ax-man in his surveying party. He continued for the next three years in railroad building in the four northern New England states in charge of location and construction. I remember his telling of the time he spent on the final location of the Bangor and Waterville Railroad, locating the bridge across the Kennebeck River with the thermometer at 13° below zero at noon.

In the spring of 1850 Father went west by what today would be considered an unduly roundabout route but which was the best available at the time. He took a ship from Bangor to Boston, then went by stage to Troy, down the Hudson River to New York by steamboat, then west by train on the Erie Railroad to Westfield, N. Y., where he stopped off to visit his sister, Anna Rich, who was teaching there. He then went by stagecoach to Erie, Pa., by steamboat to Cleveland and Detroit and then on the very new and then crude Michigan Central Railroad across the state to Michigan City, the terminus of the road. From there he travelled to Chicago on the same steam ferry that brought the first locomotive engine to reach Chicago (it was intended to run on a little strap railroad just finished from Chicago out toward Elgin). From Chicago he reached LaSalle by canal, then down the river to Naples, across by strap rail to Springfield and by stage to Alton and on to St. Louis, and then by steamboat to Cairo. There he was put in charge of locating the Illinois Central Railroad from Cairo to Centralia and the following year, after going back east to get married, he returned to take charge of the construction of his section of the railroad. His official records are now with the railroad's archives in the Newberry Library in Chicago. One day when I was at the Newberry I asked the curator of the collection if he had any material about my father. The curator reached over to a pile of papers on his desk and handed me the top one with one of Father's payrolls, with his own salary of $150.00 a month, the highest paid division engineer on the line. I have in my possession in the family archives Father's copy of the same payroll. When he completed the work in southern Illinois in 1855, he went to Chicago and handed his account books and papers over to George B. McClellan, who was then clerk in the office of the company.

In the fall of 1855, Father was asked to check on the desirability of building a railroad from Chicago to St. Paul. He got over to the Mississippi River and took a steamship to Fort Snelling, the head of navigation. There he rented a horse and rode up to the Falls, where there is now the city of Minneapolis. It was then a small unincorporated village of 250 persons. It was incorporated later in the same year. I have in my possession a copy of a letter which he wrote home to his family in Maine at the time saying, "There is going to be a great city here some day." I've been to Minneapolis many times and find that I am hard pressed to believe that it was a small unincorporated village when my father went there just before he retired from his profession. A copy of the letter is now in the Minnesota Historical Society.

As part of his salary from the railroad he acquired land in what is now the town of Duquoin, Ill., which he and Chester Keyes (from whom my first name was derived) founded and developed and which in recent years has become famous as the site of the Hambletonian trotting races.

With this background it is not surprising that I received, in the last decade of the 19th century, an 1850 upbringing which I survived as far as I know without any damage to my health or my morals. In 1856 Father lost his two oldest sons and decided that it was time to retire from his career of building railroads and to settle down and bring up a family. His second half-sister, who by this time had married Dr. Elijah DeWitt, a prominent citizen in Elyria, the county seat of Lorain County, Ohio, persuaded him to settle there, and he remained there until his death in 1898. During 1857 he bought five and a half acres of land and a house in the center of town, "kitty corner" across the street from the schoolhouse block, for $2100.00. Repairs and improvements to the house came to $1350.00 and new furniture, household implements and outdoor tools and a sewing machine cost $1780.00, making a total investment of a little over $5000.00.

The author (second from right) and his nine brothers at a 1919 family gathering

ANNE MARY STEVENS RICH METCALF, 1757–1866
Author feels source of his own stubbornness may lie in his grandmother's "strong jaw"

TWELVE OF THE THIRTEEN LIVING CHILDREN OF ISAAC STEVENS METCALF IN 1912
Standing: Isaac Stevens (Ike), Thomas Nelson (Nelson), the author (Keyes), Eliab Wright (Eli), Joseph Mayo (Mayo), Paul Harlan (Harl)
Seated: Henry Martyn (Harry), Antoinette Putnam (Nette), John Milton Putnam (John), Charles Rich (Charlie), Marion), Anne Mayo Metcalf Root (Annie)
(The names in parentheses are the names they called each other, the names the author uses when referring to his brothers and sisters in the text)

EDWIN HATFIELD ANDERSON, 1861–1947
Emphasized staff quality as New York Public Library director

HARRY MILLER LYDENBERG, 1874–1960
At the top of the author's list of great librarians

AZARIAH SMITH ROOT, 1862–1927
Oberlin librarian helped start the author on his library career

The author (left) receives from Evan Farber, president of the
Association of College and Research Libraries, the first ACRL
academic-research librarian of the year award at the first ACRL
National Convention in Boston in November, 1978. Metcalf shared
the honor with Robert B. Downs.

KEYES DeWITT METCALF
A 1955 Portrait by Karsh of Ottawa

Father's first wife, Antoinette Brigham Putnam, was the daughter of the minister at Dunbarton, N. H., whom he had seen singing in the choir one Sunday after he had walked ten miles up the hill from Henniker, where he was at work, to attend church. As already indicated, they were married a few years later and during the next 23 years twelve children were born, almost like clockwork, one every two years, except for one pair of twins. Antoinette belonged to the New England Putnam family descended from John Putnam who emigrated from Buckinghamshire, England, in 1634 (John Putnam was also the ancestor of General Israel Putnam of Revolutionary fame). She died in 1875, leaving Father with nine children, four of them teenagers and the other five ranging from two to ten in age.

After three years, doing the best he could with a first-class housekeeper, who remained a close friend of the family for the rest of her life, Father married my mother, Harriet Howes. She was born in 1850 in a 400-year old stone farm house near Gayton, England, ten to fifteen miles south of Northampton, where her mother's family had lived for 300 years. Later in the same year, together with three older brothers and a sister, she was brought to this country, where the family settled in Elyria, Ohio. Two years later (four months before another daughter was born) the father died of tuberculosis, which he had probably picked up on the immigrant ship coming over from England. This was followed a few years later by the mother's death from the same disease, and the six children were taken in by six different families in Lorain County, Ohio. In those days they were called "foster" not "adopted" children, but the six were able to keep in touch with each other throughout their lives. The oldest boy was killed at Knoxville in 1863 and a second one, after receiving a severe wound at Vicksburg, practiced medicine for a short time in Grant County in Wisconsin before succumbing to the wound in 1874. My mother lived in Elyria with Aaron and Rebecca Bullock and at sixteen began to teach school in neighboring villages. At eighteen she transferred to Elyria and taught there for ten years until Father persuaded her to marry him.

Mother was a very brave as well as a remarkable woman. Although at 28 she was only five years older than her oldest stepson, she was considered the mother and was much beloved by each of the nine stepchildren, as well as by her own six boys who were born during the next thirteen years. She managed the household successfully and led an active outside life, particularly in the family Congregational Church. Her former school students adored her. One night in December, 1913, twenty years after my mother's death, riding from Washington to Elyria, my reservation was mixed up with that of William Graves Sharp, then Chairman of the House of Representatives Ways and Means Committee and later President Wilson's Ambassador to France during the First World War. Mr. Sharp was quite provoked at me for my stubbornness in insisting that I was in the section which he thought was his. It turned out that I was right. But when in the course of discussion he discovered that I was the son of Harriet Howes Metcalf, he almost broke into tears and told me that my mother was the finest teacher he'd ever had and that he could not over-emphasize what she had done for him and the influence she had had on his life. Then he invited me to have breakfast with him the next morning on the train.

With his conservative upbringing, my father quite normally became more conservative as he grew older and saw the world moving faster and farther away from what he had been trained to believe. Yet in spite of his conservative attitude on other things, he thought that his girls (since a woman's life was bound to be more restricted than a man's) had to have at least one year farther away from home than the boys, who went to Oberlin College, only nine miles away. So one of the girls had four years at Wellesley, two had one year at Wellesley (one of them later having graduate work in Chicago), and the fourth girl had a library school degree from Pratt and an AM from Oberlin as well as a year at Carleton College.

I remember Father as an old man with a long white beard, whom you always obeyed and looked up to with respect but of whom you were not afraid. He had a kindly word of good cheer for every boy we passed on the street as we drove the farm wagon to the farm or around town.

Mother died of pneumonia in December, 1894. Father, who up to that time had been an active and comparatively young man of nearly 73, died a broken-down old man three years later, just over 76. After Mother's death my oldest sister, Marion, who had taught science at Wellesley during the 1880's and the Bible at Hampton Institute in the early 1890's, gave up her career and came home to help Father with the five surviving younger children, the oldest of the six boys having died of pneumonia only a few days after his mother.

I was born on Saturday, April 13, 1889, my father's thirteenth son and seventeenth child. I was reminded often as a boy of the saying that Saturday's child (I was born on a Saturday afternoon at about 4:30) must work for a living and this being the case and since I was born late in the day it was inevitable that I was born lazy—two things that did not fit together very well. I had, and still have, another handicap with which I was born. I was, and am, excessively lefthanded, of which more later.

I might add that my younger brother, Nelson, a college faculty member throughout his career at Oberlin, Columbia, Minnesota, Iowa State, and finally the University of Chicago (except for four years in the Navy during World War II), was born a year and a half later.

Chapter 2
Choosing a Profession

I sometimes think that I was born and bred to be a librarian. I certainly was one of those fortunate individuals who had very little trouble selecting the field in which he wanted to spend his life. I had a brother-in-law 27 years older than I was who was a successful librarian, an older sister who decided when I was still a small boy to go into library work, and a cousin who went into library school early in the century. I suppose that these facts had something to do with my decision. But as I think back on it, I'm inclined to believe that the first push that started me toward librarianship was the indirect result of my left-handedness.

From what I have been told by older members of my family, I had an unusually happy disposition as a small child and felt the world treated me well. Things came my way to such an extent that until I was nearly three I couldn't be bothered to walk or talk. Why should I walk when people would carry me? Why should I talk when I got the food that I needed without asking for it by words? It was my younger brother, Nelson, who taught me to both walk and talk (unintentionally on his part, I am sure) because I found he was getting ahead of me even though he was almost 18 months younger.

I learned to read from the Bible at home at family prayers. Aided by my mother, I began to take part when I was four. This meant that the first grade in school was easy, although I was allowed to start before I was five and a half. I had had a few months at a private kindergarten before that. I recently found the receipt for my tuition, $5.00 a month, and I have a picture of my class. Elyria, Ohio, had no public kindergarten until the following year.

In the second grade I ran into trouble. I liked my teacher, who did not match her name, Miss Cross, but she thought I should learn to write with my right hand. This confused me and did not improve my disposition. The crisis came when the class took up sewing, something that was taught in those days to both sexes in Elyria at least. We started with threading a needle and the directions were, of course, to do it right-handedly. I was never able to get my needle threaded, so I didn't get along very well in that particular course, although later, during two years alone in New York City (most of it at the West Side Y.M.C.A.), I was able to darn my own socks and sew on buttons. Miss Cross finally realized that since I didn't write legibly with my right hand, I might as well go back to the left.

I can assure you that as a result the world seemed brighter again. I was soon reading avidly, not only children's books, from the Sunday School library, for teenagers, but history, particularly American, with great enthusiasm, and spending hours with a Compendium of Human Knowledge that we called "The Red Book" because of its cover. In the second, third, and fourth grades I read among many other things Charles C. Coffin's *The Boys of '76* dealing with the American Revolution, Theodore Roosevelt's *Naval History of the War of 1812,* two two-volume works on the Civil War, J. T. Headley's *The Great Rebellion* and J. S. C. Abbot's *The Civil War,* to say nothing of his *History of Napoleon Bonaparte* and a large part of George Bancroft's ten-volume American History.

These and many other things were in our home library where I had a free hand, although I must confess that I later found that certain books which were not considered fit for my perusal had been sequestered. These included, as I learned at age twelve, Tom Sawyer and *Huckleberry Finn,* Robert Louis Stevenson's *Kidnapped* and *Treasure Island,* and Kipling's *Stalky and Co.*

During these years, school was a pleasure and went well but in the winter of 1898, when I was eight years old, my father died, a little over three years after Mother's death. My sister, Marion, was then the head of a household of seven or eight, with older brothers and sisters and their spouses dropping in from time to time. In an effort to keep the large family together, she started three things that were useful to the family and to me personally; the first lasted only until we moved to a new house nine months after Father died. This was called "The Garden Fund," in which we all pitched in to grow (on the large home garden plot as well as at one of our farms) all the market gardening produce we could (we had no difficulty selling it to neighbors). For the first time I learned something about how hard work could bring in money. That same summer I earned money directly for myself by weeding onions on a nearby farm at 5¢ an hour. In that connection, I should add that I received a weekly allowance of one cent for each of my years of age and that of that amount one cent went into the Sunday School collection, one to the Congregational Church, and at least one into a savings account.

The second temporary project was "The Family Paper" to which each of us once a week presented a written "literary" contribution consisting of a poem (which I could never accomplish however hard I tried), an essay, a review of a recently read book, or a critique of a contribution done by another member of the family for the Paper the week before. These were my first literary efforts.

The third of Marion's projects was a family letter (Circulator as we called it) to which all thirteen of us contributed, whether from Elyria; Chicago, Illinois; Lawrence, Kansas; Oberlin College; Talladega, Alabama; or DesMoines, Iowa. This letter is still being carried on with my one surviving brother and a child of each of the seven others who had one or more children. It is now, in 1980, 82 years old and makes the circuit about once in six weeks. Twenty years later Marion started a second circular letter to which there now are nearly 50 contributors, including those in the first one plus those of Father's grandchildren and great-grandchildren who have grown up. These letters have changed tremendously over the years, particularly in the political viewpoints they express (no member of the group voted for FDR in 1933, but it would be difficult to find three or four who attempted to defend Nixon after his resignation). These letters have given me a first-hand view of what has happened to the world in well over two generations as we shifted from a completely conservative family to one much less homogeneous. But I am glad to report that, as a result of being brought up in a large and closely-knit family, we have been able to disagree violently at times but without quarreling. There are now 44 of my father's great-great-grandchildren; not surprising, perhaps, since he was born 157 years ago, yet remarkable when one considers that, as a result of Father's late marriage and of the fact that his first six offspring were childless, the first of his children to have children was not born until he was 40 and he was 67 before his first grand-child arrived.

Father's death naturally upset me and I became nervous and irritable without quite realizing the cause. When the spring term came two months later, it was decided to pro-mote me from the fourth to the fifth grade, perhaps in the belief that this would keep me busy and take my mind off my loss. It may have helped but the fifth-grade teacher, Miss Phipps, could not see why I should not write with my right hand and, without malice on her part I'm sure, I was shifted again. By this time my mental and physical processes were pretty well established and the strain of the change affected my nervous system. I often say that it "addled" my brain and that I never recovered.

In the autumn of 1898 we moved into a new house in another part of town. The old house, in which the family had lived for 42 years, had neither telephone nor running water nor a bathroom and had not been satisfactory to the family for some years (except for Father). But the cost of putting it in shape would have been greater than building a new house. The old house stood in an expensive location on a 5½-acre lot which, after it was sold, was cut up into building sites for some 20 houses; the house itself, instead of being torn down, was broken up into three two-family dwellings and moved a mile away to a poorer section of town.

The excitement of the change of scene to the new house probably helped my situation but it did not correct it and in the sixth grade I was somewhat of a burden to my teacher because for the first time I did not behave as good young boys should. When the girl in front of me let her long hair hang down on my desk, I put a lock of it in my fortunately empty inkwell and then put the cap on, with a resulting scream on the girl's part. At recess one day a classmate gave me a stick of gum, something that I had never had before, and I chewed it in class because I did not know how to get rid of it.

The next year, in the seventh grade, I began to have

nervous twitches of my head. Arrangements were made to have me leave school an hour earlier in the afternoon than my classmates, with the idea that I could spend more time out of doors and that this would help. I went on to the eighth grade in September, 1900, in a new grammar school building. This again was useful in taking my mind off myself.

The next summer Marion took Nelson and me to the World's Fair in Buffalo. There we heard Sousa's band and saw many exciting exhibits, climaxed, as far as I was concerned, with our first motion picture. We had been brought up to believe the theatre was naturally wicked and not good for children (nor adults, for that matter), this in spite of the fact that by this time I had not only read with pleasure Lamb's *Tales From Shakespeare* but had heard practically all of Shakespeare's plays read aloud at home, with each of us taking a part. I should admit that, when Buffalo Bill's Wild West Show came to town, somehow my older brothers and I managed to see it without Father's knowing about it. Nelson and I had a terrible struggle to get Marion into the motion picture building in Buffalo. The program was made up of 15-minute film shorts and the first one to come on was a prize fight featuring "Kid" McCoy. Marion immediately stood up to leave but my brother and I were strong enough to pull her down and the show went on with no bloodshed at our seats or on the screen. One short, involving trick photography, showed a man walking along a railroad track. It was so hot that he took off his coat, failing to see a train coming. He was hit by the train and the cowcatcher on the engine threw him to one side. He got up and came back on the track and somehow had another coat on and this was all repeated again and again until the time was up. Nelson and I thought it was uproariously funny.

Before returning to Elyria after four days at the Fair, we visited Niagara Falls, which was very exciting; we crossed the bridge into Canada to see the Horseshoe Falls and took the excursion steamer Will of the Wisp that went as close to the Falls as possible and got us soaked with spray. We went home by boat from Buffalo to Cleveland at my request and, as we had not made a reservation, Nelson and I spent the night "sleeping" on mattresses on the deck as all the staterooms but one had already been reserved. We had a 10¢ breakfast in a Cleveland restaurant next morning (my first in a city restaurant). Breakfast consisted of an egg (5¢), two slices of toast (1¢ each), one pat of butter (1¢), and a glass of milk (2¢). As you can see, this made a great impression on me. When we got back to Elyria after less than a week's absence, I was very much surprised to find that the town had not changed and that no one seemed to realize that we had been away.

In the autumn of 1901 I was twelve and started high school. For the first time, except for the sewing lessons six years earlier, I began to have trouble with my school work. I found first-year Latin difficult. I struggled patiently, studying harder than ever before, and by the winter received what I was told was the highest mark ever given by my very good Latin teacher, Miss May Allen, who had taught at least eight of my older brothers and sisters. But I was getting more nervous and twitchy and shaking my head from time to time. In April my botany class went on a field trip to Elyria's Cascade Park, theoretically to find wild flowers but one of the boys thought it presented a good opportunity to throw rocks into the Black River, which ran through the park. One of the rocks failed to reach the river because my head got in the way. The resulting scalp wound bled copiously but otherwise did not seem to do any serious harm. By the time the bandage was off, however, I was more nervous and twitchy than ever and my habit of shaking my head seemed to be confirmed. My family must have thought I was going to have St. Vitus dance. I was taken out of school and a little later my sister, Marion, took me by train to Grand Rapids, Mich., where my brother, Harl, was acting pastor of a large Congregational Church. She left me there for some six weeks and I was kept busy in the new surroundings. At the end of that period I took the train back home. It was my first trip by myself. I had to change trains in the midst of the journey and felt quite grown up.

School was over for the year but by September my problem had not disappeared and it was decided I should not return to school until the following April, when I would go back and finish my first year of high school. This was a blow to me. Marion realized that I would be better off if I were kept busy doing something different. So my half-sister, Anna, whose husband, Azariah Smith Root, was the librarian of Oberlin College, invited me to come over to Oberlin, nine miles away, for a few weeks at the beginning of September. To keep me out of mischief I was put to work, theoretically at 5¢ an hour, in the Oberlin College library. I enjoyed the work tremendously. Azariah taught me to "read" the shelves, straighten out the books, to check in periodicals as they were received, unpack books as they arrived from Baker and Taylor in New York, from Stevens and Brown in London, and Harrassowitz in Leipzig, and to do other tasks. I'm inclined to believe that absent-mindedness on my employer's part, rather than poor work on mine, was why I never was paid for my labors but I never ventured to complain. At the end of three weeks I returned home, more content to spend the time until April, 1903, working around the home place, playing vigorously out of doors and reading everything I could lay my hands on. But while I did not recover completely and was still nervous and shaking my head, I did finish my first high school year that spring.

My brother Nelson had mastoid trouble the following summer and was far from well. I learned later that many of our family friends in Elyria were convinced that neither of us would live until we grew up. After six weeks at school in the autumn of 1903, our doctor advised Marion that she had better take both of us out of school and have us spend a winter in a place where we could have plenty of exercise out of doors. Our older brothers had all left home for college and there was nothing to keep us from making the change. We went down to Tryon, S. C., in what is known as the "thermal belt," and spent more than half of the winter there climbing in the Blue Ridge Mountains day after day. The rest of the winter we spent in Talladega, Ala. My brother John, then Acting President and later President of Talladega College (one of the first colleges set up for Negroes after the Civil War), was in the North raising money for the college. Marion taught his course in New Testament Exegesis. Nelson and I played and hiked long distances outdoors and climbed the mountain that was the end of the Appalachian chain. We were back in Elyria in May, husky and well for the first time in years, ready to face the world and full of interest in strenuous athletics.

I spent the summer of 1904 working as a hired man for my cousin, George Rich, on his nearby farm with Edward Sanford Jones, whose sister Florence a little later married my brother Mayo. Ed (after graduating from Oberlin and receiving his doctorate from the University of Chicago) became Professor of Psychology and Dean of Students at the University of Buffalo. I received $10 for the three months' work—not $10 a month. Ed and I, slight for 15-year-olds, between us did the work of one man. He was right-handed and I was left-handed, so we could put our pitchforks into the same haycock together and we had no trouble keeping up with the regular hired man, who was over 70. That fall I started my sophomore year in high school in Elyria. But within a month Marion decided that our house was much too large for the three of us. It had been built only six years earlier, when there were seven of us at home and others returning at frequent intervals, so that we needed the seven bedrooms. But now it was not only too large but too expensive. Marion decided to pull up stakes and move to Oberlin. We did so and I entered Oberlin High School a few weeks late. On the first day for my first class I had English. There were double seats in the classroom and the only place for me to sit was with Don King, the third son of the then president of Oberlin College. As a result we became good friends. I spent a week with him at the end of the next summer at the home of his mother's family, the first time I'd ever been away from my own home (except at a relative's) by myself. Don and I roomed together in my junior year at Oberlin and, as he had dropped out for a year, my brother Nelson roomed with him in their senior year. We remained good friends the rest of our lives. He went to Harvard Medical School after graduating from Oberlin, specialized in chest problems, and became one of the leading men in his specialty, with his home in a Boston suburb. He and his wife Helen, who was for many years head of the Campfire Girls Camp at Fairlie, Vermont, welcomed the Metcalfs there when we came to Harvard 26 years after graduating from Oberlin.

The next summer, in 1905, I was back at George Rich's, working on the farm, milking the cows, peddling the milk, helping to build a silo, rebuilding a barn, getting in hay and other crops. It was a very hot summer, with the thermometer up in the 90's or over 100 day after day. I received $20 for the three months' work, an increase from the $10 of the summer before. It may not be surprising that I decided, one hot day while digging in full sunshine with the temperature over 110°, that I did not want to be a farmer, and began to wonder what else I could do. I briefly considered teaching school, as many Oberlin College graduates did in those days. But I decided that I was too shy to do that successfully. I then thought back to the library work that I had done three years earlier, the only work assignment I'd ever experienced except for farming and home duties. I remembered how much I had enjoyed it and asked myself why I shouldn't be a librarian (I was convinced that librarians never *had* to make speeches or stand up in front of an audience). Then I wondered what one did to prepare for librarianship and naturally wrote to Azariah Root to ask, "How do you become a librarian?" He wrote back succinctly, "The best way to prepare for a library career is to work in a library. Do you want a job?" I replied promptly, "Yes."

When high school reopened early in September, 1905, I became *the* page and errand boy at the Oberlin College

Library. It was then, as it is now, the largest and, in my
opinion, the best college library in the United States, except
for Dartmouth, which has almost, if not quite, a university
library and is, as a result, the only college library that is a
member of the Association of Research Libraries. In order to
carry out my assignments without interfering unduly with
my school work or with desirable physical activities (I had
become very much interested in athletics) I was excused from
two of my three study periods at high school and used them
and any other time required to put away books and do
errands for the library. I was the only regular student assistant and my tasks were varied that school year and the five
that followed until I graduated from Oberlin. I enjoyed the
work from the beginning and have been doing library work
ever since except for four summers.

In 1906 I was back on the Rich farm near Elyria, receiving
$30 for the summer. In 1907 I worked as an axe man, the
junior member of a surveying party that was locating ten miles
of the Chicago, Milwaukee, St. Paul, and Pacific Transconti-
nental Railroad in Montana's Bitter Root Mountains. I received $30 a month and keep, which enabled me to return
home with no debts and 25¢ in my pocket after a roundabout
train trip home which added 10 states to the 11 (plus Canada)
that I already had been in. I had slept in tents in beds made of
wood covered with pine branches in lieu of a mattress, and
part of the time in a wide home-made bed with two other men.
I had climbed snow-topped peaks on the 4th of July in the
Bitter Root Mountains, crossed the Rockies several times,
visited my two oldest brothers in Lawrence, Kansas, and
perhaps best of all, become acquainted with types of mankind
that I never had dreamed of.

In order to take the Montana position, which had been
offered to me by telegram by my brother, Eliab Wight Metcalf (Eli to the family), who was the head of the surveying
party that I joined, I had to leave high school four full weeks
before Commencement. This, of course, meant missing final
examinations and involved various other complications but

finally I was able to arrange it. I first went to the high school principal, who sent me to the Oberlin public school superintendent, who sent me to the president of the Oberlin Board of Education, who was my brother-in-law, Azariah Smith Root, for whom I was working part-time. Professor Root, knowing that I had had a pretty restricted life in having been brought up since I was eight years of age by two unmarried sisters, said, "Go ahead and arrange with the high school principal for some way to make up the work." It was perhaps easier in those days to cut red tape than it is today and the principal said:

1) You're good enough in American History, so we will pass you on that.

2) You must write a paper acceptable to your English teacher before we give you your high school diploma. (It was decided that I should write a criticism of Rudyard Kipling as an author. My library sister sent to me in Montana such material from college duplicates as she could find and I concocted the paper during the long summer evenings.)

3) You must make a written translation of the rest of Virgil which was my Latin course. (Fortunately I was able to say that I'd already done that during my spring vacation and I turned it right in. You can see by that fact what a strange boy I was.)

4) You must finish certain physics laboratory experiments which were to be assigned in the weeks ahead but these could be done in the fall (I did them by mid-November).

When the experiments were finished I went to the principal to ask for my diploma. He said, "Go to the superintendent." I found the latter walking around the building and he said, "I can't go back to the office now but it must be somewhere on my desk, go down and try to find it." This I did and thereby had what could be properly called an "informal" commencement. I should add that, this being 1908 and not 1978, I had been admitted to Oberlin College two months earlier without a high school diploma (The World Do Change!).

In 1909 Nelson and I worked on farms in Middlefield, Mass., a rural hill town in the Berkshires, which enabled us to make an excursion to Boston and Cambridge and also to visit Warwick and Royalston, Mass., where our father and his parents had lived, as well as Amherst and Williams Colleges and to climb Mt. Greylock, the highest in Massachusetts. We raced up the mountain's eastern slope, then bare as a result of a dirt and rock slide, and ended in a dead heat, completely exhausted. But we made the trip up and back, which we had been told would take all day, by 10 o'clock in the morning. This gave us time to go to Pittsfield and call on William Stearns Davis, who had been my much-liked history teacher for two years. This call, I suppose, resulted in his reporting to his Oberlin successor, Albert Howe Lybyer, of whom I shall write later, and was at least partly responsible for my correcting papers for Professor Lybyer in my senior year.

In 1911, after graduation from Oberlin and before my library school opened in September, I was in charge of a playground in Youngstown, Ohio, in the midst of what was then called the worst slum west of the Allegheny Mountains. The playground was a comparatively small plot of bare ground belonging to the Christ Mission Settlement where I was housed. The settlement building shut it in on one side; a cheap bakery, overrun with rats, despite the fact that it operated day and night, was on a second. On the third side was a tenement house whose residents included a large black man with a head covered with bumps, resulting from his occupation of sticking his head through a hole in a padded canvas and permitting anyone who wished to throw baseballs at him from 40 feet away for five cents. Regular doses of cocaine, I was told, prevented him from suffering unduly. On the fourth side, across Dobbs Alley, was a "flop house" where a bed was available at 15¢ a night and from which strange noises emerged frequently during most nights from drunken men, often suffering from delirium tremens and generally of a quarrelsome nature. I slept in a room just across the alley from the "flop house." It was the hottest summer recorded by the U.S. Weather Bureau up to that time in that part of the country. Just a short distance away from the settlement, in opposite directions, were giant steel mills spewing out heat and pollution day and night. Frequently I would go to bed after a bath without using a towel and wake up the next morning practically black all over from the soot that had drifted in through the open windows.

The boys who used the playground were from at least 15 different nationalities, including a gypsy who was particularly combative in temperament. It was here that I learned first-hand about anti-semitic prejudice which before that I knew chiefly from my reading, beginning with Sir Walter Scott's *Ivanhoe* and Shakespeare's *Merchant of Venice*. A number of the boys from the playground were able to go to a local Fresh Air Camp for a week. One of them without hesitation or complaint slept in a double bed with a black boy but refused to be assigned to a tent occupied also by a quiet, well-behaved Jewish boy in a separate bed. In my time at Oberlin College there was only one Jewish boy among nearly 400 students and I had known of only one Jewish family in Elyria and one in Oberlin.

The five summers that I spent away from home not doing library work (I had two summers with full-time library work in the meantime) turned out very satisfactorily as far as preparation for a life-time library career was concerned. While they involved a great deal of hard work, I never regretted any of them.

Chapter 3
Page in the Oberlin College Library
1905-1911

Azariah Smith Root was the Oberlin College Librarian and also my brother-in-law, having married one of my half-sisters. He was born in 1862 in Middlefield, Mass., 27 years ahead of me. He was in one way like John Langdon Sibley, the Librarian of Harvard from 1856 to 1877, in that he ransacked the attics and houses in Lorain County for books and pamphlets as Mr. Sibley had done in Cambridge and Boston. But the comparison was not applicable beyond their collecting activities and the books they acquired with very small budgets. Sibley had a difficult streak in his disposition which tended to flare up at critical times. Azariah was always friendly and smiling and was well liked by the students, the faculty, the townspeople and the college administration. He graduated from Oberlin in 1884 and after nearly two years in law school in Boston and Cambridge he was asked to return to Oberlin to catalogue the library, which then included about 15,000 volumes. In 1887 he was appointed Librarian. He already knew the library very well, as he frequently had persuaded his predecessor to lock him in the library at night so he could continue to read. He was one of those rare individuals who seemed able to read a page at one glance. Three years after becoming Librarian, he was made Professor of Bibliography in addition to his basic position. In 1893 he became a faculty member of the Prudential Committee of the Board of Trustees that had the responsibility for administering the affairs of the College which were not specifically entrusted to other officers, a position that he held until his death 34 years later, at which time he had been its senior academic member for 18 years. He also was a member of the Trustees Investment Committee after 1915. On at least one occasion, he served as chairman of a committee to administer the College in the absence of the President. He also was for years the Chairman of the College Budget Committee, as well as president of the Town of Oberlin Board of Education. He often served as a substitute preacher in the town's Negro churches. He presided over an investigating committee that struggled with town problems and was a leader in many town affairs. He was responsible for the arrangement by which the Library became the Town as well as the College Library when the Carnegie Library was completed in 1908, making it—as far as I can learn—the first joint College and Public Library in the country. He probably was better known to the students of the College than any other professor or administrator. In addition to his library work, he taught three two-hour one-semester courses, dealing with the *Use of Libraries*, *The History of Printing*, and *Book Illustration*.

A record of Azariah Root's library career outside of Oberlin is available elsewhere. I will be content here to say that he was the Chairman of one (I think the first) Committee of the American Library Association on Education for Librarianship. He acted as Dean of the first (I believe the only) Library Correspondence School, the one sponsored by the Gaylord Brothers Company, and he was on leave from Oberlin to serve as Principal of the New York Public Library Library School in 1916-17. He had been asked to take the position by Miss Mary Wright Plummer, who had just been president of the American Library Association and who was ill and died before the year was far advanced.

Professor Root was president of the American Library Association for the year 1921-22, the second college librarian (as distinct from a university librarian) to hold that position, having been preceded 30 years earlier by William I. Fletcher of Amherst College. He spent two sabbaticals and many summers abroad studying the origins of printing from movable type but the results of his researches never were published. By 1927 he probably knew more about the subject than anyone else, as he not only had gone through all the records to be found in Mainz and elsewhere in Germany but had also read the official school and other records in Haarlem in the Netherlands where John Koster worked. There are those who believe that Koster, not Gutenberg, was the first printer. But Root found no evidence that he ever used movable type.

In addition to his library school experience in the New York Public Library and with Gaylord Brothers, Root taught in the University of Michigan Library School at Ann Arbor for several summers and was a close friend of W. W. Bishop. During his last summer, in 1927, he taught an administration course at Columbia. A few weeks later, soon after college opened at Oberlin with its first new president in 25 years, Ernest Hatch Wilkins, Professor Root died after an operation. President Wilkins, who had been dean of the faculty at the University of Chicago, told me later that he had decided to come to Oberlin largely because it had a great library and a great librarian.

Azariah Root was rather short, thick-set and heavy. He had both a mustache and a full beard, the latter grown when still young to cover up a large mole on his chin. He had a fine sense of humor and I remember his delight one day when the coatroom attendant found in a library wastebasket an English Department freshman theme about Professor Root which closed with, "He has on his face a look of almost human intelligence." Azariah frequently led the then compulsory chapel service which was held daily from Tuesday through Saturday throughout the academic year and was primarily religious in character. One day he ended the service by reciting the 23rd Psalm from memory instead of with the customary prayer and included the mixed-up phrases, "Thou anointest my cup with oil and my head runneth over." A caricature of Azariah's head under these conditions appeared in the next College Annual, to the amusement of everyone, including the victim.

Professor Root did nothing about his excessive weight until he was in his 50's when his doctor warned him that he should get more exercise and spend more time outdoors. He then tried a little backyard gardening but did not enjoy it. I think he was physically (certainly not mentally) lazy, and he was kept too busy by his chosen work to bother with exercise or dieting. On one occasion, however, he did something that few others have accomplished. He rode by streetcar from Oberlin to Boston, finding only one short stretch near Fulton, New York, where at that time there was no streetcar available. If you find it hard to believe this, look in one of the early editions of the Atlas volume of the Century Dictionary, which we had in our house early in the century and still have for that matter.

If I remember correctly, in my early time in Oberlin Azariah received a salary of $1800 a year while the regular professors were at $1600. A few years later, when I was Acting Librarian, his salary had reached $2600.

Although Professor Root was my brother-in-law and I began to see him frequently when very young and worked under his direction for eight years and probably more closely with him than any other librarian did during at least 14 more years, it never occurred to me to call him anything but Professor or Mr. Root.

I confess that during the whole period my primary ambition, if I had one, was to succeed him. But as will be seen later, this was not to be. I owe much to him from the time he taught me how to cut pages in 1902 until his death in 1927. One thing he taught me, which perhaps influenced my library career more than any other single thing, was the value of money. If I have become a "pinch-penny" and have tried to watch with perhaps too extreme caution each dollar in library budgets that have been available to me, both before my retirement and afterward while working as a consultant, the share of it that cannot be attributed to my ancestry probably finds its source in Azariah Root, one of the comparatively few great American librarians.

The full-time Oberlin Library professional staff in 1905, in addition to Professor Root, included as its senior member Miss Eoline Spaulding, who had come to the library as Assistant Cataloguer in 1892. She became Head Cataloguer three years later, a position that she held for 28 years.

Next in length of service came Miss Esther Close, who began work in the college library in 1894 and continued until 1933, except for five years — 1903 to 1908 — when she was librarian of the Union Library Association rather than a member of the staff of the college library.

William Wirt Foote was the only man, except Azariah, on the staff during my student days. He had hoped to become a concert singer but his voice and throat gave out and he worked in the library as Assistant Cataloguer and in other positions from 1901 to 1911. Later he became librarian of the Mississippi State College and finally served for many years as librarian of what is now Washington State University (then Washington State College) in Pullman, Washington. I last saw him in the late 1940's in Columbia, Missouri, at a meeting of the informal "Library Building Committee" at the University of Missouri. Mr. Foote was trying to plan a new library building for his college, fortunately with little success because the architect was insisting on a non-functional Gothic building. When the new library finally was built after Mr. Foote's retirement, it was one of our first modular buildings, from which we learned an important lesson which will be spoken of later. Mr. Foote still was afflicted even at that time with the gift of "continuous utterance." Early in my years in the Oberlin library he was given the task of underlining the author's name in each of some 40,000 uncatalogued pamphlets that had been given to the library. I then arranged them alphabetically. Mr. Foote talked all the time and it gave me a wonderful opportunity to learn to work without being unduly disturbed by others talking, something that has been useful to me for over 70 years.

Miss Mary J. Fraser worked in the book order department of the library from 1901 to 1929. She was a quiet, efficient and intelligent acquisitions librarian, from whom I picked up a good deal of information that I used later.

Miss Hattie Henderson was an Oberlin graduate who had gone to the Western Reserve Library School and was a first-class cataloguer, serving from 1904 until her premature death in 1925. She was one of the first black librarians with library school training. I remember being told that her beginning salary in the Library after graduating from library school was only $25 a month for a 44-hour week, which made my own wages of 15¢ an hour seem not unduly low, after all.

Antoinette B. P. Metcalf, my half-sister, graduated from the Pratt Institute Library School in 1902. After working as reference librarian at Pratt for two years, she came back to Oberlin, from which she had graduated in 1893 (with an AM sixteen years later), as its first reference librarian. She remained for six years before going to Wellesley in 1910 as its first reference librarian and later associate librarian. She continued there until her retirement in 1939.

"Net," as we called her, was my senior by 16 years. While she encouraged me in my library work from 1905 until her death 56 years later, she did not hesitate to criticize me when I needed it, particularly for incorrect spelling and too much colloquialism in my speech. Thus she was a helpful influence as well as a close associate and much loved sister. I remember well her calling my attention to errors in spelling in letters written to her during vacation periods and library school days. She also encouraged me to broaden my reading in the field of European history, in which I later specialized. At Wellesley she had double the salary she had received at Oberlin and worked a 35-hour week 35 weeks in the year instead of the 44 hours a week for 48 weeks in the year that had been the schedule at Oberlin. I might add that when Mary Wright Plummer started the New York Public Library Library School in 1911 my sister was her first choice as teacher of reference but she refused the offer.

Professor Root, as already noted, had chosen his library profession by the time the first library school was founded. The others mentioned on his staff who had not attended library school properly could be called "professional librarians" for that day and age. I doubt if there was as strong a college (as distinct from university) library staff to be found anywhere else in 1905.

Thanks to Professor Root's efforts, the library's collections were, as already noted, quite large for a college library early in the century. The average quality would not have been considered unusually high because such a large proportion was made up of gifts. With the help of the Union Library Association collections which met many of the students' course and recreational needs, Oberlin's holdings did make up a first-class undergraduate library, while an unusually large collection of research material helped to attract a better than average college faculty in a number of disciplines. With the limited funds that were available, the librarian had acquired more French and German books, both current and retrospective, than most other college libraries of the time.

The English and American History collections were good. A fine start had been made with manuscripts, particularly those relating to slavery. There was a remarkable college archives section, which Professor Root had brought together and organized. He was more knowledgeable in the history of the college, which had an exceptionally interesting past, than anyone else in Oberlin, which had been involved from the beginning in anti-slavery movements and other reforms.

Oberlin had been a station on what was known as the "Underground Railroad," which aided Negro slaves who had escaped and then helped them make their way to Canada. At one time in the 1850's, after the Supreme Court's Dred Scott decision, practically the whole Oberlin faculty was jailed in Cleveland for rescuing and freeing an escaped slave who had been picked up by his owners. In the years between 1837 and 1900, Oberlin graduated a full half of all the blacks who graduated from white colleges in the United States.

Students were prohibited from using liquor and tobacco. I do not remember seeing a faculty member smoke and I saw a student smoking only three times in my six years as library page—and never in the library. At one time early in the college's history, an emphasis was placed on the use of graham bread on the basis that it was more healthful and less expensive than white bread. As already noted, Oberlin was a leader in the Anti-Saloon movement.

The fact that Oberlin was the first college to admit women working for a degree had an inevitable effect on it in connection with the women's movement. I have an interesting personal sidelight in this connection. My first wife's paternal grandfather was one of the earliest settlers in the town of Oberlin. He had bought his home plot from the first settler, Peter Pindar Pease, the year the college was opened, and my granddaughter, who graduated from Oberlin in 1972, is the fifth generation of women in her family to do so. My daughter has the original deed for the place which was the family headquarters for nearly 140 years. Her great-grandmother was a classmate of Lucy Stone (Blackwell), known for her

women's rights attitude and the fact that she kept her maiden
name after her marriage. Lucy Stone's husband was a
brother-in-law of another classmate, Antoinette Brown
Blackwell, the first ordained female minister in the country,
who went through a very difficult period in obtaining a
position. Another Blackwell sister, Elizabeth, was the first
woman doctor in this country. The interesting and quite
handsome reading room in the old Hobart College library
received its name from her, for she had graduated from the
Hobart College Medical School.

The Oberlin library presented an ideal place for a boy who
was convinced that he wanted to be a librarian and to learn
about library work. By the end of my college career, I had
been engaged in practically all kinds of library work except
cataloguing, and in Professor Root's course on *The Use of
Libraries* I had learned the basic principles in that field.

The use of the library was heavy and I had a variety of
tasks. As there was no other regular student assistant, my
regular duties left me with little spare time. But I had been
brought up on the theory that "the devil finds things for idle
hands to do." Perhaps this was all for the good, although as I
look back on it I often wonder how I managed to get through
my high school and college work and also devote a good deal
of time to athletic and other interests which will be dealt with
in a later chapter. At least I learned to work steadily if not
effectively, and regularly had at least 9½ hours of sleep.

Professor Root taught three one-semester courses. I took
each of them, beginning with the one on The Use of Libraries, which I found very helpful and which would have
confirmed my choice of library work for a profession if it had
needed any confirming. It included in concentrated form
Book Selection, Cataloguing, Classification, Reference, Bibliography, and Public Service. I often have said that I learned
more from this course than I learned later in library
school—and this is not said as a complaint against the library
school.

Professor Root was a great teacher but he did embarrass
me once. The class was held at 2 in the afternoon and I sat in

the front row. One afternoon, through the combined effect of a strenuous football practice the day before and an extra big lunch, I fell sound asleep. I woke up suddenly to find Professor Root, standing some distance from where I was sitting and not at his regular place at the desk, talking in a low voice and saying that he would continue to talk in this way so as not to disturb Mr. Metcalf.

The Spear Library, which housed the main collections of Oberlin College from 1885 to 1908, was named in honor of its donor, the Reverend Charles V. Spear of Pittsfield, Mass. The stone-faced building, which cost $30,000 to construct, was five levels high, if you included the two stack levels on parts of two floors. It had no elevator. The only means of vertical transportation for its contents, from the time I started my work there in 1905 until the Carnegie Library which replaced it was ready for occupancy three years later, was Keyes Metcalf. The shipping entrance was in the basement, which was at ground level. There were more books stored on the top level than on any one of the four lower stack decks.

When I first became acquainted with it the ground floor or basement still housed among other things a zoological and botanical museum while its mezzanine had bookstacks illuminated only by open gas jets, with no Bunsen burners to protect them. This handicap was removed early in my library career, the gas jets being replaced by incandescent bulbs, protected by wire cages, on the ends of long cords.

The librarian's office was on this floor. Its chief claim to fame, besides being the office of the librarian, lay in its use 12 years earlier, in 1893, for the organization of the Anti-Saloon League of America. In 1919 the League, led by its secretary, Wayne B. Wheeler, who went to Oberlin with my librarian sister and was perhaps the most capable lobbyist the country has known, had the primary responsibility for the enactment of the 18th Amendment to the Constitution and the passing of the Volstead Act.

Other basement floor space was occupied by a shipping and receiving room where I often unpacked the large book boxes then used by our foreign agents, Stevens and Brown of London and Harrassowitz of Leipzig.

About a dozen wide and rather steep outside front steps occupied most of the central third of the south side of the building, leading halfway up to the main-floor level. There was a comparatively narrow entrance lobby with several doors, and the main floor was reached by climbing inside steps that led to another narrow lobby. The one door at its left side opened on what seemed to me at the time to be a very large main reading room. Immediately to the right, after entering the reading room, one passed in turn the circulation desk, the reserve book desk and the reference desk, with the catalogue in front of them. By turning right again you could enter an open two-level, multi-tiered iron bookstack, with the ranges running from east to west and windows on its two outside walls providing most of the light, although there was the regular stack lighting for that time with low-wattage unprotected incandescent bulbs.

A left turn from the main reading room entrance would bring one to the desk of the librarian of the Union Library Association, which was the library of the Union of Student Literary Societies. To its left was another two-level open bookstack which housed the U.L.A. collection. In those days the student literary society collections in college libraries often were almost as important as the main college library (it was in one of the Yale University student libraries that William Frederick Poole began his library work and brought out the first edition of Poole's Index; the very pleasant undergraduate reading room in the Sterling Library at Yale was called the Brothers and Linonian Room, from the Yale Student Libraries).

The Oberlin U.L.A. collection was cared for by its own librarian, except that it was my duty to put away books after they had been used. The library specialized in the fields of history, literature and the social sciences, and also had a good collection of general periodicals. Although it contained only some 25,000 volumes, they were used much more per volume than the 100,000 volumes in the regular college library. The college library and the U.L.A. had duplicate holdings of many monographs and standard periodical files called "Poole Sets" (which were indexed in Wm. F. Poole's well-known printed index volumes).

Above the building's entrance lobby, stretching out over the main inside stairs and reached by going up a few steps immediately in front of the main reading room door and following a not too wide passage, one would find a long, narrow cataloguing room.

From there steep stairs with a right-angle turn and no landing took one up to the third or top floor. This floor contained a small work room, an open book-and-newspaper stack, and a small apartment that Professor Root and his wife occupied briefly after their marriage in 1887 while waiting for their house to be completed. In my time it was occupied by two students who were the building's part-time janitors. But most of this floor was filled with wooden bookstacks, many of which went up to the ceiling, with upper shelves that could be reached only with the aid of a stool. The ceiling, beneath the many-gabled roof, was very irregular in height.

The library was the newest of the four buildings that I had known in the central, nearly square college campus. Between the first time that I worked in the library in September, 1902, and September, 1905, the largest of these buildings, the college chapel, which seated 1200, or more than the total student body, burned down. The other two buildings were small and used for classrooms.

The Spear Library and both classroom buildings were torn down some time after 1908 to carry out provisions of the Charles M. Hall will. This will, in addition to providing for a special endowment for the upkeep and beautification of the main campus, gave the college one-third of the Hall residuary estate.

Mr. Hall was the inventor of the process by which aluminum still is reduced from bauxite. He was a classmate of one of my older brothers and had the same chemistry teacher, Frank F. Jewett, whom I had 25 years later. During Mr. Hall's senior year, in 1885, Professor Jewett remarked in the course of one of his lectures that if someone could find an inexpensive method to make aluminum out of bauxite, he would make a fortune. As a result Mr. Hall, instead of going into teaching as most of his classmates did, went to work in the woodshed of his house, just a block from where I later lived, and in less than a year had worked out the basic method that is still used.

With the aid of a lawyer classmate, Mr. Hall was able to keep at least a reasonable share of the rewards and became a wealthy man, with most of his funds in stock of the Aluminum Company of America, which was controlled largely by the Mellon family. Mr. Hall never married and naturally kept up his interest in Oberlin. Upon his death, it turned out that he had, as noted, left one-third of his residuary estate, consisting of $2,000,000 in stock, to Oberlin. Another third went to Berea College in Kentucky and the final third to what later became the Yenching Institute at Harvard, in which I naturally had considerable interest during my Harvard years. One provision of Mr. Hall's will was that the aluminum company stock could not be sold for something like 12 years after his death. By then World War I and the resultant expansion of the airplane industry (Mr. Hall had died in 1914) meant that the stock had quintupled in value before Oberlin could make use of anything except the interest. The value of the Hall money has more than quintupled for a second time since the stock first was turned over to the college, a fact which has been largely responsible for Oberlin's being the great college that it is today and having the great library that it now has.

But to go back to the Spear Library—during the years 1905 to 1908 it was what could properly be called completely full and new books which were coming in at an ever-increasing rate had to be tucked in any space that could be found. As time went on, I became the only person who knew where many of the books had been placed, a matter which later proved important as far as I was concerned.

In addition to the collections in the Spear Library, a large theological library (much of which is now at Vanderbilt University in Nashville) and several small science collections as well as a very good music library in Warner Hall, the main Conservatory of Music building, made up the college library. In the attic of the music building wooden shelves had been installed to hold part of the library's large collection of duplicates for exchange. This was supplemented by an old frame house on West Lorain Street, adjacent to the site now occupied by the 1908 Carnegie Library.

In it lived a black (it was then called "Negro") family named Williams, consisting of mother, daughter and son, Henry, who helped in the library on occasions and who was a close friend of mine throughout the years. He was called "Buddha" because in school one day the name came up in a history class and he knew more about Buddha than anyone else. He graduated from Oberlin College in my class and became a high school principal in St. Louis and later in Brooklyn. The Williams family quarters became more and more cramped by the constantly increasing collection of duplicates. The floors of the house were reinforced from below but we used to say that the only reason the building stood up was that the books were piled in up to the ceiling so that it couldn't collapse.

Whenever anyone in Oberlin or nearby had more printed material than he knew what to do with, it was made clear to him that the Oberlin College Library would welcome it. When a citizen died leaving a collection of books, his heirs were encouraged to give them to the library. Although the tax laws at that time did not help as they do today, a tremendous amount of material thus was acquired. With the duplicates that resulted, the library carried on perhaps the largest exchange program in any college or university at the time. One of my early tasks was to take the library's two-wheeled hand pushcart to a house and clear out from the attic and elsewhere books, pamphlets, and magazines that were being given to the library.

From time to time, the pushcart also was useful in going to

a professor's house in order to return large quantities of books that the professor had drawn from the library—sometimes (I regret to say) without his having signed for all of them. One of the professors, whose interests were unusually broad, several times a year would send back to the library a pushcart full of books from his house in one of the more distant parts of town.

(Twenty years later, after this professor had become dean of a professional graduate school in a large eastern university, he visited the New York Public Library Reference Department. Some time later a book was found on a subway car and returned to the library. Since in theory books in the reference department never were permitted to leave the library, it was carefully checked and found that this book had been signed out for use in the library by this dean, who had come to New York to work on a research problem. He had used a temporary local address on his call slip and Harry Lydenberg, who was then the chief of the reference department, asked me to get in touch with the dean and rebuke him. This was one of the few occasions when I refused to carry out an assignment given me by a superior officer. I said that since I had gone to school under this professor, I thought it was up to Mr. Lydenberg to substitute for me.)

But my chief duty as page in the Oberlin library was to put away books that had been withdrawn from the shelves for use. The stacks were open, so stack service to bring books for readers to the circulation desk rarely was necessary. The library was more heavily used than other college libraries in those days. During rush periods I sometimes had trouble keeping up with my work but I managed well enough so that I was not discharged and indeed was encouraged to continue year after year.

Since Professor Root was my brother-in-law and since one of my older sisters was the reference librarian, I suppose Azariah might have been accused of nepotism in employing us. But as far as I have been able to learn, either then or later, this was not the case. Perhaps one of the reasons was that I received only 15¢ an hour for my work and was not given an increase in pay for the regular page work over the period of six years that I continued in the position. As I have noted, when my sister left Oberlin to become Wellesley's reference librarian in 1910, her salary was doubled and her working hours were reduced.

The library had an unusually good as well as large collection for that period. It was heavily used by the students throughout the day because they were made to feel that they were welcome and it had what they wanted to read. The evening use was exceptionally large, partly because of the prevailing (what we now call "parietal") rules. The library was the only place to which women students were allowed to go in the evening except to regular college functions (concerts, lectures, athletic contests, etc.). Otherwise, they were confined to their dormitories.

Each of the women's college dormitories had a co-educational dining room. The men at that time had no dormitory accommodations (with one minor exception) and lived in rooms in private houses scattered about the town. They had to leave the women's residential halls at 7:00 P.M. after a 5:30 evening meal. The freshman women had to leave the library no later than 7:30 but the upper-class women could stay until 9:30, when the library closed, and then go directly to their rooms. They could be accompanied at that time back to the dormitory and left at the door. I might add that at the time of my 1902 library experience the campus walks consisted of long parallel boards, two in each direction, each about 18 inches across but a foot apart so as to prevent undue intimacy.

It may be appropriate to say here that, even before college, I discovered that the best way to keep up with the times, as a generalist not as a specialist, was through reading current periodicals, although many of the periodicals that I became acquainted with were in special fields. For instance, I read or at least glanced through the *Harvard Graduate's Magazine* regularly throughout high school and college in spite of the fact that it never occurred to me that I ever would go to Harvard. I became reasonably well acquainted with all the titles included in the Reader's Guide and the F. W. Faxon Company Annual Index.

As early as my tenth year, long before high school, my sister Marion on Sunday afternoons selected what she considered the most important articles in *The Outlook, The Independent, The American Review of Reviews,* and *The World's Work* and read them aloud to her younger brothers. Probably too much of my general education might be said to be based on current periodicals and, while this may have provided only a thin veneer of an education, it has been a major influence on my life.

I should add the following on this topic: My father began his subscription to *Harper's Magazine* in 1850, before he was married, and the bound files with which I became acquainted before I was 10 interested me particularly because of its pictures. He also subscribed to the *Atlantic* from its beginning and the *Scribner's Monthly* and later, among others, *McClure's* in its early years. Kipling's Stalky and Company stories in the *McClure's* were kept out of my hands. The habit stuck; I still subscribe not only to library journals but also to some 40 other periodicals, the current issues of which piled up on a table in our living room while these pages were being written.

Even after my father's death, my sister Marion (as was the case with Father) would not have a newspaper in the house except for the local weekly town paper because of the time it took to read it and the things in it that were not thought fit for young minds. This rule was broken at the end of the last century for about a year while my oldest brother, Wilder, was in the Philippines as head of the "famous" 20th Kansas National Guard Regiment, a position in which he succeeded General Fred Funston.

Chapter 4
A New Library Building
and
My First Administrative Experiences

Sometime before my family moved to Oberlin in September, 1904, a flashily dressed and attractive young woman using the name of Mrs. Cassie Chadwick came to one of the Oberlin banks. After some conversation, she told the cashier and the president that she was an illegitimate daughter of Andrew Carnegie and needed to borrow some money for which her father would be responsible. Somehow she convinced them that she was a safe risk and was able in the months that followed to borrow large sums of money without collateral.

47

To make a long story short, she failed to repay the loans and her reference to Mr. Carnegie proved to be false. The bank failed. Those responsible lost their positions and reputations and Mrs. Chadwick went to jail. Many of the Oberlin faculty members and students lost everything they had in the bank. I remember, however, that when Azariah Root, the librarian, was questioned about it, he reported that he had lost nothing as his account was slightly overdrawn at the time.

The whole affair quite naturally came to Mr. Carnegie's attention. In spite of his blameless connection with it, he was persuaded to reimburse all members of the college community for the losses they had suffered. But the important part of the story as far as the college library was concerned was that it gave the college and Professor Root an opportunity to present their library building problem to Mr. Carnegie's agent, Mr. James Bertram. The latter wrote on January 20, 1905, to President Henry Churchill King, "With reference to your letter and subsequent correspondence, Mr. Carnegie desires me to say that he will be glad to pay for the erection of a library building for Oberlin College to the extent of $125,000, this to be conditioned upon your raising $100,000 for new endowment for Oberlin College." Before Oberlin's appeal to Mr. Carnegie, Professor Root had prepared a document entitled, "Statement in Regard to the Proposed New Library Building for Oberlin College." To the best of my knowledge, this was the earliest program for a library building drawn up by a college librarian. It is 26 pages long. It starts out with general basic requirements for the building which included:

1. It must be absolutely fireproof.
2. It should be extremely simple in its exterior.
3. Economy of administration must be kept in mind.
4. An absolutely dry basement is one of the essentials.
5. Natural light should be provided as far as possible.
6. There must be satisfactory lighting, heating and ventilating.

He went on to propose a building with an interior hollow

square above the second floor; the space beneath this, lighted by skylight, was to be used for the delivery or, as we would now call it, the circulation desk, the public catalogue, the reference desk and the current periodicals. He proposed the site for the building and then described in some detail each of the four floors.

I hope that some day the program will be printed in full, because it describes what a leader of the college librarians of his time wanted for a library early in the century and is of great interest historically. Before Eileen Thornton retired as Oberlin librarian in 1971, she checked through the library's records and found among Professor Root's papers this program, a copy of which she was good enough to send to me.

Azariah was influential enough in the college so that he had a large part (something that was unusual in those days for librarians) in planning the library from beginning to end. The architects were Patton and Miller of Chicago. Between them, with the aid of a good contractor, George Feick of Sandusky, Ohio, the resulting building was, in my considered opinion, the best college library building constructed in the United States up to the time that it was completed and dedicated in June, 1908. William Coolidge Lane, the librarian of Harvard College, gave the dedication address and made one of the early speeches on interlibrary cooperation. The library cost less for what was obtained in quality and quantity than any other library for which I have found a record at any period, and it was still in use 66 years later, until the summer of 1974, when the Seeley Mudd Learning Center replaced it. Costs were measured in cubic rather than square feet at that time and they came to 11¢, which was unbelievably low, even taking into account the fact that the main reading room, with nearly 6300 square feet, was two and one-half stack levels high and most of the rest of the building was 15 feet from floor to floor. The square footage cost was around $1.50. Some of the original battleship linoleum floor covering still was in use and in good shape after those 66 years.

During this period library requirements have, of course,
changed greatly. The Carnegie Library was added to successfully after some 25 years but is now completely outdated.
Although tentative plans for a second addition were made 45
years after the original construction, the college fortunately
did not carry them out, although this resulted in unsatisfactory congestion for many years. The 1908 building had an
unusual characteristic for that period. It was entered just one
step above the outside sidewalk and there was no basement.
The site was nearly level, with the water table close to the
surface as it is in much of Oberlin. The college had been able
to acquire land inexpensively when it was founded in 1833
because the area was almost swampy. Heating for the library
was provided by a new college central heating plant, so there
was no boiler room and the main electric switchboard occupied a very small area in the left-hand back corner of the
shipping and receiving room on the ground floor.

As was the case in most academic libraries constructed early
in this century, the central services were on the second floor.
In the right rear northeast corner of the building, there was
what today would seem an unduly small rectangular multi-tier book stack six levels high with the first, third and sixth
floors on the same level as the first, second, and fourth floors
of the building. The fifth stack level was reached by a ramp
from the third floor because the main reading room was two
and one-half stack levels high. The third floor was smaller
than the others and the ramp from it was unduly steep,
something that taught me the lesson that such ramps are
undesirable in a library, one which I hope I will never forget.
I once lost control of a loaded book truck on this ramp. It was
as unpleasant an experience as the time when I was pushing
a book truck through the reading room and it began to
squeak so badly that I fled into the book stack in embarrassment, leaving the truck in the middle of the room.

The main entrance to the building had a small vestibule
which widened into a large windowless lobby. On the right
were two rooms which were used for an open shelf library
for recreational and popular reading, available without ques-

tion to anyone, townspeople or students. There was a good selection of fiction and non-fiction and also a small general reference collection. The town of Oberlin contributed a very small sum toward the servicing of those rooms, and it became a joint college and public library, one of if not the earliest of its kind. The entrance lobby provided good space for library exhibits and bulletin boards. An inadequately sized men's toilet room opened off a small corridor leading from the right side of the lobby. Straight ahead from the front entrance was a large coatroom; at first there was an attendant but after a comparatively short time it was used unattended. In the first and second decades of the century, this was possible and even preferable because patrons did not have to queue up on rainy days when they were hurrying to go to classes, and possessions did not seem to disappear as they have done in later decades. Other and in many ways better arrangements for coatrooms have developed in later years. This taught me another lesson which was reconfirmed on my arrival at Harvard 30 years later, when I found an attended check room that was very little used and which was given up shortly thereafter, with other arrangements made for wraps, bundles and umbrellas. An academic library presents in this respect a very different problem from a public library, where users drift in and out throughout the day with no special pressure of peak loads between class hours.

Back of the check room there were two rooms, one on each side of a centrally placed back door which led to an interior staff stairway to the second floor. One of these rooms was used for temporary storage of new material and the other as a room for binding preparation, pasting, labelling, etc. In the northwest corner of the building was the small shipping and receiving room already mentioned, and next to it on the west side were the rest-room for women and then a broad main stairway. There was at the left of the front entrance a pleasant children's room and beyond it a large corner room that was used for many years for faculty meetings as the most suitable room for that purpose available in the college.

The stairway to the second floor had a wide landing where

it turned back on itself so that at the head of the stairs one
faced toward the center of the building. The second floor
front had, for the full width of the building, a large reading
room, 132 feet long, with some 6300 square feet of space. It
had, for those days, a large number of large windows in the
center third of the front but the rest of the three outside
walls and two-thirds of the fourth had book shelves for
reference books. The last ten years of "Poole sets" and other
heavily used periodicals were shelved under satisfactorily
spaced windows placed eight feet above the floor. There
were long tables separated by a wide aisle down the center of
the room. The tables had very good table lights for that time
and there were ceiling lights as well. This area was three
bookstack levels high. Back of it, under the central court
already referred to, were the public catalogue, the reference
desk and the circulation desk and the current periodicals.
One entered the stack room by passing the reference desk.
Aside from that there was no stack supervision. The reference and circulation desks facing the service area also over-
looked and thus provided supervision for the reading room,
which was considered necessary at that time. The catalogue
stretched along the back wall of this service room and much
of the wall beyond the reference desk. It was divided by a
door leading back into the acquisition and catalogue rooms,
which were over the two rear rooms on the first floor. The
catalogue trays were among the first installed that could be
pulled out from either side, making it possible for the
cataloguers and the acquisition staff to use the catalogue
without going into the public area. This was convenient except on the rare occasions when persons wanted to withdraw
the same tray on both sides at the same time. In due course
the whole catalogue had to be enlarged and this ingenious
scheme, which I next saw at Harvard's Business Administration School library 30 years later, had to be given up.

In the far left rear corner of the building on this floor were
the administrative offices, with the secretary's room and the
librarian's quarters beyond it. In the secretary's room was the

switchboard, for it had been planned to have telephone connections between all parts of the library. But this never worked out satisfactorily. The librarian's office had a small toilet room attached. The office had ceiling-high shelves along the far wall and a desk some ten feet long and three feet across. Professor Root had realized that his old desk always had been full and hoped that by having one of this size he could manage better. I will speak about it again later on but should add that it was in use in the reference area of this floor, still in good shape after 66 years, when I last saw it.

Since the reading room was nearly three stack levels high, as was necessary in those days for large rooms in order to provide adequate light and air, the third floor was reduced in size by that space and by the glass-covered court above the central services room. This made it considerably smaller than the two floors below it. It was used for seminar rooms and at the head of the stairs there was a good sized lobby from which service could be provided for the top two floors. From here there also was a good view over the main reading room and over the opaque glass ceiling in the court to the book stacks on the other side.

The fourth and top floor was, except for the open court, the same size in the center as the first two floors. It had toilet facilities, two entrances to the sixth-level stack, both of which were kept locked, and more seminar rooms. Two of the large seminar rooms on the fourth floor originally were filled partly with newspaper stacks, with shelves with rollers which I found very useful for the thickly bound newspaper volumes. During the Christmas holidays we used the corridors on the fourth floor for work space in preparing new manila rope bundles of serials. The seminar rooms on both the third and fourth floors quickly filled up with books that more properly should have been shelved in the main stack. Thus I became prejudiced against seminar rooms, something that has stayed with me ever since and has affected the planning of a considerable number of library buildings erected throughout the country since 1950.

I will tell later in this chapter of my work in connection with the Carnegie Library in the summer of 1908. I was asked by Professor Root to work in the library in the summer of 1910 after my junior year and to take a complete inventory of its printed contents, checking the shelves with the shelf list. I had a classmate as my assistant, and between us we were able to complete the task. It was a big one because it had not been done for many years, mistakes inevitably had been made in combining the ULA collection and the college library two years before, and of course books had been lost or stolen in the preceding years. My assistant, unfortunately, became dizzy when he leaned or squatted down to one of the lower shelves. So I obtained plenty of exercise that summer working at what might have been thought of as a sedentary occupation.

It was a very useful experience for me, as I had to examine every title in the library. While I did not remember them all they made an impression on me and I have remembered many of the titles ever since. The advantage of being in Oberlin all summer and the fact that there was an intensive beginning French course from 7 to 9 each morning, 5 days a week, which I took with a first-class female instructor, was useful. I learned more French in the eight weeks of summer school than I had learned German in two full years under less competent guidance. Altogether it made a useful summer for me.

When I decided to be a librarian in August, 1905, I thought of library work as something that involved primarily reading and getting acquainted with books and obtaining information from them for the readers. As a boy of seven or eight I had become fascinated by a large red bound volume published in the 1870's entitled *Compendium of Knowledge.* I was amazed by all the information that could be found in it. I am sure I must have nearly worn it out. It seemed to contain a little of everything, including a World Atlas and a great many graphic and statistical charts. The charts were pie-shaped, in blocks, and in other forms. I pored over them day after day. A

generation later, when I was at the New York Public Library, I
became acquainted with Willard Cope Brinton, a consulting
engineer who wrote *Graphic Methods of Presenting Facts* and
other books and magazine articles on graphic charts and had a
great deal to do with promoting their use and making them as
popular as they now are. If I had not remembered the *Compendium of Knowledge* and had not done a good deal of other
reading, I might have been convinced that Mr. Brinton had
invented the whole idea in which he was wrapped up so
completely.

I was enthralled by the *Compendium* in spite of the fact
that I failed to comprehend much of it. I remember the map
of the United States, which was not drawn on the Mercator
projection scale, and I did not understand what the curve of
the earth did to a map of this kind. As a result I got into a
violent argument with my next older brother when I insisted
that "Maine was farther north than Minnesota" and I
thought I could prove it by placing a ruler across the page
and showing that the northern tip of Maine was higher up on
the map of the United States than the Lake of the Woods in
Minnesota. My family was amused by my attention to the
volume, and on my eighth birthday the verse prepared for
me included "and he took the Red Book from the shelf and
studied on statistics."

But to go back to library work. My sister "Net" (Miss A. B.
P. Metcalf, Oberlin, 1893) had in September, 1904, become
reference librarian at Oberlin, and the work that she did had
attracted me very much. I am sure that the fact that librarians might be involved in administration on a large scale
never occurred to me and was farthest from my mind when I
chose my profession. I have said often in the last 50 years
that I have done almost everything relating to libraries and
librarianship except reference work but this is not quite true.
From time to time between 1910 and 1937 I did manage to
do a little of it and I served for nearly ten years as Chief of
the Reference Department of the New York Public Library.
But it was an administrative position in fact if not in name;

during that time I signed many thousands of answers to reference questions mailed to the Library but always saying that our Information Desk or the Economics Division or one of the other divisions (as the case might be) had reported the following.

In December, 1905, Professor Root told me that he had a Christmas vacation job for me. He said that the library had accumulated a great mass of back files of newspapers and periodicals (many of them incomplete) which it could not afford to bind in regular library bindings. He had purchased a large roll, perhaps five or six feet in width and several feet in diameter, of heavy, stiff, reddish-brown manila rope paper and a bale of shoe strings. With a group of boys whom I was to select and supervise, he wanted me to sew this serial material together with the shoe strings and make manila-rope-covered bundles, using awls to punch the required holes. After showing me how it was to be done, he gave me a free hand. I selected a half-dozen friends, and we set to work through the Christmas vacation, except for Christmas and New Year's Days, in the library's shipping room and the basement-level corridor. Though I was in charge, I received the same pay (15¢ an hour) as the other boys. We were all interested in the assignment and the group worked steadily and consistently.

I still remember my excitement when I found among the material a copy of the Ulster County Gazette reporting the death of George Washington. But the anti-climax came when Professor Root disillusioned me about its authenticity as an original copy.

This task was repeated for the five following Christmas holidays, the last one being in 1911, when I came home for a vacation from library school in New York to take charge. I made enough money to buy the round-trip coach fare between New York and Oberlin, amounting to $22, by coming on the Lackawanna and the Nickel Plate Railroads instead of the New York Central train that would have cost $24. I was in a coach car filled with newly arrived immigrants from Ellis

Island, laden down with bundles of all kinds, and I didn't get very much sleep.

I was interested to find when I later came to the New York Public Library that it had tens of thousands of similar manila-rope bundles in its book stack. They were not sewed in but were covered by manila rope paper and tied up carefully. There are some 325,000 of these bundles in the New York Public Library research collections today.

This assignment gave me a good idea of the problems that arise in overseeing the work of others. Rather to my surprise I found it enjoyable, not only the first year but during those that followed, to spend my time assigning details to others and keeping everyone busy and interested all the time. This assignment was my first administrative experience and had much to do with switching me in due course into a lifetime in that branch of my profession.

Nearly three years later, when the new library building described earlier in this chapter was ready for occupancy, I was assigned to the task of supervising the move. I suppose Professor Root realized that I was the only member of his staff who knew where a great many of the volumes had been stored. This was before the days when motor trucks were available. The distance for the move was only a few hundred yards across the campus and it was decided to use hand carts for it instead of horse-drawn drays. We were able to borrow a half-dozen or more carts from stores around Oberlin which were less busy in the summer than during the winter months because most of the students were out of town. These carts were used ordinarily for the delivery of groceries, and carts resembling them still can be found in the downtown areas of many of our big cities. With Professor Root a plan was worked out to have the college carpenter construct boxes three feet long and a foot wide, with solid bottom boards and ends with handles but with thin plywood sides to reduce the weight, in which to carry the books. We were able to pile six boxes at a time on a hand cart, with a number on a 3-by-5-inch card on each box so that they could be unloaded and shelved in proper order in the new building. We arranged for chutes on which to slide the boxes down from one floor to another on the first four levels of the old building. Fortunately there was an elevator in the new one. There were, however, four serious problems:

1. To find books and to send them in the order in which they were to be placed in the new building. As already stated, I was the only person who knew where they were in the old one, the library having been overcrowded for years, and books being tucked in wherever an inch of space could be found.

2. To get them down from the top or fifth level of the old library, where a steep winding stairway provided the only exit.

3. We had to keep the Union Library Association collection, shelved separately in the old building, together and place it temporarily in the new building wherever we could find space, so that later it could be merged with the college library collection where space was reserved for it. The merger could not be done in advance because of the lack of space in the old building and the necessity of changing class marks and placing new book plates in the ULA material.

4.   The final problem was cleaning the books. At that time satisfactory vacuum cleaners were not available and the books were very dusty. The solution we adopted was assigned to my younger brother, Nelson. He took a book in each hand and slapped the two together as hard as he could out of doors, of course before they were taken into the new building. The one man on the regular college staff, William W. Foote, placed the books on the shelves in the new building. He left the library for a top position elsewhere soon after this.

Since I was in charge of a rather large enterprise, during the move I received 20¢ an hour for the first time.

I also had another source of income that summer. The move into the new building was made before all the doors

had locks. We were able to lock off the bookstack to which
the books were being transferred. But it seemed wise to have
a night watchman on duty and I was assigned the task, with
the understanding that I would sleep in the building with
one eye open. The critical point was the two top levels of
what was to be a six-level multi-tier bookstack but which had
not been erected. This space was used until the books had
filled the first four levels as a "temporary" home (it lasted for
nine years) for the Olney Art collection which had just been
given to the college. Richard Olney, the donor, had been
President Cleveland's second-term Attorney General and
later Secretary of State and the collection was valued at
$150,000. After the books had been settled on the lower
floors, I was put in charge of the heavy work of hanging the
pictures on walls which were 15 feet high (two stack levels)
and moving around floor cases and other things. There was a
large collection of art objects of various kinds, including
paintings in heavy deep frames and covered by plate glass.
Some of the pictures were very large and the hanging of
them was quite a strenuous task.

A committee of the faculty supervised the work and
helped with it. This gave me an opportunity to become well
acquainted with a number of the faculty with whom I had not
dealt before, although I probably already knew as large a
percentage of them as any college student because for the
three preceding years I had been putting away books and
was in frequent contact with the professors who used the
library.

I had a cot in the middle of the floor of what later became
the fifth stack level and slept there. The only direct access to
this space, except from the stacks below which were securely
locked, was up the ramp from the third floor, where there
was to be a door—not yet installed—leading to the fifth level.
There also was a fire escape door which on hot nights I liked
to keep open because the building was not air conditioned
and northern Ohio can be very hot on August nights. I
arranged to pile unused book shelves in both of the doorways

in such a way that anyone touching them would collapse the whole pile, which I was sure would wake me up. Of course, I was unarmed but that was not the problem in 1908 that it would be today.

I had another problem to face that seemed more serious then than it would be today—bats, one of which again and again flew in the open fire escape door over the pile of shelves and then back and forth through the room full of valuable art objects. I feared they would knock down and ruin a valuable object by mistake and spent many hours trying to drive them out of the room with a broom with no great success. It was more than 30 years later that a Harvard graduate student who had been a friend of my daughter in her Oberlin days came to our house in Belmont to see her and, finding me in old clothes and looking like a hired man, asked what could be considered embarrassing questions about my daughter's father. I never saw him again but a couple of years later he became famous because he had discovered why bats are able to fly what seems to be recklessly in the dark without harming themselves or other objects. Nature has equipped them with their own radar.

After the art collection was installed and the library material was in its new home, the regular staff had time to settle down in its work. Professor Root was ready to merge the Union Library Association collection with the college library. Again, I had a special assignment. As helpers I found town girls who had been in high school with me. The library processing staff, using two shelf lists, took the books that I brought to them from the ULA collection and made such changes on the catalogue cards and the shelf-list numbers and letters as were necessary to merge the collections. Then the girls pasted the classmarks on the backs of the books and placed in each volume a book plate showing its source and beside the book plate wrote the information required to show the book's location. I then reshelved the volumes in their new locations and did the minor shifting that was, of course, required. I was kept very busy. It was my first opportunity to work with girls of my own age and it provided additional useful experience, if not in administration then in something closely approaching it: the timing of work so that a fairly large force of young women was kept busy. I found it a bit different from my work with male students and I confess I enjoyed it.

The summer was a financial bonanza. I received 20¢ an hour for 8 hours a day, 6 days a week, and 5¢ an hour for being night watchman for 12 hours a day every day. It added up to about $60 a month.

Two weeks were left before school began, and a group of more than a dozen of my high school and college friends, boys and girls, with the mother of one of the boys as chaperon, hired a farmer with a hayrack to drive us down to Vermillion on Lake Erie. We had rented two summer cottages for very little money, one for the girls and the cooking and eating of meals, and one for the boys. During the stay each of the seven girls had the responsibility of preparing five of the 35 meals, each meal with a different boy, so there was no regular pairing-off. It was a great experience for me as my social life had been confined almost exclusively to my own large family.

The September house party at Vermillion was repeated the next two years. Six years later I married one of the girls, Martha Amanda Gerrish, whose father had been the Oberlin town engineer and many years before had installed the first town water-softening plant in Ohio, if not in the United States.

Chapter 5
Non-Library Activities
in High School and College
and Decision on Library School

Professor Root's course on the *Use of Libraries* naturally brought up the question of the proper preparation for library work as far as my college courses and reading were concerned. I asked him about it. He encouraged me to select as wide a group of subjects as I could. I followed his advice and took at least one course in every discipline taught at Oberlin except geology, physics, and fine arts. I signed up for a fine arts course one year but when, at the first meeting, I discovered that all the other students in the class were girls, I shifted to another field. I did not take a geology course because I could not fit it in with my program but I acquired a copy of the then standard geology textbook by Chamberlain and Salisbury and read it carefully and with interest. Beginning physics I had had in high school but I confess that what I learned from it is of little use 70 years later.

Professor Root did not discourage me from European and other foreign history, in which I had a special interest and in which I took more courses than in other fields. Oberlin did not have majors in those days. I did not feel the need of any further work in American History because of my previous reading and the fact that the American History professor, Lyman Beecher Hall, who still opened all class sessions with prayer and who had read the 9th and 10th editions of the Encyclopedia Britannica from cover to cover and remembered every word in them, did not have a reputation as an inspiring teacher.

I followed Professor Root's advice and took enough work in other disciplines so that I hoped that I would be able to understand the special vocabularies of each and be able to do reference work in all fields. As an indirect result, I have always been a generalist rather than a specialist. In spite of this planning, I never did become a reference librarian.

I took Professor Root's courses on the *History of Printing* and *Book Illustration* which have been useful throughout my life, although I never could claim to be an authority in these fields. They made me realize that the book arts were fascinating and I was able in 1916-17, when I was acting librarian at Oberlin, to teach all three of Professor Root's courses without getting into much trouble.

My chief regret about my formal undergraduate education lies in the field of languages. After four years of Latin in high school, with Virgil in my senior year, which I greatly enjoyed, I decided to take at least a fifth year, or the first year of college Latin as it was called. This proved to be a disappointment due, I felt, to poor instruction, although I liked and admired the professor as a man. I had two years of German, having had none in high school, and while I found pronunciation comparatively easy I learned little except during one of the four semesters, when I was allowed to study the language at Oberlin Academy, where there was a better teacher than was available in the college. After that I felt that I should not waste any more time on it. I did take a full year of college French in an intensive summer school course in 1909, following my junior year while I was working full time in the library. I found French pronunciation very difficult but my five years of Latin made it comparatively easy to read.

Although I must admit that my language work was completely inadequate for one who was to work in large academic and research libraries throughout his career, what I had taken did enable me to pass the entrance examinations for library school, which at that time required a reading knowledge of French and German. For a good many years at the New York Public Library I was able to (or at least I did) take the final responsibility for book selection in all languages using the Latin alphabet and I initiated the selection for history, literature and all the humanities except the fine arts and music. I found Dutch and Portuguese particularly difficult, and to a lesser degree the Scandinavian languages.

During my senior year, at my suggestion, Professor Root permitted me to broaden my experience by taking charge of the circulation desk one evening a week and the reference desk another evening. During the latter evening there was an older assistant at the circulation desk so I was not the top staff member in the country's busiest college library during the time of its heaviest use. But I may have complicated a problem that I had to face six months later after I graduated from Oberlin, which will be related in another chapter.

Any specializing that I did was in history, particularly European and world history. Much of that interest stemmed from my early reading and was greatly increased when in the spring of 1908, in Professor William Stearns Davis' course on *Europe After the Fall of Rome,* he said to the class the morning after the announcement that Austria had taken over Bosnia and Herzegovina that this marked the beginning of a general European war. Few of us realized at that time how true it was. I remember the great impression it made on me, although most of the class seemed unconcerned. Although I was only a sophomore, Professor Davis was good enough to break the rules and let me take his seminar in Italian Renaissance the next spring, which theoretically was open only to seniors. He left Oberlin for Minnesota that next year and was succeeded by Albert Howe Lybyer, a man who had taught at Robert College in Constantinople, as it was then called, and had completed his PhD at Harvard under Archibald Cary Coolidge. Professor Coolidge in 1910 became the director of Harvard's library. I took a course with Professor Lybyer his first year at Oberlin and, probably because of what Professor Davis had told him of my work the previous year, he asked me the next year to correct the weekly reports from his students in German history since the Napoleonic Wars. I also took a Russian history seminar with him, one that had not been given before at Oberlin and in connection with which I had to prepare a bibliography. The library was not well supplied with material in the field as it had practically nothing in the Slavic languages. But in the bibliography I missed an important long article in one of the French encyclopedias and others in the big French biographical dictionary.

While I am sure it rather pleased Professor Lybyer to catch me out, it also made me feel that library school would be good for me and it took me down a bit. I had a second seminar with Professor Lybyer the summer of 1912 when I was back in Oberlin, this one on Asiatic history, which again was new for Oberlin. Both of these courses broadened my background in ways that have proved useful ever since.

I was not interested in what was thought of as "pure science" and chose dendrology, which is the identification of trees with and without leaves, evolution and first-year chemistry. Dendrology and evolution were among the first

courses in those subjects taught in American colleges and I
enjoyed them. Genes had just been discovered and caused a
good deal of excitement. Two of my closest high school and
college friends, Otis F. Curtis and Laurence MacDaniels,
were in the dendrology course. Neither one had done work
in high school that would have admitted one to a good
college today. But the dendrology instructor, Professor
Frederick Grover, got them so interested that they specialized in botany, went to Cornell University Agricultural
School and became well-known scholars and heads of their
respective departments (MacDaniels, by the way, was captain
of Oberlin's football team his senior year and in three years
playing against Cornell, one game was lost by six points, one
was tied, and the third was won by Oberlin).

My third close friend was President King's third son,
Donald S. King, of whom I have spoken already. Don, after
graduating, went to Harvard Medical School and became
one of Boston's best known specialists for pneumonia,
pleurisy and tuberculosis. Forty years later he came to my
sister Antoinette's rescue when she had a blood clot in her
lungs and he was called in, to my delight, by her general
practitioner.

I avoided physics and botany since I had had one year of
each in high school but took a first-year course in organic
chemistry and, for some reason that I cannot explain, did
well in it. My work in mathematics was confined to a year of
trigonometry and analytical geometry, which today often are
taught in secondary schools. I had some aptitude for
mathematics and would have gone on to calculus and other
advanced mathematics except that when I was working in
Montana in the summer of 1907 with a surveying party, I
heard of a fairly advanced engineer who was discharged
because he solved his problems with higher mathematics
instead of using the formulas in the engineering textbooks.
As I was not expecting to use mathematics beyond budget
making, I decided against further work in the subject.

My English courses were freshman English with Professor

Wagar, thought of as the best teacher in the college, another
one with him on Victorian literature, for which I read practically all of Ruskin, Newman and Matthew Arnold, and others
as well, and a third in Elizabethan literature under a young,
comparatively inexperienced teacher, who announced at the
first session that he never gave a mark higher than a "C" to a
member of the football team, which seemed to be directed at
me. His Elizabethan literature lectures inevitably involved
English history, an area where, wisely or not, I thought I
knew as much as or more than he. As a result we frequently
had arguments and I did well to get the "C" which he had
specified at the beginning. I found out years later, when I
was acting librarian at Oberlin, that this English literature
course, together with the senior Bible which I also will mention, resulted in my standing 23rd in my class of 176, of
whom only 22 received Phi Beta Kappa keys.

Here I might also mention the course on musical appreciation, for which I had no aptitude. Before the final examination, when I found I could not read my notes, I wickedly
borrowed those prepared by Martha Gerrish, whom I later
married and who was a born musician and an appreciator of
music. I received a higher mark than she did, which placed
her 24th in the class, immediately after my 23rd.

My philosophy and ethics courses went well enough, although I enjoyed them less than any of my other college
work except for that in foreign languages. The compulsory
freshman Bible course was enjoyed because of the unusually
fine teacher, the father of "Bob" Hutchins, who later became
president of the University of Chicago and then head of the
Center for the Study of Democratic Institutions in Santa
Barbara. My senior Bible course was taught by President
King himself. But his papers were corrected by an assistant
whom I had always disliked. Perhaps as a result I received a
low mark which helped keep me from receiving a Phi Beta
Kappa key.

I was very much interested in my social science courses in
economics, sociology, social relations and labor relations,

which were taught by A. B. Wolfe, who later went to Ohio
State University. He tried to get us interested by making
what seemed to a conservative youngster outrageous statements. But all the courses proved to be useful throughout my
library career.

Another discipline in which I was particularly interested
was government or political science, as it then was called at
Oberlin. The professor, who had a German graduate education and doctorate, was in many ways very good and inspired
more of his students to go on to graduate work than any of
his colleagues. But he often irritated me because he seemed
to lack a feeling for figures. In speaking of budgets he would
use one million dollars when he meant ten, or twenty-five
million dollars instead of two and a half. Only a few years
later when World War I broke out, he provoked numerous
faculty members and trustees because of his defense of Germany. Fortunately President King prevented his discharge.

Let me close this section by saying that my high school and
college courses and experience gave me a far better preparation to take advantage of the library school that followed
than most budding librarians receive. It never occurred to
me to take snap courses or be interested in grades but I
followed my natural interests as far as I could without going
against Professor Root's advice.

As far as my social life was concerned I will be brief. In the
winter of my junior year in high school, Martha Gerrish (the
oldest of five daughters of the village engineer) and Keyes
Metcalf apparently were the only persons in their class who
had never had a "date." I do not believe that either of us was
ugly or disagreeable; it was simply shyness. One winter day in
our junior year, as part of a conspiracy or practical joke, a
girl unknown to me sent me a note signed "Mart," the name
by which Martha Gerrish usually was known. Mart received a
note signed "Keyes." Each note said that the one writing
would be interested in a "date." As a result, we met and while
we realized it was a put-up job, we agreed that the boys in my
class already mentioned—Otis Curtis, Laurence MacDaniels

and Donald King—would spend an evening together at Mart's home and she would make fudge for all of us as well as three girls she invited. As it turned out, we all had a good time, found that we all loved to skate, and from then on very frequently had good times at the skating rink. This continued for six years with the same boys but with different girls except for Mart. In three of those years, a week or ten days was spent (as already mentioned) in two adjoining cottages on Lake Erie in September before school opened, with the girls in one cottage and the boys in the other and the mother of one of the boys as chaperon. A number of our college classmates joined us to make up a group of 10 or 12.

Each of the boys except myself finally found girls who had not been in the original group but we had fine times together dating, or "fussing" as we called it in those days, which was something that was quite different from today. In order to keep the group from breaking up into regular couples, a different boy and girl each time had the responsibility for preparing meals and three or more times during the period each of us had the opportunity to get well acquainted with a different person. In the six years before I graduated I saw more of Mart than any other girl but it never occurred to me even to hold Mart's hand, except when it was necessary for skating, or to indulge in any other form of intimacy. I probably spent an average of from three to six evenings a year at Mart's home with her (not even the movies in those days) and dancing and cards were prohibited at Oberlin at that time.

We had perhaps two class parties each year that we attended and there were several evenings (generally at Mart's) with the four boys and such girls as the other boys suggested. That was the limit of my social life except that Mart and I would often study together at the library in the evening and I would walk her home. I had promised my sister, Marion, who had seen too many college engagements fall through, that I would not become engaged before I graduated and neither Mart nor I ever talked in any way about marriage and she was genuinely surprised, I am convinced, when on

the evening of Commencement Day I asked her to marry me.
She accepted but that evening, as all too often, she had a bad
migraine headache and was quite unsure of herself later; it
took a week for me to convince her that she had accepted.

As for athletics, during the three years in high school and
four in college I tried my best to become a good football
player. I was hard muscled and reasonably fast on my feet
and loved the sport. But that wasn't enough. I did earn a
football letter in high school, although I played all of only
one game, 10 minutes in another and five in a third. In
college I played with my class team for two years and played
with the varsity team for five minutes against Ohio State
University in my sophomore year. I was a regular my last two
years, always a disappointment to the coach but kept in the
game because the coach thought I knew the rules better than
anyone else on the team. He gave me the task of protesting to
the officials when I thought that they were wrong. He even
left me in charge of the team one day when I was incapacitated with a dislocated left thumb and he had to scout Ohio
State for the game which was to decide the state championship. In that Ohio State game, my last, I was fortunate
enough to block a kick that I caught with my hands and
stomach. With a clear field in front of me and a chance to run
for the winning touchdown, I dropped the ball. The game
ended 0 to 0 but we still held the state championship because
Ohio State already had lost one game to an Ohio team, while
we had not. But I did not become a football hero.

In basketball, the only basket I made was in a game with my
class team. I was halfway down the floor with the ball
when friends rooting for the other team called out to me to
try for a basket. By some unbelievable luck—I already had
missed shot after shot—it went in without even touching the
rim.

Being left-handed I tried to be a baseball pitcher but had
to give it up because my arm went lame as the result of a
football injury.

In track, which I never really enjoyed, the results were

entirely different and I have several claims to fame. At Notre Dame's indoor track in 1910, I had dirt kicked in my face by two Notre Dame high hurdlers when they broke the world indoor record in a 50-yard race. I also tied their two high jumpers, who were the best in the country that year and regularly jumped several inches over 6 feet, at 5 feet 9 inches. At that time a group of small boys, 12 to 15 years of age, occupied the bleachers beside the jumping pit in a corner of the building. Boys of this age enrolled at Notre Dame as well as college students at that time. They were so amused by my strange, untutored jumping style (Oberlin had no track coach) that they laughed uproariously when I landed full length after each jump with my face in the dirt. The amusement was catching and the Notre Dame jumpers laughed so hard that they could not do themselves justice. I also became a runner and in my senior year, when I was captain of the track team, won both the high and low hurdles as well as the high jump in the State meet. Altogether I became known as a good track athlete, though I never felt I earned the title.

My other non-curricular college activities have been recorded, except that I was class treasurer my junior year, a member of the student senate and one of the five members of the student honor court my senior year, when the court had an unusually busy time dealing with cases of cheating in examinations reported to us. I might add that, though this was 1910-11, the college authorities always accepted our recommendations for punishment, so that in this respect Oberlin was not behind the times.

During my senior year my eyes had begun to trouble me when I read for long periods. My oculist told me that the use of a little eye stimulant could get me through my senior year without glasses. After that, he said, I probably would not be reading so much that I would have to worry about it. But I learned differently. By the time the playground where I was working in Youngstown closed on Labor Day my eyes were bothering me so much that I acquired glasses with steel frames and the small lenses that were in use at that time. I

used these until middle age, when bifocals were called for. I
was advised that glasses would trouble me less if I wore them
all day long every day, although I needed them only for
reading. I followed that advice except when I refereed football games. I have worn glasses ever since but I find now at
90 I can read comfortably without glasses for the first time in
more than 65 years. I suppose that means that I am not only
an anachronism but have reached my second childhood.

Early in my senior year I asked Professor Root for advice
about library work after graduation. He had known for six
years that I was planning a library career. He said I might
apply for work in a large library, such as the Library of
Congress, where many of the department heads had not
gone to library school, and that I could work up to a position
such as that held by Charles Martel, the library's classification
expert, for whom he had great respect. But he suggested that
it would put me several years ahead in my chosen field if I
went to library school. He said that my years of library
experience were desirable before library school. I then asked
what library school he would recommend, although I had
taken for granted that I would go to the New York State
Library School at Albany, which Melville Dewey started after
his school at Columbia was thrown out when the university
discovered that it admitted women. A large percentage of
men with library school training had, in the past, gone to
Albany and this was still the school chosen by most men.

Azariah, who was very much interested in library education, said without hesitation, "Go to Pratt" (the Pratt Institute in Brooklyn). I knew about Pratt because my sister had gone
there. Azariah continued, "Pratt is the place for you to go
because Mary Wright Plummer is in charge and she's the best
person in the field." He might have added (and I think he
undoubtedly had this in mind) that at least a year in a big city
would be a good experience for me. I am sure this turned out
to be the case because I had been brought up in a small town
and had gone to a small town college and was completely
ignorant of city life.

From my study of the different library school catalogues (there were only a handful of schools at that time) I knew that Albany based its selection of students largely on college records and that graduation with reasonably good marks was the chief requisite for admission. Pratt admitted by examination on the theory that, even as late as 1911, in an occupation where women predominated, college graduation should not be the major criterion for admission because there were good prospective candidates for library school who did not have college degrees. Pratt required good marks in five examinations—general history, general literature, general information, and a reading knowledge of French and German. I also learned from my sister that classes at Pratt were limited to 25 and that something like 75 to 85 persons applied each year and that quite a number of them who had failed the examination the previous year had spent the time in between preparing for re-examination. It apparently would be far more difficult for me to be admitted to Pratt than to Albany. Naturally I was a bit frightened. In the early spring the Pratt examination papers were sent on to Professor Root to supervise my work in taking them. I thought I did reasonably well, although I was not sure at all about my language translations, which I feared might prove inadequate.

A college faculty committee, with the dean of the faculty as chairman, made a study of the efficacy of the education it was providing in the spring of my senior year. It asked all the students to fill out questionnaires, giving among other things the time spent by each student in class, in laboratories, and in study preparing for classes. I truthfully reported that I had no laboratory work that year and was spending only 10 hours a week studying. I was not asked about extra-curricular activities. But I had been a regular on the football team, captain of the track team, a member of the student honor court, and had corrected papers for the head of the history department. In addition, I had replaced on the shelves all the books used in the country's busiest college library. Theoretically, the questionnaire was unsigned and completely anonymous but, as I learned later from Professor Root, my wretched handwriting gave me away. At least partly as a result of my answers the faculty decided that it was being unduly lenient in its whole educational program and later generations of Oberlin students suffered or gained, as the case may be.

But to go back to my library school examinations: I was notified promptly to my great pleasure, if not surprise, that I had passed them and was admitted to Pratt for the year beginning in September, 1911. A few weeks later, however, I learned that Miss Plummer (on whose account I had applied to Pratt) had resigned in order to take charge of a new library school, to be financed by the Carnegie Corporation at $15,000 a year for five years. It was to open in September at the New York Public Library, which was moving that same month, May, 1911, into its new $10,000,000 building (a tremendous sum for those days) at 476 Fifth Avenue. This building had been in planning and construction for 14 years. With Professor Root's approval, I wrote to Miss Plummer and asked if I could apply to the new school and give up Pratt.

Miss Plummer had introduced an examination system in New York similar to the one at Pratt. To my surprise and pleasure, she replied that I would be admitted to the new school and, since I had passed the Pratt examinations, would not have to take the new set. I might add that when the school opened I found out that I was the only male in a class of 40 and realized why I was admitted apparently with no hesitation. Should this be called "male chauvinism" or something else?

During the months before the close of the college year, several other opportunities presented themselves that might have taken the place of library school. Amateur Athletic Union (AAU) representatives from a half-dozen different cities in the Midwest and Eastern United States telephoned or wired to me suggesting that I agree to represent them on their track teams, promising that all my expenses in first-class hotels (along with a liberal expense account) would be paid and that I would be required to enter only one event each week instead of the four or five to which I had been accustomed. In addition, I was approached by one of the good Ohio liberal arts colleges in regard to a football coaching position (this was at a time when a college had only one coach instead of a group of them as they have today). I had no difficulty in turning down all the athletic offers, much as I was interested in athletics. For some 25 years thereafter I did referee football games regularly every fall for high schools, preparatory schools, and small colleges in Ohio, New York, New Jersey and Pennsylvania and for several years had charge of the Westchester County, New York, high school track meets. My younger brother was the head football coach at Columbia University from 1915 to 1918, and spent the rest of his time until retirement in physical education and related athletic fields. I occasionally took a Saturday off from refereeing to scout games for him while he was at Columbia, which gave me an opportunity to visit Amherst College and Wesleyan University among others. I found that while I thought I made a good football referee when my primary task was to follow the ball, I was not so successful as an umpire or scout; my primary training in football was keeping track of the ball. This did not help me to watch over the conduct of 22 active and often excited men at one time. This experience turned out to be very useful in library administration.

Officiating brought some interesting experiences. In a football game in Ada, Ohio, between what then was called Ohio Normal University and Lehigh University, I was faced by a problem not covered in the rule book which I could not figure out. It resulted from a 50-mile gale blowing a kicked ball back onto the playing field after it had landed behind the goal line on the play that decided the game. My decision was displeasing to a small mob. Another day, while refereeing at New York's Polo Grounds in the final game for the New York City area high school championship, I found that the

game between these teams the year before had ended in a
riot with the crowd piling on to the field. This year the stands
again were full but a large contingent of police surrounded
the field and the only untoward incident came when I was
mistaken for a player and had the wind knocked out of me. I
had to call "time out" for myself, which I found just a bit
embarrassing. Luckily the head linesman that day was a
former coach at Oberlin, at that time a student at Columbia's
College of Physicians and Surgeons. He brought me around
quickly (I might add that he later married a niece of mine).

I found in refereeing that the best way to avoid trouble was
to make difficult decisions without hesitation and to execute
them with no delay. I remember a Westchester County game
in which a star player became so unduly rough that I removed him from the game and got him off the field so fast
that no one had time to complain or contest my decision. The
next time I heard anything about this particular player was
when I read that he had become captain and an All-
American quarterback at Notre Dame.

I am sorely tempted to go on with my athletic reminis-
cences. I will say only that, while I received a good liberal arts
education at Oberlin, my experience in athletics, especially in
football and track, stood me in better stead in library administration than any of my college courses. I doubt that this
would be true if my library work had developed along other
lines.

I should admit that during my college years there were two
other developments besides athletics that tempted me from
library work and library school. I have always enjoyed outdoor life, even though at 16 I had chosen to become not a
farmer but a librarian. In the summer of 1908, following a
course in dendrology, I became intensely interested in forestry, which Gifford Pinchot, working with President Theodore Roosevelt, then was promoting. During my long, long
evenings as night watchman at the Oberlin library I read
everything I could find on the subject. The deeper I dug into
it, the more I realized that if I were to spend a lifetime in
forestry and were to become anything more than a field

worker, I must learn a great deal more about the basic biological sciences, something that I decided I was not prepared to do. Nor did I want to get into a position where in late middle age I might stagnate.

My other temptation came from Professor Albert H. Lybyer of the history department at Oberlin, who later occupied a similar position at the University of Illinois and for whom I corrected papers throughout my senior year. When he learned that I planned on librarianship as a career, he tried to persuade me I would make a better librarian if I went to graduate school first and acquired a PhD in History. Only a few years earlier he had received his doctorate in history at Harvard working under Archibald Cary Coolidge who, in 1910, had become the director of the Harvard University library. Professor Lybyer told me that he had written to Professor Coolidge about me and that there was a fellowship available for me in Harvard's graduate history department which would make it possible for me to go on for graduate work. If this had been 1940 or 1975 instead of 1911, I suspect Professor Lybyer would have been right. But I am not completely convinced for I feared that specializing as much as one has to do to receive a PhD in history would tend to make one so much of a specialist that it would be difficult, if not almost impossible, to give equal emphasis to other disciplines as I think a chief librarian should. At any rate, I turned down the offer and have wondered often if I would have ended my active career as director of the Harvard University library if I had gone to Harvard and taken my doctorate there before—or instead of—going to library school. To pay my expenses I would have had to work on the side while studying and undoubtedly I would have been given an opportunity to work in the library under Professor Coolidge.

I overcame all of these temptations—athletics, forestry, and graduate work in history at Harvard—and in September, 1911, I joined the first class of the Library School of the New York Public Library.

Chapter 6
Library School in 1911
and
Back to Oberlin in 1912

Late in September, 1911, I set out for New York City with a very heavy suitcase and a typewriter that dated back to the 1880s and had belonged to my future mother-in-law. As I remember it, it seemed to weigh "a large part of a ton," but I was convinced it would be useful in my library school work.

This was to be my first venture alone in a big city. I had written to one of my college friends, Donald M. Brodie, who had just started in at the Union Theological Seminary, and he had invited me to share his room until I could find a place to

78

stay. He met me at the New York Central 125th Street
Station, and we managed between us to walk a mile with my
baggage to his room near Broadway and 122nd Street, following 125th Street most of the way. That street then was a
prosperous retail center to which the large downtown retail
stores were considering moving as more convenient and
closer to their clientele than their downtown locations.
Within a very short time, with what later became a ghetto
moving in, the street changed in character and its very bright
prospects disappeared.

Don had the morning newspaper advertisements for available rooms and went with me to investigate those in the
Columbia area. We soon found a possible room on West
123rd Street, not far from a small farm complete with a cow
that often could be seen grazing on a hill-top close to Broadway. It was the area later used by the Jewish Theological
Seminary and its library. The second-floor room had one
window on a narrow inside court of a five-floor walkup and
cost $2.50 a week. I shifted a week later to a slightly larger
room at the end of the court with more air that cost $3 a
week. The landlady was a pleasant elderly Swedish woman
whom I saw only once a week when I looked her up to pay
my rent. The room was clean and the house quiet. I met
none of my neighbors. Don then introduced me to a board-
ing house primarily for Columbia graduate students where I
could get an adequate breakfast and evening meal for $3 a
week. After two nights at Union, I was ready for the library
school which I had looked in on the day before.

To reach the New York Public Library all I needed to do
was to walk half a block to Broadway, then down the hill to
the 129th Street stop of the Van Cortlandt Park branch of the
Interborough Subway or up the hill to the 116th Street
Station, catch the downtown train to Times Square and then
walk a short quarter of a mile to the 42nd Street entrance of
the New York Public Library. The library school had its
quarters in a large basement room with windows facing Fifth
Avenue and with a row of columns parallel to Fifth Avenue

which divided the room in two. Forty student desks were set in ten rows facing 40th Street, with two desks on each side of a central aisle.

Miss Plummer's desk was in a small alcove jutting out to a window on the Fifth Avenue side of the room in front of where the students sat. My first impression of her was that she was overly dignified. Though I sat within 20 feet of her, when she wanted to talk to me she would have one of her assistants bring me a note. But I found her a very capable and understanding woman, as Professor Root had said she was. Her assignment, in addition to being the principal and thus in charge of the entire enterprise, was to organize the curriculum, bring in outside speakers from literary and library fields, and then get her students interested in modern literature. That was an area in which my busy Oberlin years had left me decidedly deficient. As a result, in her foreign literature course the German, French, Italian and Russian fiction that I read in English translations during the next few months was more extensive than the English fiction I had read up to that time.

I was surprised by the frankness of these books but it contributed a good deal to my education. My previous fiction reading had been chiefly boys' books, such as practically all of G. A. Henty's historical stories (which formed the basis for my comprehension of history from early Egyptian times to the present), such standard American and English authors as William Dean Howells, Hawthorne, Scott and Dickens, and less well-known novels obtained from Sunday School libraries in Elyria and Oberlin and from our rather extensive home library.

Miss Plummer had four able full-time assistants. One was Agnes Van Valkenburgh, who had come from the Milwaukee Public Library and taught cataloguing and indexing, book selection, and, for the first years, classification and subject heading, technical French and German, and later trade and national bibliography. She was a large, heavily built woman with a good sense of humor and was a real human being. She seemed to keep a special eye on me as the only man in the class and did not hesitate to call my attention to the fact when I carelessly neglected food spots on my coat, warning me that I should watch out for my appearance. Within two weeks she announced that one of the girls and I had turned in the best catalogue cards, something that for me was understandable as I had had far more library experience than anyone else in the class. A little later she told me that my handwriting was so impossible that she was going to select me as her assistant to help correct the work of the others. Miss Van Valkenburgh stayed with the school only five years and, after a year with the H. W. Wilson Company, became librarian at Bay City, Michigan, where she died prematurely in 1920.

The next in rank was a remarkably fine woman and superb teacher, Mary Louisa Sutliff, who had had 20 years' experience with the New York State Library, teaching in the library school there for six years, before going to head the catalogue department at the California State Library at Sacramento. She stayed with the school until 1926 and then followed it to Columbia, where she continued to teach for many years, admired and loved by hundreds of her students. At the New York Public Library School, she taught reference and bibliography and later classification and other subjects. Many students came to think of her as a personal friend.

Ernestine Rose had graduated from Wesleyan in Connecticut in 1902 and was left without an alma mater when the men in the college a few years later made things so unpleasant for the women that it changed to a male institution for some 60 years before going "co-ed" again only a few years ago (will history repeat itself?). She had graduated from the New York State Library School and worked as a branch librarian in the circulation department of the New York Public Library at Chatham Square in the Chinese district before putting in five years on the library school staff as registrar and supervisor of practice work. Later, after a year as assistant principal at the Carnegie Library of Pittsburgh library school, she returned to New York to head the 135th

Street branch of the New York Public Library circulation
department and become a specialist in work with blacks,
responsible in due course for that library's famous Schom-
burg collection and a leader in the field.

Miss Plummer's fourth full-time assistant, Catherine S.
Tracy, after graduating from Pratt and gaining experience
in various libraries, including a year in the reference department of the New York Public Library, came to the school
as librarian of the school collection and school bibliographer
and taught the history of printing, cataloguing of early
printed books, technical German and French. In addition to
these four, Margaret Bennett was secretary-stenographer for
the school and instructor in typing, a field in which she had
little success with the writer of this volume.

In addition to the regular classes, most of which were held
in an inside basement room, later used by the photographic
department that developed rapidly in the 1920's, we had
talks and lectures by some of the library's division chiefs. I
remember particularly those given by Dr. Charles C. Williamson, who had recently taken over the economics division
of the library. He had received his Doctorate at Western
Reserve and had been one of Carey Thomas's "bright young
men" whom she took on for a few years at Bryn Mawr and
then passed on to other institutions. More will be said about
him later.

During the fall term of 1911 and on my return to the
school from January to June, 1913, a large number of the
senior librarians in the country spoke to us, including Herbert Putnam, William Warner Bishop of the Library of Congress, Lutie Stearns from Wisconsin, and George B. Utley,
then secretary of the American Library Association and later
librarian of the Newberry Library. Literary lights such as
Louis Underwood, Percy Mackaye, Jessie Rittenhouse and
Alfred Noyes came; most of them were good friends of Miss
Plummer and all of them were eye-openers to me.

I have always felt that the instruction and inspiration that
the library school faculty provided me was better than most

library schools give today, largely because the instructors had had a great deal of practical library experience before coming to the school, were not dogmatic, and encouraged discussion. Members of the two classes in which I had my first year's work were unusually good material with which the school had to work, as is often the case with the first classes in any school because they tend to be made up of students who have come there believing that it will be new and different. Because of my extensive earlier experience, the work was easy for me. I spent less time on school work than most of the other students but I was not critical enough by nature to become bored with doing things that were not new to me. It also gave me more time to become acquainted with the city, in which I was much interested. I believe that the New York Public Library school in its first years provided the kind of instruction that many of us in the last 65 years have complained that our library schools were not giving. I believe that the students received the kind of instruction that Dr. C. C. Williamson recommended in his famous Carnegie report years later. We were taught the basic principles but not dogmatically. Our curiosity was aroused and we went out into the library world realizing that there still was much to learn. Underlying it all was the realization that greater knowledge of books must be sought for as long as we lived.

Outside of school my life was largely spent during the months remaining in 1911 in becoming acquainted with the city as far as I could within the bounds of a slender budget. The city was very different in 1911 from what it is now. The Grand Central Station was not completed. The New York Public Library central building, which had been opened only the previous May, stood out among the neighborhood four-story brownstone front buildings that had been built as private residences. It was the tallest, as well as the largest, structure in the area. The streets were busy as they had been for years with the streetcars and buses, and, believe it or not, with more horses than automobiles. Occasionally I stood at the corner of 42nd Street and Fifth Avenue and counted the

makeup of traffic; it was in November, 1911, that I first
found more automobiles than horses, a situation that has not
been reversed since then.

I made it a point to walk from 42nd Street to my room on
123rd Street, a distance of about five miles, the five days a
week I was at the school. In spite of the traffic and the
crossings, I could make it in less than 75 minutes. While
generally I walked about half the distance in Central Park, I
often took the few extra minutes required to go other ways,
following each of the north and south avenues from Fifth to
West End from time to time. Saturdays and Sundays were
spent chiefly in walking, with frequent attendance in different churches. I counted on a good 50 miles a week in all. I
went by ferry to Staten Island, most of it then rural in
character, to Ellis Island where immigrants were taken in
large numbers before coming into the country, and to the
Statue of Liberty, which I climbed (and found the next day
that the high steps had unexpectedly made me lame), to
Washington Heights and Van Cortlandt Park, to New Jersey
and the New Jersey Palisades by the 42nd Street, Fort Lee
and Dyckman Street ferries, to Brooklyn to Prospect Park,
and out to Coney Island. I visited the wilds of Queens and
the northern part of the Bronx, in each of which I was lost at
one time or another, out of sight of human habitation. I
walked on Broadway from Columbia down to the Battery.
My lunches would be a sandwich and perhaps a chocolate bar
picked up from a street handcart on the Lower East Side or
in an Automat. It took me quite a few weeks to get up
courage enough to go into one of the Automats for the
first time. They were so brightly lighted that I feared they
would be too expensive. The subway fare was 5¢ in those
days, so carfare was not a serious matter.

I did not forget about the Metropolitan Museum and the
American Museum of Natural History, which were the first
and still the largest and most interesting ones that I have ever
seen in spite of the wonderful success of Boston's Museum of
Science. The Aquarium at the Battery, the American Geo-

graphical Society, the New York Historical Society, the Bronx Botanical Garden and the Bronx Zoo also were exciting. I particularly remember a walk on the East Side one Saturday during a garbagemen's strike, when the garbage covered the sidewalks and spilled out into the streets. For the first time in my life I began to read daily newspapers regularly, the New York Times or the Tribune in the morning and the Evening Sun or Post in the afternoon. I frequently walked up and down Riverside Drive in the evening, enjoying the handsome view of the Hudson River and both of its banks.

At library school very soon we began to have practice work. I was assigned to various divisions of the reference department; first, to file cards in the economics division under the direction of William Seaver, the first assistant there, who later became the head of the Massachusetts Institute of Technology library, and Charles C. Williamson, later director of Columbia's University Library and its library school. The second was the American History Room with Mr. Helbig, who had a strong German accent that tended to enrage American history scholars, and his young assistant, Sylvester Vigilante, an Italian boy who worked there from his schooldays until retirement some 50 years later, and who already knew the collection and readers better than anyone else in spite of his lack of formal education. I worked in the map room, where I was overwhelmed by the great collections and by the knowledge of William Elliott, again a man who had acquired that knowledge without a formal education. The climax came when, as a special favor, I was assigned an afternoon with Wilberforce Eames, the greatest bibliographer the country has produced, in the rare book division. He also had little formal education but had received numerous honorary degrees. I was awed by his knowledge of books and his remarkable memory.

Toward the end of October, Miss Plummer told me that the National Guard Armory at 33rd Street and Park Avenue was considering hiring someone to catalogue its library and asked me if I would be interested. The work could be done any time, evenings if preferred. At the beginning of November I undertook the assignment, which proved to be an easy one. There were a few military books and some fiction in English. My chief problem was writing clearly enough so the cards could be read without difficulty. The library was on the mezzanine level, immediately adjacent to the large main floor but with no window opening so I could not see what was going on there but could hear it.

My special memory of the whole experience was overhearing a dance going on one evening. It was soon after Irving Berlin had written the music for *Alexander's Ragtime Band,* which was at the height of its popularity. As soon as the dancing began that selection was played. The crowd insisted on encore after encore for at least an hour, with tremendous applause greeting each performance (I might add that after my return to the school in 1913 I went to the Armory again and saw there my first exhibition of modern art and paintings, including the Nude Descending a Staircase and a number of Picasso paintings which I, as an anachronism, must confess were even farther beyond my comprehension then than they are now, and that is saying a good deal).

Writing my recollections of this period reminds me of the Saturday when I took the 129th Street ferry across the Hudson and, on reaching the landing at Fort Lee, walked north on a path fairly close to the river at the foot of the Palisades. Just as the bank grew very steep, I heard a tremendous noise above me and in a moment a group of cowboys on horseback came rushing down the hill. Only then did I realize that I was witnessing a "Wild West" movie being made for the Biograph Company, which I believe then had its headquarters in New York or near at hand.

As the term began to draw to a close I did some careful figuring to decide whether it would be cheaper to stay in New York, paying my board and room there for two weeks, or spend train fare to Oberlin and return, living at home and working in the library, binding periodicals and newspapers into bundles as I had done during the previous six years, to say nothing of seeing my family and Mart Gerrish. It ended by my deciding to go to Oberlin which, as it turned out, had an important effect on my career.

The work in the library went along as in earlier years but I soon learned that Professor Root, the librarian, had planned to take the second semester, from the first of February until college opened in September, as a sabbatical abroad to continue his studies on the origin of printing from movable type and try to answer the question of whether Koster or Gutenberg came first with movable type. One evening my sister Anna (Mrs. Root) told me—almost whispered to me—that Azariah was afraid he could not leave because on his staff, which was then made up entirely of women, he could not find one who was willing to assume the responsibility for taking charge of the library during his absence. Between us we decided that my sister should tell her husband that I would be willing to undertake the assignment and the next day he asked me if I would give up library school for a year to serve as executive assistant in the library during his absence. I accepted immediately on condition that the school in New York would grant me leave of absence and that I could go to New York to pick up my possessions and to talk to Miss Plummer. He said he would see Miss Plummer at the American Library Association mid-winter meeting in Chicago and might be able to reach an agreement with her. So I returned to New York the last day of the year and spent the next few nights at the YMCA headquarters of the Columbia College of Physicians and Surgeons on West 57th Street, where a number of my Oberlin friends were living. Not realizing what went on in New York on New Year's Eve, I went to bed early and was wakened at midnight by a tremendous noise coming from all directions. That was my introduction to the year 1912, which was to be of interest and value to me in my work in years to come.

Professor Root saw Miss Plummer in Chicago, and on her reluctant approval of a year's leave of absence, I settled my affairs in New York, entrained for Oberlin again as soon as I could, and reported for work at the Oberlin College library before the end of the first week in January. Professor Root took me into his office to show me his 10 ft. x 3 ft. desk piled high in neat stacks averaging three feet in height and covering the whole desk except for one section at the middle of one side about two feet deep and three feet wide and occupying only one fifth of the total square footage, which he had reserved so he could sign his correspondence and write notes. Although he could write legibly with either hand, he had a stamp made with his signature on it (the right-handed one) which he told me I was authorized to use on official correspondence followed by my initials. We then plunged into the task of clearing his desk. That took us the rest of the month of January. Clearing his desk taught me a lesson about the problems that can arise from letting material pile up and putting tasks aside because there always seem to be other things to do that are more important. As a result, in future years I kept my desk reasonably clear until nearly the end of my regular library work in 1955, and at least I looked over everything on my desk every day so that I knew where I stood. More of this later.

At the end of the first semester (about the end of January) Professor Root and his wife left for Haarlem in the Netherlands and Mainz in Germany to do research on the origin of printing from movable type. The Oberlin library staff understood that I was to use his desk, carry on the necessary correspondence, sign all the letters ordering new books, etc., and work with Miss Fraser, the order assistant, on the selection of new English and American books. We were to rely on faculty recommendations for foreign book selection. My one restriction was that I must keep within the budget. I would, of course, consult with the staff on problems which arose in connection with other operations. But the final responsibility was in my hands and I was to be called the Executive Assistant.

It took less than 24 hours for me to learn why Miss Spaulding, the senior member of the staff, and all of her juniors had refused to become acting librarian. The afternoon after Professor Root's departure from Oberlin, a faculty meeting was held at 4 o'clock. After the meeting closed a telephone call came from President King asking me to come to his office. On my arrival, he told me that the faculty had discussed the library situation and had decided that the students were so accustomed to whisper and talk to each other in the large reading room that it was not a good place to study. The faculty had voted that there should be no more talking or whispering except in obtaining help from the staff. Since I was in charge I was responsible for putting the faculty's action into effect immediately.

I was too overwhelmed to protest. I knew that Professor Root was fond of the students and liked the freedom in the library, and that their talking had not disturbed him. He concentrated so easily on whatever he had in mind that he probably had not noticed what had happened in the past year and a half since my sister, Antoinette, had gone to Wellesley. She was a strict disciplinarian and by force of character had kept things under control during her regime as reference librarian. I realized that I had done most of my small amount of studying in the reading room the previous school year and had done as much talking as the others. Because of my library work I knew practically everyone in college except the freshmen; the college on the average had only about 200 in each of the three upper classes.

The president announced his new rule at chapel the next day. How was I to carry out the orders given me by the president? I immediately had large signs printed saying simply "SILENCE" in large letters. These were placed on top of the eight-foot high bookcases which surrounded much of the reading room. I confess that they tended to disappear but not at the rate they would have 65 years later.

I took my place in the reading room at 9 a. m. and stayed there except during the lunch and dinner hours until 9 p.m. I asked anyone whom I saw talking or whispering to another student to leave the library for the rest of the day. For a second offense, one day was added to the penalty, and for the third, a week. Somehow the problem was resolved without a fight or even a quarrel even though many of the victims were good friends of mine. I kept this up for six weeks, ignoring almost all my other duties.

This was one of the most terrible experiences in my life but I did quiet the room down. When I returned to Oberlin again in September, 1916, as acting librarian, the room still was quiet. I should, of course, admit that the "SILENCE" signs became collectors' items. Can you imagine a similar situation happening today without a revolution or at least a protest on the part of the students? "The world does change."

During this time Mart Gerrish was working with the Associated Charities in Cleveland, 35 miles away, with only an hour's street-car ride between her office there and Oberlin. She came home every other weekend, which made a pleasant interlude for me as the library closed at 5 on Saturdays and was closed all day Sunday. I was living with my sister Marion, who had brought me up after my parents died, so I was not completely alone during the week. My brother Nelson was a senior in the college and roomed in the new men's dormi ory with Don King, the president's son, with whom I had roomed two years before.

After the six-week-long nightmare in the reading room, things quieted down and I caught up with the book selection. As noted, I kept my desk clear then and later, a practice that proved especially useful when I went to Harvard 25 years later, where I used a desk large enough to have kneeholes on all four sides but did not do as well. (It was the desk that Justin Winsor, the first president of the American Library Association, had purchased soon after he became librarian of Harvard College in 1877 and he had chosen such a large one because he had a great interest in maps and indeed for many years had a superstructure on top of the desk which he could use in connection with the maps).

Any spare time that I found was spent in going through the 40,000 uncatalogued pamphlets that I had alphabetized seven years earlier, picking out those that I thought should be catalogued. This was a fine experience for me. I found in the lot half a dozen pamphlets in a language that I could not make out, although they had been published around the middle of the last century, in Washington State. I still can remember the gleam in Professor Root's eye when I showed them to him the next fall and his telling me that they were the first printing west of the Rockies and undoubtedly had been taken to Hawaii when the press on which they were printed was moved from what later became Washington State to the Islands. Some 40 years later the pamphlets had been picked up there by Oberlin's president, James H. Fairchild, who went to Hawaii for a visit in 1885 and on his return to Oberlin brought back with him a large amount of printed material which he had acquired by gift for the college library.

(To finish this particular story, I should say that the next year, while back at library school and doing practice work with Wilberforce Eames again, he showed me the New York Public Library copies of the same pamphlets, which had been printed for the Congregational Mission Board, the American part of which was called the American Missionary Association and the foreign part the American Board of Commissioners for Foreign Missions. These pamphlets were translations of chapters of the Bible made by our missionaries, who then printed them in an American Indian language which up to that time had never been put into writing. During my Harvard years I was able to complete arrangements for the gift by the American Board of Commissioners for Foreign Missions of its archives to Harvard. In that very valuable collection we found a third set of this series of pamphlets.)

Among my memories of the spring and summer months of 1912 three stand out. The first was learning of the sinking of the Titanic. Little did I realize that as a result of it the building in which I was to have my office 25 years later would be built. The second was something that I did not think of again until 21 years later and that did not come to mind thereafter until I was writing this chapter and read in the newspaper of the death of Raymond Moley, one of President Franklin D. Roosevelt's chief advisors. A young man, two or three years older than I, came into my office early one July day and introduced himself as Raymond Moley. He told me that he had accepted a high school teaching assignment with two conditions: that he must take some education courses, which he was doing in the Oberlin College summer school, and that part of his teaching assignment was to coach the football team. He never had played football and had no interest in the game but he had been referred to me as someone who might help him out. This I agreed to do and at a number of conferences I tried to explain some of the basic principles of the game and to give him such hints as I could about dealing with the boys. It was evident that he was not interested in the assignment and he seemed to me a bit colorless. But when the papers began to speak of him in connection with his work for President Roosevelt, I naturally looked up his quite distinguished career. Then I forgot about him again until I read of his death the day before I wrote the first draft of this paragraph.

The third event, about which I had been warned before Professor Root started on his sabbatical, follows.

He told me that nearly every year he expected to have a visit from two or more Mormon elders (The Church of the Latter Day Saints), who would ask to see a manuscript which I would find in the library safe. Some called it *The Manuscript Found.* Others called it *The Manuscript Story.* It had been written by Solomon Spalding and had been given to the Oberlin College library by Oberlin's president, James Harris Fairchild, who had received it in 1885 from a Mr. L. L. Rice. I then remembered that in April, 1899, when I was just ten years old, I came home from school with a splitting headache, the first one I can remember having had. I was reading in Henry Howe's two-volume *Historical Collections of Ohio,* which was published in 1888, while I was waiting for the doctor. He determined that I had scarlet fever and the volume was taken away and fumigated and I was told I could not see it again for a year. Quite naturally, I suppose, I forgot about it. In it was the story about *The Manuscript Found* which said that Joseph Smith had in some way got hold of the manuscript and from it wrote his *Book of Mormon* which is the Mormon Bible. This was in his New York State days.

Professor Root said that the Mormon elders would ask for this book and that I was to watch them carefully and see to it that they did not mutilate it or try to walk off with it. In due course, two Mormon elders arrived. I took the volume from the safe. They examined it and then left, saying it was very evident that it had nothing to do with Joseph Smith's *Book of Mormon.* I forgot about it for nearly sixty years.

In the early 1970's, Elinor and I were spending our vacation, as we had been accustomed to do for many years, at Beechknoll in the Catskill Mountains near Phoenecia, New York. Evelyn Craig, who was in charge there, suggested I might be interested in a volume on the Catskill Mountains. I read the book with interest and found a chapter about Solomon Spalding which repeated the story that I had read in Howe's *Historical Collections of Ohio.* This, of course, reminded me of my experience in 1912 and I wrote to Oberlin to ask if anyone there ever had looked into the problem in more detail than had been done when I saw the manuscript in 1912. The reply came that nothing had happened. But in 1978 the librarian wrote me that he had just heard of a book published in California (a paperback volume) entitled *Who Really Wrote the Book of Mormon?.* I sent for the volume and found that the authors had studied the problem and decided that there were two Solomon Spalding manuscripts, one called *The Manuscript Story,* which was the one in the Oberlin College library, and the other *The Manuscript Found,* which they claimed had been the source used by Joseph Smith in writing the Mormon Bible. This manuscript had disappeared completely and they had been unable to find it but were convinced that it had been used by Smith.

I am certainly not enough of a scholar to have any opinion

about it. I write about it here simply as an example of coincidences in which I have been involved.

When I was asked to coach the freshman football team, which took only a few hours a week as they did not practice every day, I accepted and took part in scrimmages several times, playing fullback against them to try them out. After football season I went to the gymnasium regularly and ran a mile or so around the indoor track there. This kept me in good physical condition to start the new year in New York.

During the summer before Professor Root came back I had two other interesting experiences. He gave me an opportunity to take a new seminar course under Professor Albert Lybyer whose papers I had corrected during my senior year in college; it was on Asia including both the Far East and what we now call the Near East and, with the one that I had taken the previous year on Russia, it gave me some knowledge of Asia concerning which I had been uninformed earlier except for what I had learned from the Bible, and by reading Swinton's *History of the World* and the volumes of G. A. Henty's historical novels, several of which dealt with Asiatic countries. While I greatly enjoyed the seminar and I profited by it, it did not change my attitude toward trying for a PhD in history. I did hope that an opportunity would come sometime to take one more course somewhere which would have given me an AM, a Master's Degree, but as will be seen in Chapter 3 of the second part of this volume, this never came to pass.

Professor Root came home in time for the opening of the college year in September, 1912, and my responsibilities were reduced until I returned to New York to rejoin the library school at the beginning of January, 1913. Working full time under Professor Root gave me the opportunity to learn many new things about the library and my profession.

I look back on the 18 months following my graduation from Oberlin until I returned to library school in January, 1913, as particularly valuable training for library work. They included my playground work in Youngstown in the summer of 1911, the first term of library school, and the year in Oberlin as executive assistant in charge of a very busy college library. The variety of the work, the acquaintance with new methods of life and different types of people, as well as an unusual degree of responsibility under difficult conditions, proved to be excellent training for the years ahead and I began to feel prepared to be a full-fledged professional librarian.

Chapter 7
Return to Library School
and
Work at the New York Public Library
January 1913–July 1913

When the winter term at the New York Public Library library school began in January, 1913, I started just where I had left off in December, 1911. The courses had not changed but this time there were four other men among the students, each of them very different from anyone I had been acquainted with at Oberlin or elsewhere. The senior in age in the group was Herbert Collar, a Dartmouth graduate who had been a first-class quarter-mile track man (on which he blamed his chronic dyspepsia), of whom I will have more to say later when he came to my rescue at a difficult time. He later became assistant librarian at the Grosvenor Library in Buffalo. I was particularly interested in him, in spite of his rather pessimistic disposition, perhaps because I found that his father was one of the authors of Collar and Daniel's Beginning Latin book that I had used in high school 12 years earlier and because he had a sister who was at the Pratt Institute Library School when my library sister was there. He died while still comparatively young.

The next in age and experience was Foster Stearns, an Amherst graduate with a Harvard AM. His father was a member of the R. H. Stearns Boston department store family and later was a close friend and sponsor of the man who became President Calvin Coolidge. Foster became librarian at the Boston Museum of Fine Arts immediately after finishing library school and four years later was named State Librarian of Massachusetts. This created much controversy as it was felt he obtained the position because of his father's influence. He resigned the position and volunteered for the Army in World War I and came back with his hearing severely affected by working close to the big guns. This handicapped him the rest of his life. On his return he served for a while as the librarian of the College of the Holy Cross in Worcester (he had been an Episcopal clergyman but had been converted to Catholicism). He later went into the diplomatic service and also represented New Hampshire in the United States House of Representatives for three terms. He received a number of foreign and American decorations. He was a member of the American Antiquarian Society and the Club of Odd Volumes, to which I also belong, and used the Boston Athenaeum where my second wife, formerly Elinor Gregory, became librarian in 1933. We both saw him from time to time until his death in 1956 at the age of 75.

The third of the men was Frederick Goodell, who apparently had not been to college. On completing his library school work he went to work in the circulation department of the New York Public Library as a branch librarian, as did the fourth in the group, Forrest Spaulding, who temporarily took charge of the circulation department's traveling libraries. Goodell went into War Library work when the First World War began and later entered the real estate business in Detroit; I never saw him again.

Forrest Spaulding, the youngest and in many ways the most interesting in the group (he was three years younger than I), had been expelled from a number of preparatory schools and had not gone to college but had a tremendous interest in books and already was a collector. He had had an exciting year's experience in the Newark Public Library under John Cotton Dana. After library school he served as the branch librarian in one of the busiest of the New York Public Library branches, Seward Park. He resigned that position to take the librarianship of the Des Moines Public Library and then, after some War Library work and after having been in charge of the Merchant Marine library, he accepted what seemed to be a very attractive position as Director of Libraries and Museums in Lima, Peru. This did not turn out as expected; his salary was not forthcoming. He returned to the United States and served as consulting librarian and secretary of Gaylord Brothers, a library supply house in Syracuse, N.Y., for five years, and then returned as librarian to Des Moines, where he continued for 25 years. When he was approaching retirement age he returned to the library in his home town of Nashua, N.H., where there was no mandatory retirement age and he could continue more or less indefinitely. While in Des Moines he also served successfully as a representative of the American Library Association in Washington, trying to obtain federal support for libraries; he laid the foundation for legislation passed in the 1960's. He also served a term as a member of the American Library Association Executive Board and as president of the Association's Public Libraries Division. In his Nashua days, which lasted until his death at 73 in 1965, he was a member of the Club of Odd Volumes in Boston and I saw him from time to time. He was an unusually good example of how a man interested in books but with comparatively little formal education could become a very useful librarian.

Although I had had much more library experience than any of the others, all four of these men were inclined to complain about the instruction in the library school, particularly that of Miss Van Valkenberg and Miss Tracy. They also argued in class, so that Miss Van Valkenburgh, normally easy-going, was apt to become somewhat provoked at them. In addition to our association at the school, we often lunched together on West 42nd Street, either at Drake's, where all the fresh rolls we could eat came with an inexpensive meal, or in a restaurant at the rear of a saloon in the same area, where we also could get an inexpensive meal but where we gave up going when one of us found a piece of fish in what was supposed to be Hungarian goulash.

From time to time we also had dinner together in Greenwich Village or on the Lower East Side in restaurants that O. Henry had described and where, for the first time in my life, I saw my friends consuming considerable quantities of alcoholic drinks and where once, much to their amusement, they managed to put one before me which I thought was ginger ale until I tasted it. Again my background was widened.

Whenever possible I continued to do a good deal of walking. I had a very small, plain room, just large enough for a bed, a bureau, a small table and chair and a clothes closet, opening on to an inner court and quite a walk from the only bathroom on the sixth floor at the West Side YMCA, on West 57th Street close to Columbus Circle. I could get a good, inexpensive breakfast there. My lunch generally cost more. But later on, when I went to work from 5 to 10 at night, I contented myself with a sandwich at a nearby Automat before going to work and then, when I reached my room at about 10:30 P.M. after walking the mile to the YMCA, I would consume some fruit, an apple, figs or dates purchased from a street stand on the way and often would devour part of a plain, dry loaf of bread.

Before I obtained this work, I spent my evenings reading English translations of foreign fiction, which were readily available at the YMCA library, presided over by Silas Berry (25 years later I learned that he was the father of a Harvard professor who was at one time dean of the Harvard Engineering School and lived not far from me in Belmont and with whom I became good friends). Finding that the YMCA had a track meet every Saturday evening, I took part in races on three Saturday evenings, at 600 yards, 1000 yards and two miles. I had no difficulty winning at the first two distances, running just fast enough to win. But apparently this aroused suspicion and I learned later that the organization had looked for the best two-miler they could find in the area and I was pitted against him in that race, one I never had run before. Although I was able to keep up with him until the last lap, I might say he then ran me off my feet. That was the end of my racing career, although (as noted earlier) I did referee track meets later on. One evening when I found some of the other men high-jumping, I arranged to have the cross-bar put up to an even six feet and cleared that height without difficulty. This was three inches higher than I ever had been forced to do in any of the track meets at Oberlin. So I realized that I must have been in pretty good shape.

The night work referred to earlier was obtained through Miss Plummer, who realized that I had time hanging heavy on my hands at the school. Mr. Lydenberg, the chief reference librarian, had told her that someone was needed every evening to check off the call slips for the books that had been used during the day and evening in the main reading room. I do not know who preceded me in the work but evidently whoever had the assignment had not been successful with it. My start on February 12, 1913, a day then celebrated in New York as Lincoln's Birthday, turned out to be the busiest day in the library's history up to that time. At 5 o'clock I found a large box of call slips sorted only into the 20 odd main classes. The inside shelf which ran continuously on both sides of the circulation desk was some two feet wide and I found it piled high with books. The pages, taking advantage of the evening meal hour, had cleared the tables in the 768-seat reading room of the books left there by readers. I went to work to arrange the books roughly by class mark and then arranged the call slips the same way and checked them off. The books were placed on book trucks which were four feet long, with one or more of the shelves on each side corresponding to the upper stack levels from which they had come. When a shelf was full, I placed the books on one of the four book lifts that connected the stacks with the reading room and notified the boys on each level to call the lift and remove the books. What happened to them after that will be related in a later chapter.

At the same time I watched the pneumatic tubes in which the call slips came through from the information desk, as the reference desk in the public catalogue room was called, and when there was no one else around (which was much of the time) I divided the slips by stack level and sent them down to the stacks. The books continued to pour in and I kept the pages, who apparently had been accustomed to standing around waiting for someone to ask them to do something, at work helping me. The Swedish evening supervisor, Einar Dekke, was very helpful and somewhat amazed at the way things went.

There were two book check-out stations, one on each side, as the reading room was divided in two by the desk, with 384 seats on each half. Each of these desks had a regular assistant who took the books brought by the pages from the book lifts, compared them with the call slips, and stamped the slip with the time that he had received the book. The slips had been stamped at the information desk when they had been turned in so that the time spent in making a book available could be checked. The window on one side was manned by a very capable, pleasant young man named Harry Haskell, and the other by a "moonlighter," Leroy Jeffers, who was in charge of book purchases for the circulation department and who worked nights to earn enough money so that he could

afford a mountain-climbing vacation. Jeffers had the reputation of buying standard American books, such as are regularly
acquired by public libraries, with a one to five percent larger
discount than anyone else in the country. The result, as I
found out six years later when I took charge of the reference
department order division, was that dealers were irritated to
such an extent that he was not notified when special bargains
were available, and in the long run it was not a profitable
arrangement for the library. This taught me a lesson which
proved useful in subsequent years. To go back to the evening
of February 12, I was able to get the pages interested in what I
was trying to do and, to the surprise of all concerned, we
cleared up the accumulated books and left only a small shelf of
unchecked ones which could be dealt with easily the next
morning by the day-time staff. My experience with the boys at
the Oberlin library in moving the books into the new building,
plus my years in athletic contests with boys playing together as
a team, had stood me in good stead.

The evening work continued to go successfully and the
Sundays, from 1 to 10 instead of 5 to 10, were always busy
because of the large number of persons who had extra time
at their disposal on that day, to which were added many
students from local colleges which in 1913 were not open on
Sundays.

I kept up this schedule of 38 hours a week, in addition to
my full library school work, until April, when I caught a cold
which I had a hard time shaking off. Miss Van Valkenburgh
and Miss Sutliff realized that I was below par physically and
suggested that I ask Herbert Collar, my classmate, to take the
evening hours three days a week, which he was glad to do.
For the rest of the term, which ended in mid-June, he took
my place every other week-day night, much to my relief in
spite of its effect on my thin pocketbook. I was getting $50 a
month for this work when I worked the 38-hour week, or
approximately 30¢ an hour, but it was very good experience.
On one Saturday that I had off Miss Van Valkenburgh and
Miss Sutliff, realizing that I liked to walk, suggested that we

spend the afternoon together walking in the fields that could be found near Englewood, N.J. I remember with great plea-sure the afternoon and their kindness to me.

With Collar's help, I finished the library school year in good shape and with enough acquaintance with the school and the library so that I had no question about continuing for the second year of library school if I could find a satisfac-tory position and so could afford to go on with it. For the first school year, I received a certificate. If I took the second year, I would be given a diploma for carrying out the following series of assignments:

1. Attendance at a comparatively small number of clas-ses, with a good many outside lecturers who sometimes gave a series of talks.

2. A considerable amount of practice work in various parts of the central library, much of which my position (if I had one in the reference department) would fulfill.

3. A lesser amount of extra unpaid work in the various parts of the circulation department. These included cen-tral circulation, the busiest of the branches, which was in the main building, some work in the central children's room, which had a large collection of books used chiefly by parents looking for material their children might use from the collections in the branches, and work in two of the busiest downtown East Side branch libraries, Tompkins Square and Seward Park, where the population at that time was largely Jewish and where I had my first all-kosher meal in a local restaurant.

4. I was also to visit branches in other parts of the city.

5. In addition to this practice work, I would have to write a thesis and visit libraries in Washington and Boston, going either by myself or with the rest of the class (I chose to go alone and will write of it later).

I was told I could do the required work without its interfer-ing with my regular library assignments by working in the stack on my regular half-day off and some extra evenings and Sundays as well, thus leaving time for the other school assignments. The story of my obtaining the position of Chief of Stacks is told in a later chapter. I took it with reluctance as I had hoped for a regular reference assignment and at the same time decided to go on with the second year of library work. You might say I had no other choice as no other position had been offered me either at the New York Public Library or elsewhere. At any rate I decided that my basic training had been completed and that when I became Chief of Stacks I would be a full fledged librarian beginning a professional career.

Part II

Part II
The New York Public Library—1913 to 1937

Introduction

The New York Public Library, Astor, Lenox and Tilden
Foundations, dates from 1895 and was the result of the
consolidation of
   (1) The Astor Library, founded by the bequest of John
Jacob Astor in 1848 as a public reference library. It was one
of the four largest reference libraries in the United States in
1895.

(2) The Lenox Library, given by James Lenox for use by the public in 1870, ten years before his death. He had gathered together a remarkably fine collection of rare books. The library was used primarily as a museum for the exhibition of important books, specializing in early editions of the Bible, the history of the American Revolution, and various other limited fields. Shortly before the consolidation it had been opened for limited use by scholars.

(3) The Tilden Trust, which came from the bequest of Samuel J. Tilden, after a law suit by members of the Tilden family who had broken his will. Following long litigation, it provided $2,000,000 out of the $8,000,000 estate and a collection of 20,000 volumes to start a new public library.

Each of the three institutions had funds that were inadequate to provide for the purposes of the donors. However, if the Lenox and Astor buildings and the land on which they stood were sold, and their endowments combined with the $2,000,000 in the Tilden Trust, and if the city would agree to build a building which could be occupied rent-free, a reference library for the city could be provided with more than 450,000 volumes and what seemed at that time an adequate endowment. The consolidation took place after several years of discussion by the trustees of the three groups, led by John Cadwalader, Lewis Cass Ledyard and John Bigelow. A state charter was obtained and the city agreed to build a library in Bryant Park between Fifth and Sixth Avenues and 40th and 42nd Streets on the site that had previously been used for the Croton Reservoir. John Shaw Billings, who had been librarian of the Surgeon General's Library in Washington and later, between 1885 and 1895, was largely responsible for building up the great medical schools at John Hopkins University and the University of Pennsylvania, became the director of the newly-established institution.

The building which the city agreed to construct in 1897 took 14 years to complete from the time the contract was signed. During that time Dr. Billings strengthened the combined staff, added a great many books and pamphlets, and developed an acquisition program which has continued with comparatively few changes to this day.

Between 1900 and 1903 Dr. Billings was able to arrange with ten public circulating libraries in the boroughs of Manhattan, the Bronx, and Staten Island, most of which had branches, to join together and become the Circulation Department of the New York Public Library, supported by city funds. Andrew Carnegie agreed to provide funds for building 40 branch libraries to replace some of those already in existence and to build new ones. Separate libraries with their own trustees were organized about this time in Queensborough and Brooklyn. Arthur Bostwick, previously the librarian of the Brooklyn Public Library, became chief of the circulation department of the New York Public Library.

In 1896, Dr. Billings persuaded Harry M. Lydenberg to come to the New York Public Library instead of staying at Harvard, where he had worked during his college days with Justin Winsor. Mr. Lydenberg was given a variety of assignments in the Reference Department and, some time before the new central building was completed, he was appointed Chief Reference Librarian. In 1908 Edwin H. Anderson was brought from the New York State Library and Library School in Albany as Associate Director. In May 1911, Mr. Anderson arranged with Mr. Carnegie to finance a library school for the next five years and have its quarters in the new building at 42nd Street and Fifth Avenue. I enrolled in this school when it opened in September 1911, and finished my first year's work at the school two years later because I had spent the calendar year 1912 in the Oberlin College Library as Executive Assistant during the absence of Azariah S. Root, who was on sabbatical for nine of the twelve months. In July 1913, after five months as part-time assistant at the main reading room desk, I began working full time. This followed eight years of preparation, seven at Oberlin and one in the New York Public Library, as well as summer work which had given me a variety of experience. I had spent four summers as a hired man on farms in Ohio or in Massachusetts, one on a railroad location surveying party in Montana in the Bitter Root Mountains, one running a playground in Youngstown, Ohio, and two in the Oberlin College Library. Each of the two Oberlin summers had provided challenging assignment, one in moving into a new building, and the other in taking an inventory of the library.

The chapters in the second part of this volume will deal with my work in the New York Public Library and outside assignments between July 1913 and August 1937, when I went to Harvard.

CHAPTER 1
The Men I Worked Under
in the
New York Public Library
from 1913 to 1937

Mr. Anderson and Mr. Lydenberg, to whom I reported during the 24 years after the beginning of what I considered my professional career as a full-time member of the staff of the New York Public Library, worked closely with the board of trustees. I reported to both of them until Mr. Anderson retired in 1934, and then to Mr. Lydenberg only.

The Trustees

I never met formally with the trustees, even after I became Chief of the Reference Department in January 1928. I think it never occurred to Mr. Anderson or to Mr. Lydenberg to ask me to attend the trustees' meetings, and I never ventured to bring up the matter. My informal contacts with individual trustees were few and far between. I had no opportunity to see the first three presidents of the board. The first, John Bigelow, died in December 1911, at the age of 95, just as I was completing my first term in the library school, and the next two died after serving only short terms. The fourth president, Lewis Cass Ledyard, took office in 1917 and continued until his death 15 years later. He had taken a leading part in the consolidation of the Astor, Lenox and Tilden Foundations and was one of the most influential men in New York and perhaps the country at large. He worked quietly behind the scenes, and kept out of the newspapers. He probably had as much to do with stopping the 1908 depression as any other individual, by insisting that the J. P. Morgan Company, with its large resources, enter the stock market when it was rapidly falling and the country was in despair. In the 1920's he refused to permit the library to conduct money-raising campaigns, although there was considerable pressure from the staff in that direction. At that time he said that the library would be better off by obtaining large gifts, which would amount to more than could be obtained through a public campaign. He approached well-to-do individuals and as a result many millions came to the library, seeming to prove that he was correct.

Six million dollars came in 1922, and my indirect connection with that will be dealt with later. The 1920's closed with a $14,000,000 bequest from the Payne Whitney estate. Mr. Ledyard had been largely responsible for Mr. Whitney's will. There were a number of other gifts of $1,000,000 or more between the two large ones just mentioned. Mr. Ledyard left $3,000,000 in his own will, which I understood was the sum that he received as Payne Whitney's lawyer. One of my recollections of personal contact with Mr. Ledyard is of the occasion when a library doorman did not recognize him and asked him to open his brief-case at the Fifth Avenue exit. I

had a difficult time cooling both of them down and preventing the discharge of the doorman. I also remember that I
took some papers to his apartment for his signature and he
offered me a cigar. I declined, saying that I did not smoke.
He looked up at me and said, "What, no vices?"

During the nearly 19 years that I was in the administrative
suite of the library from 1919 to 1937, I went to the treasurer's office at the United States Trust Company from time
to time. It was perhaps New York's most conservative bank. I
did not see Mr. Sheldon, the library's treasurer, but many
years later I became acquainted with his nephew, who arranged with his mother to provide funds for Harvard's Sheldon collection, which made possible the construction of a
special theatre exhibition room in the Houghton Library in
memory of Edward Sheldon, the dramatist, who was another
nephew. This room since has been transferred to the Pusey
Library. Mr. Sheldon's assistant, with whom I talked at the
United States Trust Company, always stood up at his old-
fashioned accountant's sloping desk as was the custom in the
19th century.

I did meet Elihu Root, Senior, when he came into the
library's 40th Street entrance for a trustees' meeting and lost
his way. I found him wandering about in the bookstacks,
recognized him from newspaper pictures and escorted him
to the trustees' room.

John Finley, the father of Harvard's well-known professor
of the same name, whom I later came to know, was then a
trustee and also editor of the *New York Times*. He often came
in the 40th Street entrance before the library opened in the
morning and would stop at my desk to ask for suggestions as
to where to find information for which he was looking. Mr.
Finley had the custom of walking all the way around Manhattan Island on his birthday each year, even after he was 70
years of age.

My other direct contacts with the trustees were not completely satisfactory. Samuel Greenbaum, a very useful trustee, came in to see Mr. Lydenberg on behalf of a young

woman who had complained to him that she had applied for
a position for which she was sure she was well qualified, but
had been turned down because she was Jewish. As the personnel officer to whom she had applied, I was questioned
and was able to produce the application blank,
which gave no indication that she was Jewish and said she had
been born in Spain. I also had a list of the persons employed
during the preceding six months, and their names indicated
that nearly half of them were Jewish. Then I showed that
there had been at the time no vacancy of the kind for which
the young woman had applied and that there still was none.

Another trustee came to my office one day, saying that he
had been told that one of the fine reference assistants, a
woman, was not paid as high a salary as men with similiar
qualifications. At the time and for a good many years later,
the Reference Department had no official graded system for
the staff. But I had one in my desk, based on education and
other qualifications, that I used when I talked with each
professional member of the staff about salary and prospects
for the future, as I made a point of doing once every year.
Without disclosing the salaries of others, I was able to show
where the staff members fitted into the salary scale. I gave to
the trustee the salaries of the male librarians of similar education and training. I was able to tell him from memory the
salary of the person with whom he was concerned and who
the others were who had the same salary or one a little higher
or a little lower, and I then showed him my graded system
sheet and he was satisfied.

I might add at this point, with the full realization that 1930
presented a very different situation from the 1970's, that it
was during the 30's that New York City regulations for employees paid by the city had forced an open payroll for the
Circulation Department and that one of the senior members
of its staff had to spend practically full time talking with staff
members who were unhappy because their salaries were
lower than those of some of their friends. The Circulation
Department had an official printed graded system and an

open payroll. But as I have already indicated, the 1920's and 1930's were a different world from today, as I think most of us now realize.

My other contact with a trustee is reported in the chapter on my deciding to go to Harvard in 1937.

Edwin Hatfield Anderson

When I began work checking off books on their return from use in the main reading room in February 1913, Dr. John Shaw Billings was director of the library, but he went to the hospital for a cancer operation later that week and died within a month. I remember Mr. Lydenberg's telling me years later that when Dr. Billings left his office for the last time, they quietly shook hands, both apparently feeling that the director would not return. It was Mr. Lydenberg who asked me if I would be interested in the reading room position and he arranged for the full-time position that I took as Chief of Stacks in July that year. But it was Mr. Anderson who proposed both positions after consultation with Miss Plummer, the principal of the library school.

Edwin Hatfield Anderson was Director of the New York Public Library from May 1913 to November 1934, when he retired voluntarily two months after his 73rd birthday. There was no set retirement plan at that time and no pension plan. Mr. Anderson lived on until 1947, when he was almost 86. He was born on September 27, 1861, in the little town of Zionsville in central Indiana, not far from Wabash College, from which he was graduated in 1883 and later received one of his five honorary degrees.

I never learned what E.H.A. (as we called him behind his back) did between college graduation and attending Melville Dewey's New York State Library School, where he spent most of the academic year 1890-91. (During the 23 years that I knew him, for 16 of which I was in his office daily, we never talked about personal matters and I went to his house only twice, and then on library business.) He left library school before the end of the year without waiting to receive a degree because he had the offer of a position as cataloguer in the new Newberry Library in Chicago from William F. Poole (of Poole's Index fame). This was followed by three years as librarian of the Carnegie Free Library, Braddock, Pennsylvania, after which he shifted to Pittsburgh, where in ten years he gathered together as fine a staff as could be found in any public library in the United States. He printed the library's catalogue, one of the last and best printed catalogues to appear in book form until recent years and one which was much used by other libraries for book-selection purposes. For some reason, again unknown to me, he then left library work for a year or more to take employment with a zinc and copper mining company in Missouri; in 1906 he was asked to take Melville Dewey's place as librarian of the New York State Library and to be head of its Library School.

Mr. Dewey, who had been responsible for many developments that helped to bring about important features of the present American library system, had been discharged from his position at the New York State Library under controversial circumstances about which librarians still disagree and which I shall not try to go into, although I could write a long chapter of gossip about them. At any rate, Mr. Anderson was asked to take Mr. Dewey's place, which he did. He stayed only two and a half years, during which he brought to the library and the school three men: James Ingersoll Wyer, who replaced him; Frank K. Walter, who helped keep the school at the top of the country's library schools during the next 12 years, and Frank L. Tolman, who stayed on in various capacities for 40 years.

In 1926 the Library School was shifted back to Columbia, whence it had come when Mr. Dewey directed it there. I have been told that Mr. Dewey had been discharged from his Columbia position when the trustees of the university discovered that through his efforts the Library School (which was the first in America if not the world) had been admitting

women. Columbia was then for males only. It was soon after
this that its affiliates, Barnard College and Teachers College
(to which women were admitted), opened.

At the end of two and a half years at the New York State
Library, Mr. Anderson, then 47, again had shown himself to
be an able administrator and staff builder. He was asked by
John Shaw Billings, director of the New York Public Library,
to become assistant director of that library. Billings thereby
apparently made it clear that he (now nearly 70) did not
expect Arthur Bostwick, who had been Chief of the Circulation Department since its founding in 1901, to succeed him.
It was because of this, I suppose, that Mr. Bostwick resigned
and became the Librarian of the St. Louis Public Library, a
position he filled very successfully for 30 years. I might add
that Mr. Bostwick spoke extemporaneously more easily than
any other man I have met, and I was always amazed at the
way words (and they were well chosen words and to the
point) poured out of his mouth with no apparent effort on
his part.

With Mr. Bostwick's departure, Mr. Anderson concentrated on the Circulation Department, leaving much of the
operation of the Reference Department to Dr. Billings and
Harry Miller Lydenberg, both of whose special interests had
always been directed toward the library's research collections
and their use. The Fifth Avenue and 42nd Street building of
the New York Public Library was opened to the public on
May 2, 1911.

Although Dr. Billings had known Mr. Carnegie and obtained from him the funds for the construction of some 40 of
the New York Public Library branch libraries, Mr. Anderson
apparently knew him better through his work at the Carnegie Libraries in Braddock and Pittsburgh and he was the
one who took the initiative on May 8, 1911, and called at Mr.
Carnegie's office with a proposal for a library school at the
New York Public Library in quarters that were available in
the new building which opened that month. He indicated
that $15,000 a year would take care of the financial needs.

Mr. Carnegie showed immediate interest and agreed to provide the funds for five years. On May 10, only two days later,
the Board of Trustees accepted the contribution "with sin-
cere appreciation and thanks" and authorized its executive
committee to take steps at once for the establishment of the
school. Mr. Anderson lost no time in persuading Mary
Wright Plummer, who had directed the Pratt Institute
School in Brooklyn for the preceding 15 years, to accept the
new position and build up the school. As I have already
noted, Professor Root had convinced me before I applied for
admission to Pratt that Miss Plummer was the ablest person
in her field. I should go on to say that Miss Plummer was Mr.
Anderson's sister-in-law, but I am sure that this had nothing
to do with the appointment. She brought together a remarkable staff in the short time remaining and acquired the
equipment; all was ready when the school was opened in
September of the same year and I joined it as the only man in
the first class of 40 at the beginning of the year.

Mr. Anderson kept up his interest in the school and, as I
have written in the account of my library school years and
work during much of the same time, he was the one who
arranged indirectly for my appointment to the staff after my
graduation in 1913 with a certificate for the first year's work
in the library school. I saw him only occasionally until the fall
of 1918, when he put me in temporary charge of the Economics and Documents Division after the discharge of Miss
Hasse in November 1918, of which more later.

I was in daily contact with Mr. Anderson from the time I
entered his office as executive assistant in January 1919 until
his retirement in June 1934. During that period I remember
only two times when he spoke to me harshly, once when the
Hasse crisis occurred while he was suffering badly from
lumbago and I had been slow in coming to his office after he
sent for me, and once in my early days in the office in 1919
when, in addition to having temporary charge of the order
department, I was serving both him and Mr. Lydenberg as

executive assistant and my work on the first of these assignments kept me from carrying out one of his requests as rapidly as he had counted on.

Mr. Anderson was of medium height with a strong, handsome face. He always stood very erect and made a good impression on those he met. Four things stand out particularly in my memory of him; two of them were occasions when I disagreed with him. The first was when I interrupted my first year in library school to go back to Oberlin College to take the administrative responsibility for the library in January 1912, and he advised against it. I think this was because he was very anxious to keep at least one man in the first class of the school. He said I would not like the Oberlin work because college students would seem so young and immature.

The second thing that bothered me was that it seemed to me, perhaps mistakenly, that he was too subservient to the trustees. There were times when I wished that he would disagree with their decisions and try to persuade them to change their minds. But he seemed unwilling to do so. Mr. Lydenberg followed Mr. Anderson in this respect. While I have no first-hand knowledge of the matter, I believe that Dr. Billings felt himself equal to the trustees, at least to the point where he would argue against their decisions if he disagreed. Mr. Lydenberg's successor, Franklin F. Hopper, followed Dr. Billings' practice rather than that of Mr. Anderson and Mr. Lydenberg. In fact, later directors became members of the Board of Trustees and in that way their equals. In spite of this, I thought very highly of Mr. Anderson and still do, as he was, in my opinion, more responsible for improving the quality of library personnel than anyone else in his generation. I owe a great deal to E.H.A. for what I learned from him.

While at Pittsburgh Mr. Anderson had much to do with book selection and was responsible for building up a good library printing plant. He brought the chief men from this plant to the New York Public Library six years after he left

Pittsburgh. So that he could spend his time on policy decisions, Mr. Anderson turned over this part of the work to Mr.
Lydenberg, who was particularly interested in it.

E.H.A. was extremely careful in the way he wrote and
often rewrote his important letters. He did not write easily,
and I had the same failing. He was accustomed to write the
Reference Department budget letter to the trustees over and
over again to be sure that it was entirely clear and within the
limits that they had set for him. I worked with him on these
letters for the first time in 1919 and 1920. For the next 14
years I drafted the letter and then he went over it word by
word, checking the figures as well as the wording. I remember well my feeling of pride when he approved my draft
without a single change.

My most important memory of Mr. Anderson was his
personnel policy. I shall write later about some of the persons
whom I brought to the library as a result of his constant
reiteration of the importance of improving staff quality. During the more than 15 years that I worked as his assistant, I
was in his office on the average of an hour a day, and he
never let a day pass without emphasizing the fact that the
most important task for a top administrator was to build up
his staff. His obsession, as some people would call it, with this
part of his work places him, in my opinion, in the top rank of
influential individuals in American library history. As already noted, the Carnegie Library of Pittsburgh, of which he
was the first librarian, ranked within ten years as one of our
best public libraries, along with Cleveland in the services that
it gave and only below the Boston Public Library and the
New York Public Library in its reference collections. In Boston the collection had been due to its early start, to the work
of Justin Winsor from 1868 to 1877 and later of Herbert
Putnam during the 1890's. By the time Mr. Anderson came
to the New York Public Library, its collections, through the
genius of John Shaw Billings and his predecessors, Joseph
Green Cogswell and James Lenox, had put that library ahead
of all the others as a reference and research library, on a par

with Harvard's and at that time probably above the Library of Congress in the quality of its collections if not their quantity. Mr. Anderson's influence brought first-class librarians to any library where he was in charge and the results were demonstrated by the fact that among the American Library Association presidents from 1910 to 1960, if you add Mr. Anderson himself, there were 22 of the 50 (13 of them between 1938 and 1960, after he had retired) who had worked with him at Pittsburgh, Albany, or the New York Public Library.

Mr. Anderson's closest friend of his own generation was Harrison W. Craver, who had been with him at the Carnegie Library of Pittsburgh, had succeeded him there, and later came to New York to take charge of the Engineering Societies Library on West 39th Street from 1917 to 1945. They were accustomed to lunch together at the Century Association several days in the week and Mr. Craver came to Mr. Anderson's office to pick him up and would keep him in continuous gales of laughter. Someone who had known both Mark Twain and Harrison Craver well, E.H.A. once told me, said that Craver was far and away the greater humorist.

Day in and day out for 16 years I probably spent more time with Mr. Anderson than anyone else at the Library. I had the advantage of coming from the Middle West, as he had, and I always felt that he liked and trusted me and my judgment. But we concerned ourselves only with library matters and I did not feel that he was a close friend, as Mr. Lydenberg became. I believe that Mr. Lydenberg's relationship with E.H.A resembled mine. The two often disagreed but Mr. Lydenberg never would argue with his superior and would leave the office quietly; often Mr. Anderson would ask me to take charge and carry out the matter under discussion. This might have placed me in a difficult position but I was saved from embarrassment by H.M.L.'s even temperament. In spite of any disagreements, Mr. Anderson felt that there was no question but that H.M.L. should succeed him. In December 1927, when he had a severe heart attack, he did what he could to insure this by appointing Mr. Lydenberg Assistant Director, which left Mr. Lydenberg's position open for me. While E.H.A. still was confined to his apartment, he called for me one day and told me what he had done and said that he was very glad I had not gone to Oberlin a few months earlier when the librarianship there was offered to me. I assumed my new position at the beginning of January 1928.

I am proud to be able to say that when I turned down each of the positions recounted in a later chapter, I carefully refrained from telling either of my superiors of the higher salaries I had been offered so that they would not feel that I was "holding them up" and looking for an increase.

Mr. Anderson's recovery from his heart attack was quite rapid and he returned to the library in a few weeks and continued for six and one-half years more. Thereafter Mr. Anderson's health was reasonably good but he did not come into the library and I saw him only once after his retirement. My wife and I were in Williamsburg, Virginia, on our return from an assignment in Western North Carolina and had called on James Thayer Gerould and his wife, the former Winifred Gregory. They told me that Mr. and Mrs. Anderson were staying at the Williamsburg Inn. I telephoned to him and he said that Mrs. Anderson was not able to see me but he came down and we had a visit in the lobby. He looked very frail but was still standing straight as a ramrod. He died at his home in Dorset, Vermont, in April 1946. His great contribution to his profession is not remembered as it should be.

Harry Miller Lydenberg

Harry Miller Lydenberg was born in Dayton, Ohio, in November 1874. His father had been injured in the Civil War, never fully recovered, and died young. Harry went to work as a newsboy at an early age and when old enough became a page in the Dayton Public Library. He knew the

Wright brothers (who 15 years later became the airplane pioneers) as members of a boys' gang with which he had frequent clashes. He told me that he had planned to go to Oberlin College but when he found that he would not be permitted to smoke his pipe there he made up his mind to go to Harvard; in spite of a shortage of funds, he managed to do so, working in the Gore Hall Library (Harvard's Central Library) under Justin Winsor and graduating in three years, in 1896, as with the Class of 1897, *magna cum laude.*

Justin Winsor asked H.M.L. to stay on in the Harvard Library but John Shaw Billings, who had become director of the newly consolidated New York Public Library a short time before, persuaded him that the NYPL would give him more exciting and useful experience than Harvard could in the years immediately ahead. Although Harry always remained a loyal Harvard man, he decided to go to the new library. There, within a few years, he had unusual and valuable experiences in various parts of the two older libraries—the Astor and the Lenox. Among other things he had the opportunity to decide what should be done with the very large and important Gordon Lester Ford collection, consisting of what we would now call American social history, which had come to the library in 1899. It was given by Ford's sons, Paul Leicester Ford (author of the best sellers, *Janice Meredith* and *The Honorable Peter Sterling*) and Worthington Chauncey Ford, who was for years director of the Massachusetts Historical Society and later in charge of the manuscript division of the Library of Congress. Later still, as that library's European representative, he sent back to Washington in the 1920's the first extensive collection (from various European sources) of microfilm of archives relating to this country. The two brothers had published some 50 volumes of source material from their father's collections through their Historical Printing Club. They were worried by the cost of storing the collection and turned it over to the New York Public Library. Mr. Lydenberg worked through the collection of well over 100,000 volumes and several times that many pamphlets;

those that he felt the library could afford to catalogue were
dealt with and the remainder, consisting of some 200,000
pamphlets, were tied up in heavy brown paper bundles, each
at least two feet high, and stored in the basement in one of
the old libraries and later the new one for nearly 25 years.

H.M.L. worked with Wilberforce Eames, the greatest of
American bibliographers, and then, as Dr. Billings' assistant,
worked on planning the new library building that was under
construction at 42nd Street and Fifth Avenue from 1897 to
1911. He then had a major part in the difficult operation of
moving into the new building. He stayed on in the library
until his retirement in 1941, having served as assistant, chief
reference librarian, assistant director, and director.

H.M.L., as he was called and as he signed his notes to his
staff, was somewhat below today's average height, slender,
wiry, and vigorous. It always amazed me to see him climb the
library stairs two or three steps at a time in spite of his
comparatively short legs. When I first became acquainted
with him, he was in his late thirties, fourteen years older
than I.

With this background, I will go back to his 45 years in the
New York Public Library. Dr. Billings was director of the
library from 1895 until his death in March 1913. During this
period he had a greater influence on Lydenberg than anyone
else. Dr. Billings was a very remarkable man in many fields;
as a surgeon, a public health officer, bookman, bibliographer, administrator, medical school and library building
planner and organizer. Soon after he graduated from the
Miami University School of Medicine in Oxford, Ohio, he
entered the Army Medical Service, which was then in the
midst of the Civil War. He established a reputation as a
surgeon and administrator. Before 1864 he was invalided
back to Washington and then transferred to the Surgeon
General's Office, where he remained until his retirement
from Army duty 30 years later. He had become interested in
medical literature at medical school while writing his thesis,
and when he was put in charge of the Surgeon General's

library, he went to work building it up. Some ten years later, he began to have its catalogue printed; in addition to listing the books, which had grown in number rapidly, it indexed the major medical periodical articles. There was an annual supplement.

In addition to continuing his work with the Surgeon General's Office and the library, Dr. Billings served as a medical advisor to the trustees of the new Johns Hopkins University Medical School and Hospital, where he made the sketched building plans and outlined a philosophy for operation of the school. Both were accepted and marked a step forward in medical training in the United States; moreover, Dr. Billings selected William H. Welch, William Osler, and many others for the faculty. In 1891, while still attached to the Surgeon General's Office, he had an even greater responsibility at the University of Pennsylvania Medical School and Hospital and as professor of hygiene. One year after his retirement from the Army in 1894 (and with the reluctant consent of the University of Pennsylvania), he transferred to the New York Public Library to be the director of that newly organized institution.

To go back to H.M.L., he joined the New York Public Library soon after Dr. Billings came and quite naturally fell under his influence, perhaps unconsciously adopting Billings' military approach to administration. While he was a good judge of persons of both sexes and very careful in the selection of his senior staff, he may have felt, like Dr. Billings, that his time was too valuable to spend on selection of junior help. When he saw that there was a job to be done he was inclined to do as Dr. Billings did with the library's card catalogue. The Astor Library had two large sets of catalogues in book form—the Cogswell and the Nelson—and the Lenox had various lists of special collections. Dr. Billings said, "We must have a card catalogue." And there was a card catalogue; almost as in the first chapter of Genesis—"God said, 'Let there be light' and there was light." The entries were clipped from the printed volumes of the book-form catalogues and lists and pasted on cards. He said there should be a subject catalogue and in due course there was one; parts of it at least made up by staff members who took home with them at night the author entries from the old book catalogue and assigned subject headings to them as best they could. Of course, this did not make a catalogue that would satisfy a perfectionist but at least you can say this about it: very quickly a catalogue which was greatly needed was provided, and it was hard to think of any subject heading under which you would not find one or more entries, so not many inquirers had to leave empty-handed.

Dr. Billings, with H.M.L., devised a classification very different from the Dewey and the Cutter classifications already in use throughout this country and abroad. It was one especially adapted to the New York Public Library, with its large closed-stack collections. This classification, with minor exceptions, had no more than two or three letters. For instance, AB for Biography and NCW for English and American Fiction. This classification is still in use for much of the collections. In recent years additions to the Main Stack collections have been shelved by size in order to save space, with each size arranged numerically as books are catalogued. The older classified books are shelved in full shelves without space for additions. But shelf space still is inadequate and the library has been unable to obtain an addition from the city. It has stored much of its collections elsewhere, first in a warehouse on West 24th Street in the garment district, and later on West 43rd Street, close to the river.

Mr. Lydenberg was greatly influenced by Dr. Billings, whom—with good reason—he believed to be a great man, a great librarian, and a great builder of library collections. H.M.L. was a conservative by nature and when I first became acquainted with him he seemed to me to be one of the most conservative men I had ever known, politically and in other ways. He believed that the library was on the right track, thanks to Dr. Billings' influence, but he was ready to consider changes or improvements and made them without hesitation when he was convinced that they were right. His conservatism and hard common sense are illustrated, in a way, by the short conversation that I had with him one day in early August 1914, just before the outbreak of World War I. I met him outside the 42nd Street entrance of the library and, in passing, he remarked, "Things look pretty black." I replied, "I am still optimistic. The world is controlled by big business and big business is not so foolish as to permit war to start, realizing that in the long run it will be harmful." He looked at me with sadness in his eyes and simply said, "Metcalf, human nature has not changed very much in the last 3000 years," and then walked on. I was young and ignorant enough to be unconvinced until I remembered that William Stearns Davis, my freshman and sophomore history teacher in Oberlin, had remarked one morning in early October 1908, when the news came that Austria had taken over Bosnia and Herzegovina, "This is the beginning of a world war."

In my considered opinion, after an acquaintance with Harry Lydenberg for nearly 50 years, of all the librarians whom I have known in this country and abroad (and my acquaintance has been large), he stands, all things considered, at the top of my list of great librarians. I was in very close touch with him during the 24 years I worked under his direction at the New York Public Library and nearly 20 years more when we kept in touch by correspondence and by occasional visits, including, for most of that time, an annual weekend together with other librarians in the Catskill Mountains.

I first met H.M.L. (we did not call him "Harry" until after he retired) during my early days in library school at a Halloween party for the library staff when he was drawing cider from a keg into paper cups. My next contact came when he asked me in early February 1913, soon after I had returned to the library school following my year in Oberlin, if I would accept a part-time evening post in the Main Reading Room. It was for 38 hours a week, 5 P.M. to 10 P.M. for six days a week and 1 P.M. to 10 P.M. (with an hour off) on Sundays and is described in another chapter. I accepted the position with pleasure at $50 a month.

In May of the same year, Miss Plummer sent me to Mr. Anderson's office (he was about to be appointed director after Dr. Billings' death in March of that year) and he told me that there would be a regular full-time assignment waiting for me after I had completed the first year of library school in June and had my certificate. Then he said, "Come and see me again in a couple of weeks and I can make a definite offer." I went, of course, but found that Mr. Anderson was busy, and was referred to Mr. Lydenberg, who said immediately that they did have a position for me and added that he thought I was not yet ready to work directly with the public but would be put in charge of the main bookstack. I meekly agreed, although my pride was hurt by his remark that I was not yet ready to work with the public. I had had far more library experience than anyone else in my class and had been responsible for the busiest college—as distinct from university—library in the United States for eight months, had been very closely involved with the student body, as shown in a preceding chapter, and had somehow managed "to get away with it." Mr. Lydenberg went on to say that I would receive $75.00 a month instead of the $50 that I had been getting for the 38-hour-a-week schedule that I had previously. I had received $100 a month in Oberlin the year before. This did not bother me at the time; I was much more interested in the job and the experience than in the salary, and knew that I could live on it and save a bit of money.

But when I took over the new assignment in July at the same time that Charles McCombs was put in charge of the Main Reading Room under the Chief of the Readers Division, C. H. A. Bjerregaard, I found that McCombs was to receive $125 a month and I confess that I was provoked to put it mildly. I knew that Charles had dealt with Mr. Anderson and not with H.M.L. and I felt that the latter had taken advantage of me. McCombs had also had library experience working in the Ohio State University library throughout his

college career and before graduating from the Albany library school, and had a year at the main reading room desk
in the Library of Congress under William Warner Bishop.
The grievance gave me a poor start with Mr. Lydenberg
which was not improved during the months that followed.

Mr. Bjerregaard and the man who had ranked next to him
at the reading room desk before Charles McCombs arrived
took a dislike to McCombs and kept complaining about him
to his chief. Mr. Bjerregaard was quite lame and was unable
to get down in the bookstack, which theoretically also came
under his supervision, so I had no trouble with him. But he
did not like Charles and seemed to take every opportunity to
complain about his actions. The situation was made even
more difficult for McCombs because the daytime assistant,
already mentioned, followed his chief's lead and did everything he could to make matters more difficult and unpleasant. Charles had a brilliant mind and dealt well with readers
but he was not naturally an administrator and became terri-
bly upset. I felt strongly that he was being abused and finally
went to Mr. Lydenberg and told him what I thought of the
situation and said that I wished he would do something about
it. Mr. Lydenberg, hardly looking up from his work (it was
his custom, while talking with someone, to check periodicals
for items to be listed in the public catalogue, and then the
telephone would ring and he would seem to be doing three
things at once), quietly and unemotionally answered, "If
McCombs is the man we want there, he will pull through."
He did pull through, in fact, although the situation was
helped when the troublesome assistant was transferred a
little later.

After I went into the office in 1919 and was personnel
officer, among other duties, the assistant who had been
largely responsible for McCombs' trouble said to me one day,
"You know, Metcalf, I am one of those persons who is never
his real self in the morning and I am inclined until noon to be
cross and difficult. After noon, the world seems to change
and I become a normal individual." I am sure that this was

true and we saw to it for the years that followed that his contacts with other staff members and the public were kept to a minimum until after lunch. The response from Mr. Lydenberg did not satisfy me at the time. But I came to realize later that he knew a great deal more about human nature than I then thought and actually was testing McCombs because he was not sure that he was tough enough "to make the grade" in an extremely difficult assignment.

My next problem with H.M.L. came when I found that the building's janitors were filling the stack staff's cold-water cooler by simply attaching a rubber hose, which they kept on the floor in the janitors' closet, to the faucet. When the building superintendent did not object to this practice, I went to Mr. Lydenberg and complained; the only acknowledgment that I received was a gruff, "When are you going to grow up?" but the desired change took place.

Sometime during the next six months, I made the only complaint in my life about my salary: I told H.M.L. that I was beginning to wonder if I had not chosen the wrong profession and would not do better as a policeman, that I believed I could do a good job in that position. He made no reply. But on January 1, 1914, my salary was increased to $100 a month (McCombs stayed at $125) and I learned to my surprise that the women who had been in library school with me had started in at $55 a month if they had had no previous experience, had gone up to $60, and that I probably was doing better than any of the women who had graduated with me. Two of the men had become branch librarians at a higher salary and another one had been appointed librarian at the Boston Museum of Fine Arts. Women were being discriminated against.

Before my first year in the stack was over, calls from H.M.L., some of which will be related in more detail in another chapter, came frequently and I began to have more contact with him. He called me one day to say that the library had purchased a photostat machine the previous year. This, so far as I know, was one of the first three in a library in the

United States. The others were at the Library of Congress and the John Carter Brown Library at Brown University. The New York Public Library machine was beginning to be used enough so that the record-keeping was too much for the young man who had been assigned the task of making the prints.

Not long after this, H.M.L. called me again to say that the library had decided it should undertake to make a shelf-card list and take an inventory for the first time. I was to select the person to do the work under my direction, as it would affect primarily the main bookstack for which I had the responsibility. His advice was to find someone I was sure could do the job satisfactorily and not to worry if the person chosen decided to spend most of his time down in the basement furnace room sitting in a chair with the furnace door open and his feet resting on the door sill. I was such a serious young man that I was shocked at the idea and it took me some time to realize that he was simply indicating that he wanted the job done and that he was indirectly (as in the matters of the cold water and McCombs) trying me out.

I had begun to get along better with Mr. Lydenberg and was able to talk to him freely, standing behind his rolltop desk while he sat there indexing periodicals. If we had not become good friends, at least we no longer were at loggerheads as far as I was concerned. From his point of view I am sure it never occurred to him that I had been unhappy about our relationship. This situation continued, except for the year when I was back in Oberlin, until the end of 1918, when Mr. Lydenberg and Mr. Anderson asked me to come into the main office as an assistant to both of them. From January 1, 1919 until December 1927, I was responsible to both Edwin Hatfield Anderson, the director, and Harry Miller Lydenberg, the chief reference librarian. It worried me that I might be unable to serve two masters but fortunately no serious problems occurred. As I wrote earlier, Mr. Anderson and Mr. Lydenberg did not always agree but when they disagreed, Mr. Lydenberg always refrained from complaining and simply stopped talking and I would go ahead and follow Mr. Anderson's direction.

This continued until December 1927, when Mr. Anderson asked the trustees to appoint Mr. Lydenberg assistant director and suggested that, beginning January 1, 1928, I be given the title of Chief of the Reference Department instead of Chief Reference Librarian, which had been H. M. L.'s title. I received an office of my own next door to Mr. Lydenberg's and there was practically no change in my work except for small steps as I gradually assumed more and more responsibility for the reference department. A new executive assistant, Charles Shaw, took my place in the director's outer office. Mr. Anderson retired six years later in the middle of 1934 at the age of 73. Mr. Lydenberg then became director and moved into Mr. Anderson's office and I moved into Mr. Lydenberg's and took over his roll-top desk and most of the small collection of reference books which he had kept there (no new assistant director was appointed). I remember particularly among the reference material the copy of Appleton's seven-volume *Cyclopedia of American Biography* in which H.M.L. had identified and marked the names and biographies and lists of publications of fictitious South American scientists whom contributors to the *Cyclopedia* had found it profitable to invent. This was one of the great scandals of the time, which was not discovered until years after publication.

Between the years 1919 and 1937 H.M.L. and I became closer friends. I had talked with him daily from 1919 on, always deferring to his judgment on the purchase of valuable and questionable books, since it was part of my task to make decisions with his help on expensive purchases. I remember only two occasions when we had problems. The first was when I had missed the review of an important work on anthropology in the *London Times Literary Supplement.* Instead of rebuking me, he quietly asked me how in the world it had happened. The second was when I insisted on a subscription to the *Reader's Digest* when it first appeared and he objected, saying that it was simply a reprint of articles to be found in magazines that we already received. In my opinion it was going to be an important periodical that would be called for constantly and ought to be in the library. I won that battle. We did have other disagreements which at the time seemed important. One was about the official catalogue file of serials, which was under the charge of Miss Tompkins, who had been in the library since the consolidation and had kept it in different alphabets according to the country of origin. I insisted that it would simplify matters to put the cards all in one alphabet as our subscriptions were not always directly from the country of origin, particularly since in the Order Division separate files were kept for the subscriptions from each dealer. I won again but I am sure that I have forgotten many cases where it was evident that his judgment was better than mine and I accepted his decisions without question.

I should add in this connection that during the late 20's and early 30's, when Mr. Lydenberg had more and more responsibility for the library as a whole, I gradually took over the indexing of some 4,000 periodicals as well as the book selection, except for expensive items. Mr. Lydenberg never authorized me to do this but when for illness or any reason he was away and I took over more and more duties, he rarely would ask me to return one to him. I continued, however, to put the important decisions before him.

Beginning in the early 1920's a half dozen of the library's division chiefs formed the custom of taking the Columbus Day weekend to hike in the Catskill Mountains at the peak of the brilliant autumn coloring. C. C. Williamson was one of the group from the beginning, although during most of this time he was no longer at 42nd Street and Fifth Avenue but working for the Rockefeller Foundation or the Carnegie Corporation and later as director of the Columbia University Library and Dean of its School of Library Service. The second senior member of the group was Frank Waite. The others included Paul North Rice, Charles McCombs, and Carl Cannon. I filled out the group. Others were with us from time to time.

We tried in the beginning to persuade Ernest Reece and

Mr. Lydenberg to come with us but failed. The latter's excuse was that he used October as his vacation month and had to put his garden to bed for the winter. Finally, in the autumn of 1929, when he was again asked to join us, H.M.L. said that he did not like to be away from home two nights at a time. I now owned my first car at the age of 40, and offered to pick him up early Saturday morning and drive him to join the others in time for breakfast at Beechknoll in Woodland Valley near Phoenicia, New York, and then have two full days of mountain climbing before our return late Sunday afternoon. H.M.L., to the delight of the whole group, accepted. I remember well the trips before daylight when he would rhapsodize about the stars, which he said reminded him of the days when he used to deliver morning newspapers as a boy before daybreak. I always suspected that he was more thrilled by this idea in 1930 than he had been in the 1880's. This was grape season and Mr. Lydenberg had fine Concord grapes in his garden and he would always bring along a number of bunches. These trips continued until Carl Cannon shifted to Yale and McCombs died. Dr. Williamson, Frank Waite, Paul Rice, Harry Lydenberg, and I continued until none of us could climb mountains any more but we could drive around and see the color and have a weekend together with interesting shop talk combined with fine scenery and brilliant foliage. This went on into the 1950's when Mr. Lydenberg (as will be told in more detail later), after periods in Mexico City, Washington, and Greensboro, North Carolina, moved to Ohio to be next door to his daughter. While he was still able to drive from Greensboro to the Catskills with Mrs. Lydenberg, he did so. Williamson, Paul Rice, and I, with our wives, continued a few years more and I stopped only after more than 50 years and some years after the other men had died.

Perhaps it is not yet clear why I think Mr. Lydenberg was one of our great librarians. I have spoken of the fact that when I first knew him he was ultra-conservative, to put it mildly, and that he was not particularly interested in administration, although he had great ability in that direction. He was wrapped up in book selection and other matters which interested him more than administration, and gave it less time than it required. He directed the book selection of the New York Public Library for well over 40 years, keeping the same ends in view during that long period. As a result, the library acquired the most well-rounded collection of books in its fields to be found anywhere. An example of the results appeared in an article in the *Library Quarterly* by Professor Douglas Waples of the University of Chicago Graduate Library School, who was interested in the quality of book selection in research libraries. He spent a summer in Europe and came back with lists provided by European scholars for the most important books for research libraries published in England, France, and Germany in 1929 in each of the social sciences, the term being broadly interpreted. This was long enough after the publication of the material so that there had been time for the libraries to have acquired and catalogued the books if they were going to do so. The titles were checked in four of our top academic libraries, as well as at the Library of Congress and the New York Public Library. Three of the four university libraries had about 50 percent of the books, the Library of Congress and Harvard had 60 to 62 percent, but the New York Public Library (with the exception of the field of law, which the library did not attempt to cover except for official gazettes and Statute Law because the Bar Association Library was only two blocks away) had 92 percent. This gives some idea of the book-selection work at the New York Public Library under Mr. Lydenberg's direction, in which he had the aid of 14 specialists on the library staff. He followed the pattern that John Shaw Billings started in 1895 and 1896. This was perhaps Mr. Lydenberg's greatest library contribution, but far from the only one.

H.M.L.'s work on the library's classification and subject headings also was noteworthy, and while the results were not always consistent, we used to say that one of the great things about the catalogue was that, whatever heading you looked

under, you would find something which would give you a
lead with which to go further. H.M.L. was very much interested in good printing and a number of the books printed
in the library's Printing Office under his direction were
selected by the Society of Graphic Arts for its 50 books of the
year. Here he had the help of John Archer, a very able
craftsman, who was in charge of the Printing and Binding
Division.

Mr. Lydenberg and Dr. William Warner Bishop, head of
the Readers Service of the Library of Congress and later
director of the University of Michigan library, were perhaps
the first librarians to become intensely worried about the
poor paper on which many books and newspapers were
printed during the last third of the 19th century. The problem for libraries has become more and more serious. H.M.L.
was the first to see what could be done about it. During the
second decade of the century he carried out more than 20
different experiments, which were described in the New
York Public Library *Bulletin,* looking for ways to preserve
books printed on poor paper. He thought during the First
World War that he had found it by pasting Japanese tissue
with rice paste on both sides of the sheets of New York City
newspapers. Funds for the work were provided by the newspapers. This seemed to be effective, although it nearly doubled the bulk of the papers and increased the cost of binding.
But within less than 20 years disintegration of the wood-pulp
paper began to show up again and it was evident that this
method was a failure. Fortunately, it was about this time that
microfilm became available and his library was the first to
adopt it for current use on a large scale, for newspapers at
the start and as time went on for other material.

In the 1920's Mr. Lydenberg became more and more active in the work of the American Library Association and was
president for 1932-33. He also was one of the founders of
the Association of Research Libraries.

Mr. Lydenberg was influential with both the Rockefeller
Foundation and the Carnegie Corporation and worked

closely with Raymond Fosdick and David Stevens of the former and Dr. Keppel and his assistants at the latter. As a result the American Library Association was aided greatly for many years by these foundations. The important part that Carl Milam played in this should not be forgotten, and Mr. Lydenberg came to realize the great value of Milam's work for the Association. He was a strong admirer of Milam but realized that opposition to him by younger librarians had grown to such an extent by the time of Milam's retirement from the ALA and transfer to the United Nations Library that it would be unwise for him to run for president of the ALA, something that I in my admiration for Milam did not realize.

The points that have just been made have been mentioned simply to indicate the breadth of Mr. Lydenberg's interests and influence. While he had a seemingly gruff exterior, his kindness to those who knew him was almost unbelievable. I remember very well when I was struggling to find a way to borrow money so that I could build a house in White Plains that he offered to let me use securities that he had accumulated for collateral. Although I refused the offer, I am sure that he would have been glad to have it accepted. I kept learning of little kindnesses that he had done for other members of the staff without anyone realizing what had happened.

One of his habits was always to leave a clean desk behind him when he left the library at night, this in spite of the fact that he had a rolltop desk where leftovers could be covered up. One day in the early spring of 1924, he was called away before his desk was clear in order to attend a meeting of the Scarsdale School Board, of which he was a member. As he was walking home after the meeting along the side of the dark road, he was struck by a hit-and-run driver and his head struck a rail on the adjoining streetcar track. Fortunately, a few minutes later another driver saw Harry staggering down the road, rushed him to the White Plains Hospital, and called his doctor, who was a skilled surgeon as well as a family doctor and close friend (I might add that he was my family doctor also). The doctor, realizing that Harry's skull had been crushed and there was no time to lose, operated immediately. The operation seemed to be a success, but the next day Mr. Lydenberg kept insisting that he must see Keyes Metcalf and refused to be quieted. The doctor called me at the library and I rushed out to the hospital, where Mr. Lydenberg said quietly, "You'll find on my desk the following things which I unfortunately left last night before going to the train." Then he gave me directions as to what to do with them. After that, he settled down and was a perfect patient and within a few weeks was on his feet again, apparently as well as ever. In fact, one Sunday within the next two months he and others from the library walked from Suffern to Nyack, New York, a distance of more than 20 miles, mostly on the top of the ridge that culminated at High Tor, where you could look down on Haverstraw and the Hudson River. At least one of the group was so tired by the end of the day that he vowed he never would go on a library walk again. But Mr. Lydenberg was at his office at 9 o'clock the next morning, none the worse for wear. I might admit that it had rained hard the night before and the fresh leaves on the bushes past which we walked were soaking wet; I was very careful to walk ahead of Mr. Lydenberg, hoping that he would not get as wet as I did.

H.M.L. retired from the New York Public Library in 1941, a few months before he was 67. He told me that this was to happen when he came up to my wedding to Elinor Gregory in June of that summer. There was no set retirement age for him at that time and his two predecessors had continued well into their 70's but he told me he was convinced that he could not deal satisfactorily with the unrest that was rising in his staff (and at many other libraries at that time because of depression salaries). He felt Franklin Hopper, who succeeded him, could do better. I have always had a suspicion that he was influenced by the fact that he knew Hopper was not well and wanted to give him the chance while he was able to take it. Hopper had been in the library for 27 years and chief of the circulation department for 22 of them, and I understand that he had the opportunity to become the librarian at Princeton about a year before that but had turned it down, probably in the hope of becoming director of the New York Public Library. Five years was all that Hopper was able to serve, but he made his mark in that time.

Mr. Lydenberg did not actually retire. Almost immediately he took over the task of organizing the Biblioteca Benjamin Franklin in Mexico City. He helped plan and had built a satisfactory library building for it and selected its stock of books. It proved to be very successful as the first of the American Information Libraries in underdeveloped countries.

In 1943 Mr. Lydenberg was called to head the American Library Association office in Washington, where again he was successful and, with the aid of two groups that had been financed by the Carnegie Corporation and the Rockefeller Foundation, did a magnificent job in providing American books and periodicals for war-damaged libraries throughout the world as soon as possible after the war. Before this time Flora Belle Ludington, the librarian at Mount Holyoke College, who was doing fine work as Chairman of the American Library Association's International Relations Committee, resigned in order to go to India and elsewhere to start American Information Libraries. I accepted her post as chairman of the committee, more in order to protect Mr. Lydenberg than anything else, because I realized there were librarians who were objecting to the emphasis that the Association was putting on international affairs.

A third retirement assignment began early in 1946 when Mr. Lydenberg became a member of a group called the Library of Congress Mission, headed by Reuben Peiss, formerly a member of the Harvard staff, who had become a successful OSS agent in Europe during the war. H.M.L. played a large part in bringing back to the United States more than a million volumes published in Germany, France, Italy, and the Low Countries during the Second World War which had been unavailable for acquisition earlier and which were distributed at about one dollar a volume to some 60 American libraries. H.M.L., in spite of his 71 years, took a leading part in the work, tiring out other members of the party who were half his age and then being fresh enough in the evening to see the things which interested him. This mission was accomplished without ransacking the European book market and taking advantage of hard-up university professors, something which had occurred, often shamelessly, after World War I. In this work he was accompanied by David Clift and Fred Kilgour, with both of whom I had worked earlier.

Mr. Lydenberg's health was vigorous. I remember one October day five years later in the early 1950's when he was in his late 70's, climbing the steep slope of Wittenberg Mountain in the Catskills with him and Paul North Rice, who was approximately my age. When Paul called for a "breather," Harry and I took our pulses and found them still in the 80's.

On his return to Washington after the successful completion of the Library of Congress mission, he resumed his work for a while at the American Library Association International Relations Office. He reached his Washington apartment from Europe one evening and without thought of a vacation walked his regular five miles to his office in the Library of Congress in time for its opening at 9 o'clock the next morning. Shortly after this he finally retired to Greensboro, North Carolina, where he purchased a small house with a good garden space such as he had enjoyed in Scarsdale earlier. He regretted that a lack of severe frosts made it impossible to grow the rhubarb and parsnips that he loved. Realizing this, I sent him one year a good-sized box of parsnips from my garden. At Greensboro there was the North Carolina College for Women, now a branch of the University of North Carolina, which was presided over by one of his good friends and former employees, Charles Adams. Harry gave up extensive travelling but each October for a time he and his wife, Madeleine, who before her marriage was Madeleine

Day, chief of the periodicals division of the New York Public Library, joined our group in the Catskills. She was a sister of Benjamin Day, who was prominent in New York City administration; an aunt of Eleanor Mitchell, a well-known librarian, and a cousin of Clarence Day, of "Life With Father" fame.

Later, when Harry's health began to fail, he moved to Otterbein, near Columbus, Ohio, and "next door" to his daughter, Mary, and her husband, who was a doctor. Harry finally was felled by a stroke, which completely incapacitated him, something that he had always feared. He died in early 1960 at age 85.

My love and respect for Harry Lydenberg as a man and as a librarian were and still are too great for any words that I can write and I shall never forget nor cease to regret my early lack of understanding of the work he was doing. Further reference to him will be made later in this volume. But I should mention here one of his most remarkable traits. While he was ultra-conservative by nature when I first worked with him, he became less conservative year by year. By the 1930's he could be called properly "middle of the road" and by the time he retired from the New York Public Library in 1941, then almost 67, he still was looking for new ideas as much as any librarian I knew. During his final five years in library work he was opening new paths and could be called a leader among our forward-looking young men, looking for ways to make our profession more useful. If this were typical among our older experienced librarians, librarianship would progress more rapidly and successfully. Without his influence, Keyes Metcalf would be even more of an anachronism than he is.

Chapter 2
Chief of Stacks
July 1913-August 1916

The story of my appointment to the position of Chief of Stacks is told in Chapter I of this part. I accepted the position with reluctance, because I had hoped for a regular reference assignment. After a month's vacation without pay because my evening work from January to June 1913 had not been regarded as counting toward a vacation, I went to Oberlin for a visit with Mart Gerrish, my sister Marion, and the Roots. I came back to New York in July and took charge of the bookstack about the same time that Charles McCombs, who had just completed his degree work at the New York State Library School, took a similar position in the main reading room. Both of us were working, theoretically at least, under C. H. A. Bjerregaard, who was 69 years old and had had 34 years with the New York Public Library and the Astor Library. I remained in this position from July 1913 through December 1918, five and a half years in all, minus 10 months when I was on leave to serve as acting librarian at Oberlin. During my first year as full-time Chief of Stacks, I kept my room at the West Side Y.M.C.A. where I had been since my return from Oberlin at the beginning of January 1913. But since I now had a full-time position with a regular salary of $75 a month, my room rent was raised from $3 to $3.50 a week.

Mr. Bjerregaard was so lame that he never, as far as I remember, tried to go down into the bookstacks, which were below the Reading Room. As a result, he did not become involved with my work in any way but did interfere with that of McCombs, as has been told earlier. Mr. Bjerregaard was born in Denmark in 1844 and graduated from the Military Academy there in 1866; he came to the United States for political reasons in 1873 and went to work in the Astor Library in 1879. His chief interest seemed to be in mysticism and he had published on a large scale in that field. He frequently was called on at his desk by elderly women also interested in mysticism.

My new assignment was to be in charge of the upper five levels of the seven-story bookstack under the big main reading room. The first level of the stack was used by the Central Circulation Branch Library and the Circulation Department's central collections, which were available to any of the branches on request. Duplicates for exchange or sale were stored on the second floor, where some vacant shelves still were available.

I was scheduled to work from 9 a.m. to 5 p.m., five and a half days a week, or their equivalent, with an hour off for lunch each day. On the half-day off during the library school

year 1913-14 I worked on my school assignments. At least
every third Sunday I also worked from 1 p.m. to 10 p.m.,
which theoretically added up to 42 to 43 hours a week. With
additional evening time to make up for the time spent at
lectures and practice work in the branch libraries it meant a
long week. I enjoyed it all and profited by it.

I found that the bookstack had no shelf list and was not in
good condition, although a short time before the staff finally
had succeeded in getting all the books off the floors, where
some of them had been since the Library opened more than
two years earlier. Many volumes still were misplaced on the
shelves, and we were not giving good service. No inventory
had been taken because of the lack of a shelf-list. Very often
books were called for that could not be found and simply
were reported on the back of the call slip "N.O.S." (Not on
Shelf).

I had been preceded in this position by two persons. The
first was Frank A. Waite, who left, after improving the situation considerably, in order to help Charles C. Williamson
organize the Economics Division. He then had taken charge
of the information desk when his predecessor at that post,
Everett Perry, left to become librarian of the Los Angeles
Public Library. More about Mr. Waite later.

Mr. Waite had been succeeded in the stacks by an acting
chief, Harry Lips, a very heavy man about my age who had
gone to work in the Astor Library building as a page at 13;
the law did not permit this but he had given his age as 14, the
age when working papers were available in New York. Harry
apparently was as stout when he started as he was later on,
and he told me that when he looked for books on the bottom
shelves, he had to lie on the floor and roll over so that he
could see the shelf and the books. He was very pleasant and
capable, easy to work with, and glad to be relieved of the
responsibilities of supervision because he was about the same
age as the young men in charge of each of the stack levels
and they were inclined to resent him. He continued as my
first assistant, a job in which I found him satisfactory. Harry
filled in wherever needed on any of the floors. We became

good friends. I remember visiting him one evening at his home between the Brooklyn end of the Brooklyn and Williamsburg Bridges. While there was running water in the apartment building, there were no flush toilets but there was a privy in the backyard. He lived with his mother, who was rapidly becoming blind, and he was in constant fear that she might set herself on fire at the gas stove. After she died he married a girl whom he had known most of his life and they moved to Westfield, New Jersey. This was after he had been promoted to the office of shipping clerk for the library. He died while still in his 30's, following a heart attack brought on, I am afraid, by his over-weight.

There was a special force for evening work made up of boys going to school and presided over by a red-headed young man named Moses Finkelstein. Moe, as he was called, left the library not long after I left the stack and I did not see him again until 1961, at the 50th anniversary celebration of the opening of the library, when he came in the 40th Street entrance and I had an opportunity to have a word with him. I asked him what he was doing and he replied, "Oh, I made my pile and retired."

Lips, Finkelstein and I took turns working Sundays, as did the other members of the day and evening staff. Sunday generally was the busiest day of the week. I found that I was often kept so busy on those days that I did not have an opportunity to sit down from 1 to 10 p.m., and a hastily eaten sandwich was the extent of my evening meal.

I might sum up my stack assignment by saying that, in spite of the fact that it was hard physical work climbing up and down stairs day after day and that when the position was offered to me I was disappointed because it was not reference work, I found that it was the most rewarding position I could have taken in the library at that time. I became acquainted with the institution's workings from top to bottom and was in touch with and came to know all the senior and most of the junior members of the staff throughout the building.

Each of the stack levels had its own chief, who had been in

the library for some years going back to the days of the Astor Library building and had worked up to his position. They were all fine, capable young men. A Scotsman, Thomas Thomson, who was in charge of the fourth level, was the most agreeable of them and the only one who stayed on in the library for many years. He later became a valuable member of the Science and Technology Division staff. He suffered, however, from having easily hurt feelings. A Scandinavian, Knut Swenson, was older than the others, and, perhaps partly because of the fact that his third stack was less busy than the fourth, fifth, and seventh levels, he was inclined to take things easy. A German, Eddie Sidler, was in charge of the busy fifth level. He was very quiet, so quiet that I never felt that I knew him well. The sixth level chief was also quiet, a Hungarian named Margolis. The seventh level was busiest of all and its chief, Verdi, was of Italian descent.

My desk was on the sixth-stack level, with doors to what was called the second building floor, since the 42nd Street entrance level was designated the ground floor. It was theoretically the quietest of all as far as stack work was concerned. Part of it was occupied by shelving for the document, oriental and Jewish division collections and other parts by the noisier sections of the accessions and catalogue divisions. On this level there was a horizontal, conveyor-belt carrier which took books to and from the document division and the book lifts in the center of the stack where they were transferred by hand to or from the book lifts. This conveyor broke down continually as most horizontal conveyors did in those days.

Since my position put me in touch with all the special reference divisions of the library, I did not have to spend as much time in them for library school practice work as would have been the case otherwise. But I did get enough experience in the print and the map rooms, the art, rare book (called reserve book), manuscripts, music, and current periodical divisions, none of which had parts of their collections in the main bookstack, so that I was able to become somewhat acquainted with their collections and staff. With all this added to the main reading rooms and collections that I had worked in during my first library school year, by the end of 1918 there was no one on the staff, except Mr. Lydenberg, who was better acquainted than I with the Reference Department as a whole, which would not have been possible with any other assignment. I also was in direct contact with the order, catalogue and accession divisions, which were on the same floor of the building as my desk.

During my first year in the stack, I was kept so busy that I was unable to take advantage of the Y.M.C.A. swimming pool and gymnasium. But in good weather I did manage to go on occasional long walks on the Sunday afternoons that I did not work, to distant and lightly populated parts of the city and the surrounding towns which could be reached with the low carfare then charged. I was able from time to time to go to the theater; this included the Hippodrome. I saw John Barrymore in *Hamlet* one evening with Azariah Root, who had come to New York on library business. I was able to obtain a room for him at the Y.M.C.A. where in 1913, with his full beard, he seemed strangely out of place.

Charles McCombs was in charge of the reading room under Mr. Bjerregaard, and we naturally had a good deal to do with each other. I remember especially one evening when, almost against my will, I accepted his invitation to the opera at the Century Opera House, which was next door to what is now the city's Cultural Center.

Forrest Spaulding and Fred Goodell were in the second year of library school with me but I saw them only during classes. Foster Stearns and Herbert Collar had gone on to positions elsewhere.

I became well acquainted with Frank Waite who, next to Harry Lydenberg, was more responsible than any other individual for giving me a good start in the library and to whom I owe a great deal. Waite—it was nearly 30 years before I began to call him "Frank"—was a farm boy from Michigan and a graduate of the University of Michigan at Ann Arbor. He had had part of his college years at Olivet College, where

he met his wife, Ginevra. Seven years at the St. Louis
Public Library followed and, during his last years there, he
worked closely with Arthur Bostwick, who earlier had been
chief of the circulation department of the New York Public
Library. Waite came to the New York Public Library early in
1911 in time to help with moving into the 42nd Street building, and proved to be very useful to Mr. Lydenberg in that
connection. He was now in charge of the information desk,
where he remained until his retirement in the 1940's. During
his more than 30 years there, he came into close contact with
more promising young men than any other librarian I know
of (with the possible exception of myself) and also with a
considerable number of women reference librarians. Many
of these went on to important positions all over the country.
Mr. Waite had a genius for becoming well acquainted with
the younger men and for 20 years was as good a judge of
them as anyone I knew.

   Frank Waite was also a born conservative who objected
vigorously to shifting from the position he was in to another.
He drew away in later years from those he did not know well
and his judgment of their ability was affected. He was one of
the group of librarians, generally six in number including
myself, who spent weekends hiking in the Catskills during
the autumn color season around Columbus Day for 40 years.
He had three daughters, each of whom married a New York
Public Library librarian, and thereby his usefulness to the
library became even greater. He never was suitably appreciated because of the idiosyncrasies which he developed
as the years went by.

   I speak of Frank Waite in detail because he helped me in
my first year at the library in a way that was invaluable. He
talked with me about my problems, and, whenever it seemed
to be needed, encouraged me. He was the first member of
the staff to invite me to his home to meet his very pleasant
wife and his three girls, who then were quite young. The
oldest daughter, Beatrice, married Andrew Osborn, who for
a long time worked with me at Harvard and lived in Bel-

mont, Massachusetts, which has been my home town for the past 40 years. Beatrice worked for a time in the Belmont Public Library while I was serving several three-year terms on that library's board of trustees. The second daughter, Virginia, married Robert Hill, who became chief of the manuscript division. The third daughter, Jane, after working in the New York Public Library for years, married Norwood Vail, who was a member of the library's art division. This was where Jane had been, so she moved to a supervisory position in the library's annex on West 43rd Street.

Robert W. Henderson (Rob) was working at the information desk in 1913. He had come from South Shields, England, near Newcastle-on-Tyne, where in his teens he had worked in the local library. He was unable to go to college in England and wanted to come to the United States. He had written to Andrew Keogh about doing library work in this country. Keogh had come here from Newcastle-on-Tyne and in due course became the distinguished librarian of Yale University. Dr. Keogh referred him to Dr. Billings of the New York Public Library and Henderson came to New York in 1910 as a cataloguer. Although he lacked a full formal education, in 1912 he joined the staff in the information division, where he was successful. In 1919, when I shifted to the director's office, he became chief of stacks and, after Charles McCombs' shift to book selection, took over the main reading room as well, holding the position that C. H. A. Bjerregaard had held earlier. We became good friends soon after my arrival in New York and an invitation to his house was the second one I had from a library staff member. There I met his delightful, auburn-haired wife, Lucy, whom Mart and I came to know intimately in the 20's and 30's when we were neighbors in White Plains and the Hendersons looked out on the same magnificent view that we had. Our gardens adjoined each other and he became an avid and skilled gardener. Early in his New York Public Library career he took over on the side the task of serving as librarian of the New York Racquet and Tennis Club. He became THE authority on the origin and history of a number of sports and a successful bibliographer and author in their fields, and was still at work at the club part-time until he retired—at 90—in December, 1978.

In addition to attending lectures and doing practice work in many parts of the library, during the year 1913-14 before receiving my diploma, I had to complete a thesis and make trips to Washington to visit the Library of Congress and to Boston to see the Harvard University library and the Boston Public Library.

I went to Washington during Christmas vacation, staying at the home of an Oberlin classmate who took me to visit the House of Representatives during the debate on whether there should be a Federal Reserve Bank. There I saw sitting nearby Mary E. Walker, one of the earliest woman doctors, who was the first woman commissioned on the surgeon's staff of our army during the Civil War and who was an early advocate of woman's suffrage and of dress reform—the first woman I ever saw dressed in trousers. I also was taken to the Senate, where a discussion was being held on the budget for Howard University, and I was interested in the way the Senators from the South took the lead in advocating its increase.

As I was looking in the catalogue in the large central reading room of the Library of Congress, Herbert Putnam, whom I had met when he spoke at the library school in New York in the fall of 1911, passed down the main aisle with his head erect, looking neither to the left nor right but apparently a bit embarrassed. I glanced down to his feet and found that one of his stocking garters had come loose and was dragging along the floor and he was trying to get out of the room without it being noticed.

From Washington I took the night train to Oberlin to be with my family and Martha Gerrish during the holidays. After I had sat down in the Pullman section where a berth had been assigned to me, an important looking man came along, looked at the section, and said to me, "This is my

section. What are you doing here?" I pulled out my ticket
and told him that I believed the section had been assigned to
me. We waited until the conductor came along and confirmed my opinion. By this time I had realized that the
contender for the place was William Graves Sharp, chairman
of the Ways and Means Committee of the House of Representatives, a resident of Elyria, and a long-time friend of my
family. A little later he became our ambassador to France
during the war. I ventured to tell him who I was. He then
greeted me cordially and with tears in his eyes said that my
mother had been the finest schoolteacher he had ever had.
He then invited me to have breakfast with him in the dining
car the next morning.

In Boston in April 1914 I visited for the second time the
Boston Public Library, which I had seen in 1909, and then
went out to Cambridge, wondering whether I could get up
courage enough to ask to see William Coolidge Lane, the
librarian, or Archibald Cary Coolidge, the director of the
Harvard Library. On my way from the subway station to the
library, which was temporarily occupying quarters in Randall
Hall, I met my Oberlin football coach. He asked me what I
was doing and I asked him what he was doing. He had come
on to help with the Harvard spring football practice, which
was still held at that time before the formation of the "Ivy
League," and I told him that I was going to the library and
did not know whom to ask for—Mr. Lane or Mr. Coolidge.
The coach, Harvey Snyder, who had been a football star at
Harvard ten years earlier, said, "I wouldn't ask for either of
them. Frank Carney is the man for you to see. He knows
more about the library than anyone else."

This, as you can imagine, was a great relief to me. I went
on to the library and asked for Frank Carney. He greeted me
cordially, pointing out Mr. Lane and Mr. Coolidge in the
distance. I had seen Mr. Lane at Oberlin in 1908 when he
gave the dedication address for the Carnegie Library there.
Carney then said to me, "I have just received word that the
structure for the new Widener Library is finished and you

may want to go with me to see the building. The inside, of course, is not yet completed." I accepted the invitation gladly. We went to all floors of the building and up on to the roof. When I came to Widener as director of the University Library and librarian of Harvard College a little more than 23 years later, Frank Carney had retired and I found that I had been through the building and on the roof before anyone then on the staff.

The subject of my thesis, "The Administration of a Large Library Bookstack," was based on my experiences during the year. Charles McCombs helped me edit it because I knew I was not a skillful writer. I failed to realize that it should have been typewritten, and it was handwritten in the best script I was able to produce. But it was not accepted and my diploma was held up until another year. In the spring of 1915, after my marriage, my mother-in-law came to visit us. She typed the thesis for me. This thesis is now in the library of the Columbia University School of Library Service, if I am not mistaken, and I still have the original manuscript copy in my wretched handwriting.

In June 1914, immediately after my class received their diplomas, I took my summer vacation and went back to Oberlin. I had been told that I would receive $125 a month on my return and Martha Gerrish and I had decided that we could live on that amount. In 1914 the question of her working did not occur to us. I had completed one full year as a regular full-time employee of the library and had been successful enough so that I was having special duties assigned to me which will be recorded later. I had had nine years of library experience, including two years in library school, the full year in Oberlin, for eight months of which I had been in charge of its very busy library, and in addition I had had considerable experience in various types of library work in both college and public libraries. I cannot imagine a better background and training and I gradually came to realize that, whatever my motive had been in selecting my profession, I was to be an administrator, not a reference librarian. I stopped worrying about this, although I still thought that being a reference librarian and helping people was the most important part of my chosen profession.

Staff Selection

As has been reported earlier, in June 1914 I completed my second library school year at the New York Public Library, during which I worked full time as chief of the stacks. I left the next day for Oberlin on a train that was combined at Albany with the Boston train, on which I joined my sister, Antoinette, who was reference librarian at Wellesley. We travelled by day coach because she was old-fashioned enough to be unwilling to take a Pullman sleeper; she was too modest to change her clothes and sleep in such a public place.

We arrived in Oberlin the next morning. Two days later Martha Gerrish and I were married at her home at 143 East College Street, Oberlin, where her grandfather had built a house in 1833, the year the college opened, on a lot that he had purchased from the first Oberlin settler, Peter Pindar Pease. After a reception at the house, we took off by the only taxi in town (there was still only one 60 years later) for a summer cottage on the banks of Lake Erie, some 15 miles away. There were no other cottages there and the owner's house was quite a distance away. We spent a quiet, restful time, broken only by one trip to Oberlin for our third class reunion and the third anniversary of our engagement.

We then went to New York. In the two remaining weeks of the five-week vacation I had that year (the fifth week was without pay), we found an apartment on University Avenue, between the 181st Street bridge over the Harlem River and the New York University Heights campus. It was a fourth-floor, four-room, walkup apartment, looking out on the Morris House, (named for Gouverneur Morris of Revolutionary fame). We were not quite in sight of the Hall of Fame that surrounded the river side of the NYU campus, but we felt almost out in the country. The rent was $20 a month and the building had just been completed. We considered that we were very fortunate. With the thousand dollars that I had saved in addition to supporting myself after my freshman year in college, we were able to buy furniture for the small apartment, including a desk that I still use and at which I sit as this chapter is dictated. We had funds left over so that I could buy an Ivers and Pond piano as a wedding present for Mart.

I went back to work the first of August. I considered that my formal academic and professional training had been completed and that I had had an unusual amount and variety of in-service training in a number of different types of libraries. I had a library position that was giving me good experience and I felt prepared for my professional life.

During my student days and my year at Oberlin in administrative work I had nothing to do with staff selection except to gather together the students who had helped with the manila rope bundles during eight Christmas holiday seasons, the group that helped move to the new library in 1908, and finally the girls who had worked on combining the Student Library Societies collection with the college library in the summer of 1908. This had been good experience but all those involved were individuals whom I had known personally and I had some idea of their fitness for the work for which they were selected. I made no regular staff appointments during the calendar year that I spent at Oberlin in 1912 while I stood in for Professor Root and the same held true for the spring of 1913 in the New York Public Library, when I was in charge of checking off book returns. But in each of these cases I had valuable experience in trying to obtain good service from those with whom I was associated.

Beginning in the summer of 1913 when I became chief of the bookstacks at the New York Public Library, I found a new situation. There was no regular personnel officer in the Reference Department at that time and while the director's office under Mr. Anderson was working hard to build up the professional staff, the errand boys (or pages, as we called them) who applied for work were sent from the office to any division chief who had a vacancy. Fortunately, just before I began this work the standard pay for the beginning page had been advanced from $15 to $20 a month for full-time stack boys. They worked 39 hours between Monday and Saturday and every other Sunday from 1 to 10 p.m. Saturdays and Sundays were generally the busiest days of the week. The part-time evening boys worked from 5 to 10 p.m. six nights a week and then took every other Sunday from 1 to 10 p.m. and were considered full-time workers. They could go to high school in the daytime and often would continue in the library while going to college or even to law school. Of course, when they stayed on they were promoted if possible and their pay was increased. But except for the stack chiefs at each of the five levels from which books were sent to the reading room, I found that there were very few boys who had been there long enough to receive more than the starting pay of $20 a month and I had an opportunity to promote the better ones from time to time.

The five stack-level chiefs received $45 a month. Each of them was a young man who had probably graduated from high school and had worked in the library for a number of years, going back to the old Astor and Lenox buildings. They have been listed in detail earlier in this chapter. The year 1913-1914 had been a comparatively quiet one in the library although its use was increasing rapidly. The stack boys seemed to be happy and the general situation was quite stable with comparatively few changes. We carried out one experiment during the year: when two vacancies occurred at once it was suggested that the two boys be replaced by one older man to see if he could do as much work as two boys. We tried to find men about 30 years of age and paid them $40 a month. The first one was named McGann. He was nearly 40 and bald, very well-meaning and anxious to do whatever he was told. But it was evident that he could not keep up with the work that had been done by two boys, and I assigned him to the level of the stack where I had my desk and helped him when I could. The other was named McGee. Though he did much better, he was not quite as useful as two boys but was kept on because he seemed a good prospect to replace one of the division chiefs if we had a vacancy.

This comparatively stable situation could not be expected to continue. When the war in Europe started the next year, just after I was married, staff changes began to occur more often and it was difficult to find replacements. The applicants for vacancies who were sent in from the director's office were not adequate in number or quality and I asked permission to place an advertisement in the *New York Times* when I had one or more vacant positions. This was granted. As time went on, these advertisements appeared in the *Times* almost every Monday morning. I had been told that was the best day in the week for this type of position. The advertisement simply said that the New York Public Library was looking for pages for errand-boy work, preferably boys of high school age. It stated the beginning salary and directed the applicants to come to the library's 40th Street entrance at 10 o'clock that morning.

In the years that followed, there were almost weekly advertisements. The results varied according to the economic situation in the city at the time; some Mondays only a handful of boys would appear and sometimes they came in tremendous numbers. I remember days when there would be a solid line of them, completely surrounding the 80-foot-square South Court, a line more than 300 feet long. I made it a practice to interview each boy very briefly so that he would not feel completely neglected. But with as many as 150 applicants at a time you can imagine how brief it sometimes had to be with each one. I asked his age, whether he could reach the library easily from his home, whether he was prepared to take his turn on Sundays and holidays, where he went or had gone to school, and what were his plans for the future, since there would be little chance for promotion in the library. I would be the first to admit that I could not be sure that my choices were always wise ones. But it was wonderful experience for me in sizing up young boys quickly and I hope I learned by experience to recognize the mistakes I had made. We had to drop comparatively few of those selected. They often realized on their own that they should not stay.

It might be helpful to other librarians to report some of the problems that arose with the boys whom I selected over the years. But before that, my success in obtaining enough boys to keep the stack work going resulted in my being asked within a short time to select boys for other parts of the library. These included those who worked in the Main Reading Room, in the 14 special-subject reading rooms, and the order, accessions and cataloguing divisions. Between these and the bookstack, which had the largest single group, this came to more than 100 individuals. I should add that they were all males at this time although, of course, the library had girls in clerical positions in practically all of the reading and work rooms. At a later period, after I had left the library, girls were used for stack work for a time and I found when I went to Harvard that a shift had already been made there from boys to girls. That situation has shifted back and forth since then, changing with the market. I do not feel in a position to say which is best under general circumstances. But I believe that it is easier to push boys and keep them on the run than girls and, though this might present a legal problem in the 1970's, I would prefer to avoid having both sexes at the same time in a large bookstack.

The most notorious of the group for which I had responsibility was a young man named Whitaker Chambers, who was attending Columbia University. I haven't a distinct memory of him except that during the Alger Hiss trial the fact came out that he had worked in the New York Public Library and had been discharged. Chambers had been assigned to the newspaper room and I discharged him when it was found that his coat locker (each member of the staff had one and understood that it could be opened with a master key without notice) had an armful of Columbia Library books in it which he had taken out without authorization; in many cases he had at least tried to destroy the identification marks. He was, of course, discharged by my direction and the books were returned to Columbia with information about him.

Four other disciplinary cases during my stack days come to mind, at least two of which taught me lessons which I hope I have not forgotten. The first was in connection with a tall, lanky, raw-boned, very likeable, reliable young man named Matthew Janeiro, whose family had come from part of what is now Yugoslavia and who lived in the West Side area in the Manhattan 50's, known as San Juan Hill. Janeiro was one of the most capable boys who worked with me in the bookstacks. I was looking for an opportunity to promote him. But one day I asked him to perform some service which seemed to me to be a simple duty and to my surprise he simply said, "No." I thought I knew how to handle boys and I said, "But I asked you to do it. Go and do it." He still refused and I unwisely delivered an ultimatum, "Do it or take your hat and go home and stay there." He took the latter course and I saw him only once after that. He came into the library to call on some of his old friends, including me. When I asked him what he was doing now, he replied, not in a bragging fashion, that he was the manager of one of the National City branch banks. I then came to realize that one should be very careful in giving ultimatums and should learn all the circumstances involved first. If I had done so in the case of Janeiro, I am sure I would have found the reason for his refusal and that it was a reasonable one.

The second case was in some ways similar but in others quite different. A youngster, whose name I will not give, refused to take his turn working on a holiday. The library's contract with the city included an agreement that it would be open every day in the year except Christmas and the Fourth of July. The other holidays were always very busy ones in the Main Reading Room and bookstacks as they provided opportunities for using the library to persons who could not come

on other days. I insisted on this young man taking his turn on
a holiday, one when I worked also. In revenge, as he told
me later, he took a typewriter that was assigned to a
cataloguer who had a desk in the bookstack, tied a rope
around it and let it out of one of the stack windows from an
alcove at one end of the stack that opened into a dark corner
of Bryant Park. When he left the building he retrieved it and
the next day took it to a typewriter shop and sold it. When its
loss was discovered, we notified the police, the nearby shops
that bought or sold typewriters, and the pawnshops of our
loss and the number of the machine. The police were able to
locate it and trace it back to our employee. We discharged the
boy, of course, but did not take him to court.

The third case has always been a little on my conscience.
Like the fourth, it involved what might be called obscene or
at least "off-color" books, of the kind that were kept in a
special "cage" surrounded by heavy wire grating on the sixth
level of the bookstack near my desk. They were available to
persons asking for them but they had to be used inside the
Main Reading Room desk under the supervision of the staff
to prevent their theft or mutilation. Only Charles McCombs
and I had keys to the "cage". We were careful to see that the
books or pamphlets were returned safely after their use. Use
was limited because readers were discouraged by the fact that
the books had to be used under supervision. I had been told
that Anthony Comstock of the Society for the Prevention
of Vice had been the heaviest user of the collection until his
death at about the time of which I write and that later his
successor, Mr. Sumner, had followed in his footsteps. The
collection included other material than obscene but of the
type that had a tendency to disappear when used. It included
atheistic pamphlets condemning the Bible and making fun of
passages in it. Through the gift of one of our readers, the
library had acquired a large collection of such material and
also of "free love" pamphlets, which today would be much
safer than they were 60 years ago.

But to go back to our story. One of the "cage" pamphlets, a

poem written probably as a stunt by a well-known American author, failed to reach me to be put back after its use inside the reading room desk, and we knew that the theft must be an inside job. With my strict Puritan up-bringing, I was particularly disturbed, because I realized that the guilty party must have been one of the stack attendants on my floor. I asked him about it. It seemed evident to me, while he denied it, that he was guilty. Following the practice of E. W. Gaillard, of whom more will be written later, I told the boy that I was sure that he had done it, in spite of the fact that I had no proof. I said that if he would return the pamphlet and promise to go to his priest and confess to him, that I would simply discharge him and not tell his mother, something that he begged me not to do. We would not take him to court and prosecute him. My bluff called his, and he confessed, and this has been on my conscience ever since.

The other case of a missing "cage" book was different in character except that it came up when another pamphlet was called for and could not be found. This was a poem by another distinguished American author. It was an item for which a considerable number of men who made collections of erotica were ready to pay a large sum. I was in despair as I had no lead of any kind. But that afternoon, while going home to the Bronx on the subway, I had the unusual good fortune of finding a seat on the Lexington Avenue subway train when I got on at its 42nd Street station. As I was adjusting my newspaper, which I had learned to do without interfering with my neighbors, I happened to note that there was a young man sitting beside me reading a small book. I suddenly realized two things: that it was the book that had disappeared from the "cage", and that the young man was one of the stack boys. I said nothing but instead of getting off at my regular stop I continued to the next one, where the young man got off. I followed him, and when he got away from the crowd I spoke to him and told him that I had seen him reading the stolen book and that I was going home with him to see what else he had there.

We got to the house and, perhaps fortunately for both of us, there was no one of his family at home. He took me through the house, including his own room. There were practically no books or papers to be found. He convinced me that this was his first offense. He told me that he had obtained the book by taking a rod from a shelf-list drawer and pushing the volume under the grating on to the stack aisle floor, and then with a broom handle taken from the janitor's closet he had been able to push it along and work it out under the door into the main stack aisle. The book was thin and was easy to push under the door. I told him not to come back to the library and that the case would not be taken to court.

Another story about a mistake that I made in selecting boys for the library will be told later in the chapter on G. William Bergquist. But I will write briefly of several other boys whom I did select before I turned the stack over to my successor, Rob Henderson, and went into the administrative office in 1919. Henderson was wise enough to add at least one more point to the qualifications which applicants for stack work had to meet: they had to be tall enough to reach the books on the top shelves in the stacks without stepping on the lower shelves, an obvious point but one I cannot recall including on my list of qualifications.

One of the boys referred to above was Daniel Welle, an unusually bright, capable, and likeable boy who was promoted rapidly and was ready to be made a stack chief when a vacancy occurred. But he was threatened with tuberculosis and had to give up his position. He was fortunate enough to be able to go up to the Catskills and live outdoors and eventually recovered his health but did not come back to the library except as a visitor.

Two of the boys were Czechoslovakians (Bohemians, as we called them), one named Nemecek and the other Novotny. They were capable, even tempered, and hard working. Both became stack chiefs but I never heard from them after I left the library. Quite possibly they are no longer living but I ask anyone who reads this book and knows anything about them to let me know.

The fourth boy came to the library in 1917 when he was in college and stayed only a year. But he did so well that I did not hesitate to give him a recommendation when he applied for law school. He left the library at that time and I heard nothing more about him until the 50th anniversary of the opening of the library in May 1961, when he saw my name in the *New York Times*. He wrote me a letter, asking me if I remembered him, and telling me that he was now president of the Board of Education of the City of New York. His name was Gustav Rosenberg.

Another page was a Greek boy named George Ladas, who later went back to Greece and taught there in a school which a cousin of mine had been able to help financially. He wrote me 50 years after leaving the library, asking if the two Metcalfs that he had known were related.

I wish I could give some words of wisdom about how to select pages for a library. I can say that it was not a pleasant experience during hard times when, week after week, I had to reject an average of a hundred boys who were deeply disappointed because they needed work so badly.

When I left the stack for the office, I was almost 30 years old, and I realized that while I did not feel my years, the time was not too far away when it would be better to put the work of selecting pages in the hands of a younger person. This is not to criticize the work that Rob Henderson did in the years that followed but simply to say that as far as I was concerned, staff selection, except in unusual cases, should be made by persons who are not much more than 20 years older than those who are being selected, unless the selector has his judgment checked by an assistant who is younger than he is. I found this true when it came to selecting new library school graduates after I reached 45 and was glad to be able to call on Quincy Mumford and Ed Freehafer for help between 1932 and 1937. I still wanted to have a hand in it but not the only hand.

Shelf List and Inventory

Quite early in my stack career, Mr. Lydenberg asked me to take charge of the library's photostat work. The previous year, 1912, he had arranged for the purchase of one of the first machines of its kind to be used in an American library. During the previous year this operation had taken most of the full time of a young man who had shown promise in the bookstack before I joined the staff there. The record keeping had become too much for him and I was delighted to have an opportunity to take part in this new photographic development. The process preceded the use by libraries of microphotography and in recent years has been replaced by what we have come to call Xeroxing, from the name of a leading manufacturer. These copying developments have been among the most important innovations in libraries throughout the world in this century.

The new photostat machine proved its usefulness very soon and work increased in volume so much that within a few years I had to turn the enterprise over to a separate unit with a full-time trained head, a clerical assistant, and an enlarged copying staff. Improved equipment included the use of microform cameras in the early 1930's. Photographic copying had become a $250,000-a-year business by the time I left the New York Public Library in 1937.

But to go back to 1913: the young man in charge of the photostat machine appeared for work one morning with a black eye and I found that he had taken part in a professional prizefight the night before and had been knocked out in the first round. He reported that the five dollars he had received for the fight was not worth the pain and he was giving up that part of his career.

By the end of my first year in the bookstack, Mr. Lydenberg had another task for me in connection with the photostat machine. The library had never had a shelf-list in either book or card form for the materials acquired when the three libraries were consolidated in 1895 or for those received thereafter before 1911. It seemed to be an almost insoluble problem. But a start had been made when the new building opened its printing office in May 1911 with a competent staff printing cards, including those for a shelf-list for all the books catalogued from then on.

Mr. Lydenberg had seen the advantage of comparatively easy copying with the photostat machine and asked the president of the photostat company to come to the library to talk with us about copying catalogue cards. Our machine was large enough to copy nine cards per exposure with the cards arranged on a special 10"x14" form. The form had narrow ridges between the cards and the cards were placed between the ridges, which kept them in place. The next step was to acquire photostat paper of suitable quality and thickness so that the cards could be filed with the regular NYPL or LC printed cards, that is, 7½x12½ centimeters (approximately 3"x5"). After several trials, this was accomplished with the library paying a premium for the special paper stock. We were then ready for the work.

The next task was selecting the cards to copy. The only way we could think of was to go through the public catalogue with its millions of author, subject, title, cross reference, and analytical cards, and pick out all the main entry cards for the books that were shelved in the main stack, except those for which we had had our own cards printed starting in 1911. It was a tremendous task to pick out the cards and, after they had been copied, to refile them accurately and promptly. Fortunately, Mr. Lydenberg had been able to find a young woman who had been a superbly good filer before she had left the library for marriage and who was ready to come back for a year.

We found that each day she could select 1,000 cards to be copied the following day and refile the cards that had been photostated the previous day. The cards she selected came to me and I went through them to make sure that no cards were included that should not be there. The 1,000 (999) cards for the day's work were in the photostat room at 9 o'clock in the morning and the 111 sheets that it took were copied by midmorning. Only negatives were made in order to save an extra step in the labor and reduce paper costs.

The negative photostat sheets, each with reproductions of nine cards, were piled in the order in which they were made. Then the cards were cut up by an electric cutter, with each card the exact size of the printed shelf-list cards, and were sent to me for another examination. I went through them again to make sure that each one was a suitable copy for filing and preservation. I found that white on black seemed just as easy to read as regular black on white printing but that going through 1,000 of these photostat cards each day resulted in slight eye aches, something that I had not experienced since I began wearing glasses before going to library school in September 1911. Whether this was my imagination or not, I have never been able to prove, but I believe that the cards were not always in exact focus and that the headaches were astigmatic in origin. The cards were interfiled by classmark with the printed ones already available and kept in the closed stack, with catalogue cases on each of the stack levels for the books that were shelved there.

I had the good fortune to be involved in the selection of the catalogue cases to be used. They were purchased from the Library Bureau and made up what was then a standard case, just over 33″ wide, holding drawers five high and six wide, with 30 drawers to a case. These cases could be placed on a regular card catalogue stand or on shelves in a standard double-faced, three-foot-wide stack section. They were purchased at $63 for each 30-tray case, or just over one-fifth of a cent for each card, since we had no trouble placing a thousand cards in a drawer. The present cost per tray is from $15 up instead of the $2 in 1913. This increase in cost has forced many of us to use plastic cases, metal ones having proved undesirable because of the noise and the damage to them when dropped.

The photostated cards were 207,000 in number. When the task was finished, in less than a year, we had a reasonably complete shelf-list at hand, and were ready for the library's first inventory.

Selection of the person to head up the inventory is recorded in Chapter 1 dealing with Mr. Lydenberg. Miss A. Florence Muzzy, a graduate of Wellesley, who had previously been the head of one of our busiest branch libraries, was chosen. She proved to be a perfect choice and, with her knowledge of the circulation department personnel, she selected as an assistant a Miss Cannon. Both were very careful workers who preferred this type of work to "struggling" with an often difficult public in a branch library. Both stayed with the inventory until I brought Miss Muzzy to my next assignment in the order department, some five years later, and she was succeeded by Miss Cannon. As had been expected, they found that in many cases the shelf-list did not match the books as they stood on the shelves. Some books were missing and others were found for which no shelf-list card was available. Each group had to be checked carefully in both the public and the official catalogues. A careful "reading" of the shelves—checking the volumes as they stood—was necessary to make sure that the missing ones had not been mis-shelved. In due course, many of the "missing" volumes turned up. The books for which no cards were found were re-catalogued or perhaps it would be more accurate to say that they were catalogued for the first time.

I do not remember the total number of missing books. The exact figure was amazingly small and I took the cards for them to Mr. Lydenberg in two files. One contained those that I thought should be replaced. The other listed books that I thought need not be replaced; but the cards for these should be withdrawn and placed in a separate file marked "missing". I was amazed how often Mr. Lydenberg would speak of a book that was missing, saying that he remembered how and when it came to the library, given by a certain person whom he remembered or ordered after a recommendation by someone he named. How I wished I had that kind of memory, although I soon found that while his memory for books and authors was remarkable, it was not so good for people whom he had met.

In this connection, I might add that this also held true for William A. Jackson, who many years later was in charge of rare books at Harvard. He had an uncanny photographic memory for title pages and authors and the location of copies of rare books but was not equally successful in remembering names of persons whom he had met at one time or another. I wish a good psychologist could explain this satisfactorily. I might add that this was the first large-scale use of photostated cards, and took place more than 15 years before Yale astonished the world by copying its catalogue photographically before it entered the Sterling Library. I do not know whether Yale's cards stood up better than the New York Public Library ones. The latter had begun to deteriorate by the time I went to Harvard in 1937. Some of them had become brittle and the corners tended to break off. In addition, part of the text on some of the cards had flaked off, probably because of inadequate developing. The photostat company had been unable to provide card stock of a quality equal to that used by the library. Mr. Lydenberg, as has been reported, was one of the first librarians to become vitally interested in the quality of paper and particularly of card stock and the New York Public Library cards that were printed at the library were of as fine a stock as was available at that time.

The inventory, even for a closed-stack library, seemed important enough to be worth continuing and it was kept up at least until 1937 with a staff of two going on with a continuous inventory. This task has been simplified by the current NYPL practice of shelving its new books by size and date of acquisition instead of by a subject classification mark. With the completion of the inventory and the correction of the records which resulted, we finally had one day when the stack produced every one of the 4,000 or 5,000 books called for by readers or was able to report that the volume was in use by another person, in the bindery, being recatalogued, or known to be missing. This was a record never repeated in the New York Public Library, or as far as I can learn in any other large research library, and you can imagine how proud I was, since it demonstrated a great improvement over the situation I had found when I came to the bookstack in July 1913, at a time when the collection had not recovered from the consolidation of the three libraries and the move into the new building. It must be realized that such a record can not be equalled in an open-stack collection.

Chapter 3
Acting Librarian at Oberlin
September 1916 Through June 1917

Mary Wright Plummer, the principal of the New York Public Library Library School, was elected president of the American Library Association for the year 1915-16; she was the second woman to hold that office. With this added to her regular assignments, the year was an unusually busy and hard one for her. On that account and for other reasons, she put off a cancer operation. In the summer of 1916, it became evident that she must have the operation and take a year's leave of absence to insure recovery. She and Mr. Anderson talked the matter over and decided to ask Professor Root to substitute for her during the year. Mr. Anderson wrote to A.S.R. to that effect. The answer came back promptly that he would like to come; he was very much interested in education for librarianship, but, because it was only four years since his sabbatical (the spring and summer of 1912, when I had substituted for him), he felt he could not leave Oberlin unless I could be released again to take his place.

Mr. Anderson called me to his office and asked if I would be willing to go to Oberlin for the year; to my amusement, he failed to try to discourage me as he had four years earlier, when he said that I would find the students very young and immature and it would not be worth my while. I understood the situation, realizing how anxious he was to persuade Mr. Root to come because he felt that the library school needed him badly. I accepted the proposal. I was to have the title of acting librarian at Oberlin, be a regular member of the faculty, and receive a salary of $150 a month for the year, which was the same that I was paid at the New York Public Library and, I think, the amount paid to associate professors at Oberlin at that time. I would occupy Professor Root's house, rent-free, but would, of course, pay for the utilities, and he would occupy my apartment in the Bronx and pay the rent there. I am sure that his salary in New York was enough higher than his Oberlin salary to make up the difference, and my $150 would go further in Oberlin than in New York. I knew that he must be interested in his salary because he was worried about the future; he had told me in 1912 on his return to Oberlin that he had been 50 years old the previous February and, while he owned his house free and clear, he had no savings of any kind and nothing to look forward to at retirement except his Carnegie pension. This pension, as I remember it, was to be one-half of his regular salary plus $100 a year, which would be inadequate for him and his wife.

This temporary change in position pleased me. My oldest child, Margaret, had been born in May in Oberlin, where I spent my vacation as soon as I received word of Margaret's arrival and we had all returned before the end of June. Meanwhile the terrible 1916 polio epidemic had broken out in New York. But our Oberlin doctor said that small infants were immune and Margaret would be likely to stay at home for the months immediately following until cold weather stopped the epidemic, so she would not be in danger of catching the disease. Back we went to New York, and we were glad to be there because our New York doctor increased Margaret's milk formula and she became much better behaved. We had been at home for only a short time when the decision on the change in Professor Root's position and mine was made, so Margaret, after ten weeks in New York, had her second night on the train before she was three months old. We had a difficult time getting her out of New York because medical regulations required a doctor's certificate obtained within a few hours before departure showing freedom of all signs of polio.

Both parties involved found themselves settled in their new positions and housing on September 1 and both had interesting times ahead of them. The Roots enjoyed spending a year in the big city, something they had never expected to be able to do. Mart, Margaret, and I used only the first floor of the Roots' big house. It was all we needed and we were glad of it because, during the extremely severe winter that followed, there was not enough gas available to heat the first floor, to say nothing of the whole house. We used fireplaces as much as we could; the locally produced natural gas was insufficient in quantity in the below-zero weather, which came often. Even with the kitchen stove going full blast, it sometimes took an hour to heat the baby's milk in the daytime. Toward morning the heat would come on suddenly and, with no thermostat to regulate the furnace, we would wake up perspiring. I remember that in 1917 the cost of gas for the month of January took two-thirds of my salary for that month.

We had a happy but busy year. Mart could push Margaret in the baby carriage down to her parents' home, three-

quarters of a mile away, whenever she wanted to. It was only
half that distance to the shopping area and she still had many
friends in town. My oldest sister, who had brought me up
after my parents died in the 1890's, lived only a hundred
yards away and was available as a baby sitter. The library was
about the same distance. Indeed, I found that getting to the
library and back did not provide my accustomed exercise and
I began to put on weight, just as I had immediately after my
marriage, though the work in the library stack had taken care
of the problem at that time. However, the college gymnasium
was at my disposal, as well as other exercise when I could find
time to take it.

The Oberlin football coach, Howard Curtis, expected to
find an exceedingly difficult task ahead of him because all
but one of the previous year's returning players had been
"fired" for starting a fraternity, something that was against
the Oberlin rules. The one remaining experienced player,
"Red" Hudson, became captain and did remarkably well
under difficult circumstances. He was killed in the fighting
near Verdun only two years later. But the college's unex-
pected problem in September was the fact that Howard Curtis came down with an infection that put him out of action for
months. It was evident that he could not coach the team that
fall. I was asked to take his place, but with the busiest college
library in the country on my hands, to say nothing of teaching Professor Root's three courses (two for one semester and
one for the other), I did not dare to undertake it. The
position was accepted by a star player from the University of
Chicago who had just graduated, and he did well with almost
no material, until the season ended with the regular Ohio
State game. Oberlin had broken even in this series over the
preceding eight years, but lost this time by a score of 128 to 0.

Freshmen were not allowed to play on the varsity team in
Oberlin at that time. I consented to coach the freshman
team, which had a number of players who in later years
turned out well and with whom I became friends, but this
coaching took only part of two afternoons a week, followed

by a Monday morning game. After the football season was over, I got my exercise running around the gymnasium's indoor track two or three days a week and in the spring I went out for track practice. Although I had not jumped over a hurdle for six years, I ran a high hurdle race against Oberlin's best hurdler and won it. Also in the spring, after war with Germany was proclaimed, I joined the more or less informal group that practiced military drill several afternoons a week.

There had been little change in the library since 1912 except that there was a new reference librarian, and the reading room was as quiet as I had left it. The new reference librarian was too much like the "old maid" librarian that mis-informed persons have come to consider typical, whose likeness has been shown again and again in the press, and whom children (among them my daughter) came to think of as one of the lowest forms of humanity. I failed to understand this until Margaret told me about it when she was 45 years old and had become a librarian herself in the Long Island town where she lives. The students did not take a fancy to the Oberlin reference librarian and began to tease her; one day, to her horror, when she returned from a trip to the bookstack she found her overshoes (rubbers) on the top of her desk. She reported it to me angrily and I calmed her down as best I could. A little later a popular professor and a good friend of mine dropped by and asked me how things were going. I told him the story of the rubbers and said I feared that the reference librarian had no sense of humor. You can see why I have not given the professor's name (since this happened in a co-educational college) when I tell you that he replied with sadness in his tone, "Keyes, you know, no woman has." Many years later, when I was chairman of an Oberlin alumni committee to select someone each year to add to the list of those who had made special contributions to the college, we chose this professor. Most of the committee were women but I did not tell them of his opinion.

The library part of my work went well. The faculty library

committee met occasionally but was so used to being domi-
nated by A.S.R. that there were no complications even in
connection with book selection. They approved the request
left by Professor Root that his daughter Marion (Polly, a
senior at Oberlin that year) be appointed to the staff for one
year following her graduation from Oberlin. She then went
to library school at the New York Public Library and later
joined its staff. Fortunately this was just before I went into
the office and took over the personnel work, so I had nothing to do with employing her and she worked in the reference department of the library until her retirement. Many
academic institutions were warned about nepotism in the
early part of the century, although Oberlin, because of co-
education, had a number of married couples on its staff at
that time, as many institutions have come to have in recent
years.

There was no problem in keeping the reading room quiet
during the year but Dean Cole, who had been the most
powerful member of the faculty since Azariah's absence in
1912, came to me in mid-winter and said that he hoped that I
would consider remaining at Oberlin after Professor Root's
return in September, to serve as assistant librarian. He said
he had a hard time talking with A.S.R., particularly on
budget matters, something that did not surprise me. Professor Root had been chairman of the budget committee for a
good many years and had also been a faculty representative
for 25 years on the prudential (executive) committee of the
Board of Trustees, where he had great influence. Dean Cole
urged me to consider the matter carefully, which I agreed to
do. He noted that this would be my last opportunity to be
included in the Carnegie Pension Plan as the Carnegie Corporation had come to realize that, with the increase in
salaries and the number of professors, they would have to
offer a new plan which had not yet been announced but
would be a contributory one with equal contributions by the
institution and the faculty members.

I considered Dean Cole's offer seriously. Mart's parents

and my sister Marion were getting well along in their 50's. We liked the town and the college. But I felt that I needed wider experience than I had had so far and that I would be very unhappy if it turned out that Dean Cole would want to consult with me about library matters behind Azariah's back. The latter was just 55 and the college at that time had no definite retirement age, so I might work with him for 15 years before taking over his position, something that I looked forward to doing ultimately. I was ready to say "no" when Professor Cole came to me again in late April to say that he would have to withdraw the proposal because of the college's financial pinch which was sure to result from the war that the United States had just entered and the resulting smaller student body which was ahead of us.

Four things took place during the year that contributed to my training and proved to be helpful to me thereafter.

1. As already indicated, I taught Professor Root's three two-hour-a-week courses during the year, one during the first semester and two during the second. First came the *History of Printing;* during the second semester there was one on *Book Illustration* and another on the *Use of Libraries.* Each of the three had a large number of students, from 20 to 40, made up from the four college classes. This, I confess, surprised me because the students easily could have learned that Professor Root would be back next year and they could have worked with him.

I had Professor Root's rough notes to work with but as I have already implied, Azariah was not particularly systematic and was so knowledgeable in the field that he did not require detailed notes. I remembered from my college days nine or ten years earlier that for the *History of Printing* I could use George Haven Putnam's *Books and Their Makers During the Middle Ages* and Joseph Moxon's *Mechanical Exercises,* published originally in the 17th century and reproduced by Theodore L. DeVinne. It was too early to take advantage of the work of Daniel Berkeley Updike which would have been of great help. I did have the rough notes that A.S.R. had made during his year's study of the Beginning of Printing from Movable Type in Göttingen and Mainz in 1898-9.

During the second semester I had more trouble but less reading to do for the course on book illustration. Azariah had left a great number of illustrations taken from available books showing the development of illustration from ancient times to the present. As part of their tests the students had to identify the method used in making these. My difficulty resulted from the fact that I had problems of my own in identifying the pictures and could not correct mistakes easily. This made me realize that I had been wise in not choosing teaching as a profession but it was good experience in learning how to bluff one's way through a difficult situation.

The third course on the Use of Libraries was comparatively easy; I had more than ten years of experience behind me as well as two years of library school, and felt that I managed reasonably well. But all this was hard on my family; in my efforts to prepare for teaching, I read through all my meals and was poor company.

2. My second valuable experience came from being a full-fledged member of the faculty. It was my first exposure to faculty meetings and I saw some of the problems that result when a president has to face a faculty which is in almost complete control, even in financial matters, but with many of its members unable to understand the financial implications of their actions. As has been noted, the faculty budget committee was not powerful enough to dare grade its colleagues, and all full professors received the same salary, no matter how long they had been there or how well they taught. A similar situation held for those in the other grades.

3. The third problem was dealing with the library budget and doing my best to provide salaries commensurate with the work done. Here I was able to be reasonably successful because it was known that Professor Root would back me. The budget committee did not provide a fixed scale for library salaries.

4. The fourth "learning experience" stemmed from the

fact that during the college year the Allen Art building was completed under the guidance of a new and competent art professor, Clarence Ward, who had just come from Rutgers and Princeton. The art collection was based on the one which had been housed on the two top stack levels of the Carnegie Library, older material, and new acquisitions which he was successful in obtaining. He now was provided with a building and eventually put together one of this country's great college art book collections. Under Professor Ward's direction the art books were moved from the library into the new building, leaving badly needed stack space in the library. Since it was known that I had helped install the Olney collection when it first came to Oberlin in 1908, I was called upon to help in the move. The serious problem, as far as I was concerned, was that Professor Ward was bound to establish a special art library in the new building and I had been taught in library school that departmental libraries should be avoided in colleges as far as possible, although we already had separate theology, music, and chemistry libraries at Oberlin.

I wrote to Professor Root in New York to tell him that I was very unhappy about the situation, and was astonished and, I must confess, vastly relieved when he wrote back that I should not worry and that Professor Ward was right. A.S.R. added, perhaps to salve my conscience, that "while I had been right in principle there should be exceptions to every rule."

This taught me a lesson about a problem which I did not have to face again until I went to Harvard 20 years later. I should add that the departmental library situation had been dealt with in the New York Public Library, where there were 14 special subject reading rooms and collections in the same building with the main reading room and the stack which had been under my charge. I shall not attempt to comment at this time on departmental libraries in college and research institutions except to say "circumstances alter cases." Sometimes they are desirable and sometimes they are not. Of course, it is almost self-evident that they tend to increase the total library budget and thus present a financial problem, particularly because of additional staff required to serve them. But libraries in other buildings can relieve the shelf space in the central building and at least postpone the necessity for a large addition to it or for a new main library building.

I had expected to complete the academic year—September 1, 1916, to August 31, 1917—at Oberlin, including a month's vacation with pay, but in June a call came from New York. Paul North Rice, who was substituting for me in the New York Public Library stack, had joined the Plattsburgh Officer Training Group, set up by Theodore Roosevelt, Grenville Clark, and General Leonard Wood. There was no suitable person available to take his place and many staff members had enlisted. I was asked if I would return to New York as soon as possible. Professor Root had finished his school year and could return to Oberlin, so I went back to New York with my family and returned to my old apartment on 174th Street in the Bronx, which I found none the worse for wear from the Roots. Oberlin cut off my salary without allowing any vacation and I received no vacation from New York, so I had a 23-month period with no holiday and no holiday pay. I did not complain. I felt that it was part of my war effort. I did not expect to volunteer, as I had a wife and child on my hands and felt I had a worth-while job.

In this connection I should add that my brother, Nelson, who had coached football and track at Oberlin after his graduation in 1912, had gone to Columbia to coach, with courses also at the Columbia College of Physicians and Surgeons. He was married during the Christmas holidays in 1915 after coaching the first Columbia football season since football had been given up there as a result of criticism of the sport by Theodore Roosevelt, the promoter of the strenuous life. Nelson had found an apartment in the same apartment house that we had been in since November 1915. There was only 17 months difference between Nelson's age and mine. We had been brought up almost as twins and were very glad to be in the same house again. Soon after my return to New York we went together to the local draft board and were told that we would not be called because of our work and our family situation. Nelson continued coaching the Columbia football team. I went back to my bookstack work in the library, finding little change from the previous year, except that we had lost members who had volunteered or been drafted. We found it almost impossible to keep together a stack force large enough to give good service.

The year in Oberlin was perhaps as valuable for me as the one in 1912 had been. It provided my first teaching experience and membership in a college faculty gave me some insight of what goes on with a dominant faculty. It made me feel more confident that when Professor Root would retire in 15 years, I might be asked to take over and the faculty would not object to my appointment. The year's sudden ending brought one disappointment which I never succeeded in overcoming. I had counted on a summer-school course in history with Professor Lybyer in Oberlin; this, with a thesis, would have given me an earned M.A. degree, something which I never obtained in spite of nearly three years of graduate work.

Chapter 4
The Stack Again
July 1917-December 1918

The Staff Association

The 18 months following my return to the New York Public Library in July 1917 proved to be one of the most trying, exasperating periods in my career. It seemed impossible to keep together a large enough stack staff to give good service. New stack boys came and old ones left seemingly every day. I was beginning to feel that I had all the experience in that particular assignment that I needed, and was more anxious than ever to get into reference work, although I realized that I was needed where I was.

A similar situation prevailed throughout the staff in the central building and the branches. Each year during the war, staff unrest in the library increased; there were not enough employees to do the work satisfactorily. Low salaries resulted from the strained financial situation. Many staff members who did not leave to join the armed services became restless and dissatisfied, and the professional staff on its own initiative started one of the first library staff associations. I remember well the meeting I attended when the speakers were two members of the staff who had been in Europe when World War I began in August 1914. Adelaide Hasse, to whom I have devoted another part of this chapter, was German in origin and had been in Germany in August 1914; she spoke on the German side. Dr. Richard Gottheil, who had a French background, was the chief of the Oriental Division, an expert on the Arab world, and Professor of Semitic languages at Columbia. He had spent the summer of 1914 in France and reported on the French side. As could be expected, the argument between the two speakers became rather heated.

Considerably later, in the autumn of 1918, under the leadership of Franklin Hopper, the association began to pay more attention to the staff situation. He decided to appoint a committee to suggest ways in which the library administration might alleviate reference department staff restlessness. Charles McCombs was appointed chairman of the committee. He talked with me about it; our work in the reading room and stack brought us closely together. I said that one of the great needs was to have someone in the main office whom members of the staff would feel free to talk with when they had problems or were dissatisfied about something in connection with their work. Such a person also could serve as personnel officer and help the library's division chiefs try to find new junior and senior assistants when they were required. I wrote out this proposal in detail and turned it over to McCombs. I never asked him if he revised it but I do know that the proposal went to Mr. Anderson's office, anonymously as far as I was concerned.

Quite a few weeks later, in early December 1918, Mr. Anderson and Mr. Lydenberg called me and said they had decided that they needed another person in the main office who would make himself generally useful to them in connection with any tasks that came up (I realized that I had written the specifications for the position that I was to undertake, but said nothing about it to anyone, and doubt if anyone except McCombs knew it). Mr. Anderson added that Mr. Hopper, the chief of the reference department's order division, was to become chief of Circulation Department in place of Benjamin Adams, who was resigning at the end of December for personal reasons. He went on to say that Carl Cannon, who had worked for Mr. Waite at the information desk before enlisting, would take Mr. Hopper's place, but that he had been severely wounded in France by shrapnel in the upper leg and would not be able to leave the hospital and assume his new duties before July 1, 1919. I was to carry on this work during the first six months of the year in addition to my position in the main office. I was somewhat taken aback by this sudden change and what it would mean to me professionally but, of course, was pleased.

Adelaide Hasse

Adelaide R. Hasse was the chief of the document division when I first came to the New York Public Library in September 1911. She had come to the library in 1897 under Dr. Billings to deal with the rapidly growing document collection. This followed work at the Library of Congress and the Los Angeles Public Library. Miss Hasse continued in the document division until nearly the end of 1918. In 1914, she had added to her responsibilities the title of chief of the economics division when Dr. Charles C. Williamson became librarian of the Municipal Reference Library.

This is the story of Miss Hasse and not of Dr. Williamson, except indirectly. She was, in my opinion, the greatest public document bibliographer in American library history and this applies not only to United States public documents but to those of the world as a whole. Her bibliographical output was tremendous in quantity and superb in quality. I believe that Dr. Childs, formerly of the Library of Congress, who was her runner-up in document work, would have agreed with this statement. Miss Hasse was an extremely capable administrator and organizer.

But Miss Hasse had other traits. She was ambitious, as I suppose many of us are. She had a sharp tongue and she did not "suffer fools gladly." In July 1913, when I became chief of the stacks with my desk in the center of the sixth-stack level, I found that a goodly portion of that level was occupied by public documents for which there was not room in the document division area, and that a noisy book conveyor which frequently went out of order was close to my desk and ran to the public documents room. My contact with this room was bound to be extensive as both the document and stack staffs were involved with the shelving and binding of volumes in the document collection and in the use of the conveyor.

As one of my daily assignments, I regularly selected a large truckload with 24 running feet of books to go to the bindery in the library basement. They went by way of the accessions division, where records of them were kept and directions were prepared for the labelling of the volumes. From time to time Miss Hasse objected to the lettering on the document volumes when they were returned and made it as difficult as she could for W. B. A. Taylor, the chief of the accessions division. He was thoroughly intimidated, and Miss Hasse angrily showed me the volumes and complained about their lettering. This was the beginning of a series of complaints she brought to my attention in regard to the bookstacks and I found very quickly that the easiest way to deal with her was to refuse to argue but simply to say, "I think this is something to refer to the man to whom we both report." I suggested that

we go together to Mr. Lydenberg's office. This happened
perhaps once or twice a year during the years which followed
while I was in charge of the main stack. In each case, Mr.
Lydenberg supported me and Miss Hasse left practically
boiling with rage. At least once Mr. Lydenberg signalled me
to wait after one of these confrontations and he said very
quietly, "I wish you could find a way to avoid this type of
situation."

As time went on, Miss Hasse became more and more
unpopular with the senior members of the library staff who
came into contact with her and this naturally did not improve
her attitude toward them. However, her own staff in the
document and economics division stood by her.

The beginning of the climax of this affair came in the early
autumn of 1918, when letters appeared in a New York
municipal staff organ and elsewhere regarding the terrible
conditions in the New York Public Library and the inadequ-
acy of the chief reference librarian, Harry Miller Lydenberg;
the document division was praised as the only efficient part
of the reference department. One of these letters was signed
by a former employee and protege of Miss Hasse and it was
clear that Miss Hasse was responsible for it. The letter came
to my attention and I immediately took it to Mr. Lydenberg
and said that I believed that the reference department staff
had complete confidence in him and that something must be
done to prevent this kind of abuse. He quietly said that he
was not in a position to defend himself and nothing could be
done unless the staff agreed with my attitude. I replied by
saying that I personally did not want to work in a place where
such statements were published about the person under
whom I was working, and I repeated that something must be
done.

I then went back to my desk and drafted a letter to Mr.
Anderson, to whom Mr. Lydenberg reported. I took the
draft to Charles McCombs, who had a far better command of
English than I and was a good editor. McCombs revised and
strengthened my statement and we took it to other division

chiefs who, we were sure, would sign it. We obtained the signatures of every division chief but one—Miss Hasse, of course. In addition, we then went to Miss Minnie Sears, the first assistant in the catalogue division, and three senior women on the staff who had been in the library for 20 years or more, and they all gladly added their signatures. The letter was then sent to Mr. Anderson. It read as follows:

"Dear Mr. Anderson:

"The Chief of the Economics Division, Miss Adelaide R. Hasse, has been conducting through newspapers and periodicals a campaign which is injuring the Library, misrepresenting the library profession, and is definitely calculated to bring discredit upon us as librarians.

"Furthermore we believe that she is systematically working to undermine your administration and to cause discord and dissatisfaction among the staff, and we also believe that ample proof of these activities exists.

"We are convinced that her conception of library service, and its practice as exemplified in the administration of the Economics Division, her frequent refusal to cooperate fairly with other divisions, her frequent disregard of the interests of other divisions and of the rights of her colleagues, and her habitual rudeness to members of the staff, interfere seriously with the work of the division chiefs, and are detrimental to the work and usefulness of the whole Library and to the spirit and welfare of the staff.

"Considering the harm that she is doing to the Library, we protest against the continuance of Miss Hasse as an employee of the New York Public Library, and place ourselves on record as ready to support you in any steps which you think it wise and necessary to take in regard to her, for the good of the service."

This letter was then signed by all of the reference department division chiefs except Henryk Arctowski, the chief of the science division. Others who signed were Edwin White Gaillard, special investigator of the reference and circulation departments, and the four senior women on the staff. A

record was made of the number of years of service of each of
those signing, including one who had been in the library for
39 years, one for 37, one for 24, two for 22, and two for 21.

Dr. Arctowski, who did not sign the document, wrote to
Mr. Anderson three days later as follows:

"A letter addressed to you and signed by the division chiefs
of the New York Public Library has been submitted to me on
Friday.

"I have been asked to sign it. I refused on the ground that
I could not agree on all the points mentioned in this letter.
In reality however, my point of view is that this letter in
question will do more harm than good - making a 'public
martyr' of a person whose motives are or may be purely
political and anti-patriotic. If I am right, the case should be
investigated and carried out by the proper authorities and
not discussed, neither privately nor publicly."

On the same day that the division chiefs' letter went to Mr.
Anderson, Mr. William B. Gamble, the chief of the division
of technology, also wrote to Anderson. His letter read:

"There has recently been sent to you a letter signed by
several members of the Reference Department staff, arraign-
ing Miss Adelaide R. Hasse, Chief of the Economics Division,
for lack of courtesy and for disloyalty to the Library. While I
have signed this letter I wish to make my position clear to you
on one point, namely: that I do not intend to convey the idea
that *I*, personally, have suffered from Miss Hasse's habitual
rudeness. I have never, with one possible exception, had
such an experience. I think it is only fair to her that I say this
to you. However, I fully appreciate the feelings of the other
signers of the joint letter.

"On the other hand, I am inclined to express even more
strongly than the joint letter my opinion concerning Miss
Hasse's disloyalty to the Library. I very much resent her
campaign for what seems to be her own aggrandizement. I
resent her poisoning of the public mind into the belief that
the Economics Division is the only efficient section of this
institution. I do not believe that a discussion of the Library's

administration should find a place in the public print - much less from the pen of a member of the staff.

"I resent her advertisement of the Library as a fount for favors which have nothing to do with legitimate library work, thereby placing the other divisions in the awkward position of explaining why they cannot 'deliver the goods.' I resent her attitude of defiance to you and to the Chief of the Reference Department as shown in a lamentable attempt to organize a Reference Staff organization in place of the one presided over by yourself. In short I resent her continuous spirit of disloyalty. If I, myself, were ever guilty of such insubordination I would certainly expect to offer a letter of resignation or to be asked to present one. I do not feel that Miss Hasse should be an exception. I feel that her continued service on the staff is a menace to the good name and to the usefulness of the Library.

"These are my personal opinions and I trust they will be accepted in the kindly spirit in which they are offered. I have no desire to obtrude my views upon matters which do not concern me, but I do believe this matter concerns me both personally and professionally. I regard Miss Hasse's public attacks as attacks upon me and upon the Division under my charge.

"With the explanation offered in the first paragraph above I subscribe most willingly to the letter which the members of the staff have sent to you. Faithfully yours, William B. Gamble, Chief of the Division of Technology."

I suppose that Mr. Anderson referred the staff's statement to the Board of Trustees or at least to the Executive Committee. Their action was decisive. Miss Hasse was discharged about November 15, just after the signing of the Armistice, and dismissal took place immediately (I do not remember the exact date). Her salary was continued until the end of the calendar year and she was given the intervening time to go through her files and clear up her desk.

The next step, to my surprise and you might say my dismay, came when I was called into Mr. Anderson's office

and told that since Miss Hasse's division should not be left
even temporarily without a head and since no one of her
assistants (a staff of some 10 persons) was up to the assignment, I was to take charge of the division while continuing to
direct the work in the bookstack, until her successor, Dr.
Williamson, who was then working with the Carnegie Corporation, would be available for duty at the beginning of the
new year. Miss Hasse's desk was in the farthest corner of a
long, narrow room and I took a desk about 15 feet in front
of her with my back toward her. I spent part of each day for
the next six weeks feeling that Miss Hasse's eyes were boring
holes through my back but I survived. Miss Hasse did not
speak to me or interfere in any way. There was no trouble
with the staff and all went smoothly. On January 2, Dr.
Williamson, who had served as Municipal Reference Librarian, then had made a special study for the Carnegie Corporation dealing among other things with library schools, took
Miss Hasse's place and remained until he resigned in 1921.
Thereafter he worked for five years for the Rockefeller
Foundation before going to Columbia University as Director
of the Library and Dean of the Library School.

As you can imagine, the six weeks before January 1919
were not easy for me, physically or mentally, and my situation was not helped by the fact that Mr. Anderson had a
severe attack of lumbago which increased the tension.

But to go back to Adelaide Hasse. To everyone's relief,
she left the library with no flare-up. She went to Washinton
and there found interesting and valuable work for the next
22 years with a variety of organizations, including the U. S.
Navy and the Brookings Institution.

A year later, at Christmas 1919, Miss Hasse sent each of
the New York Public Library division chiefs a Christmas
message, listing the members of Congress, the cabinet members, and other important Washington personages she had
worked with during the year, and thanking us for having
been responsible for this.

But this was not the last that we heard from Miss Hasse.

More than 17 years later, in May 1936, at the American Library Association's annual conference in Richmond, Virginia, Dr. Frederick Keppel, who had been a good friend of the New York Public Library for years, and of its then-director, Harry Miller Lydenberg, was nominated for honorary membership in the association. The association's Executive Board had always been very careful in nominations of this kind. The by-laws stated that honorary members could be elected only by the unanimous vote of all members present at a general session. Those in favor of Dr. Keppel were asked to stand and it looked as though everyone had done so; then those opposed were called for and Adelaide Hasse, who had a tall, stately figure, stood up alone. Therefore Dr. Keppel was not elected. It might be said that in this way she had the last word. The whole affair left a bad taste in my mouth. I am convinced that I did the right thing but it was a shame to have Miss Hasse's library career end in this way. During her 21 years in the New York Public Library, she had built up the finest public document collection to be found anywhere and had gone a long way toward making the material in an important and difficult field easier to deal with bibliographically than it had ever been before.

The Spanish Flu and a Personal Problem

This section may not seem to belong in a volume entitled *Seventy-Five Years of Library Work* but I hope it will help others who go through difficult personal periods to realize that many problems can be overcome with a little effort (and I confess more than a little luck). As noted in the previous chapter, Mart, Margaret, and I returned to our apartment in the Bronx in July 1917 and the Roots went back to Oberlin. My brother Nelson was still in the same apartment house with his wife Helen. Columbia, against his advice, had decided to go back into "big time" football with what later became the Ivy League universities, instead of playing with Amherst, Wil-

liams, Wesleyan, and other institutions having about the same
number of male undergraduates that it had. Columbia had
become primarily a graduate school. As a result, Nelson's
1917 season was less successful than previous seasons had
been, and the Columbia authorities told him that one of his
duties was to bring players to Columbia as well as to coach
them. This was a task in which he was not interested and of
which he did not approve. He continued at Columbia
throughout the academic year, coaching the track team in the
spring, but left on August 31, 1918, and returned to Oberlin.

The year 1917-18 was hard for me because it was almost
impossible to find satisfactory junior help for the library as a
whole, for which I was responsible, and it was difficult to
keep up with the demands on us, continue with the inventory,
and deal with the weekend and Sunday crowds that came in
spite of war conditions. I will report later on the study that I
made in the 1930's on the way economic conditions affect the
use of a great research library.

Nelson and Helen's first child was due in May 1918 and the
doctor for both Metcalf families selected what he thought
was a good local hospital. However, because of the war and
through no one's fault, so far as we could tell, Helen did not
receive satisfactory care. As a result of this the doctor told us -
Mart and I were expecting a child about August 1 - that he
could find a first-class English nurse who could take care of
Mart; he suggested that the child be born in our apartment.

About the first of July I went into the library one Saturday
morning and then proceeded to a playground belonging to
one of the West Side schools where we had made a reservation to put on a track meet for the boys and young men of the
library staff, believing that it would help to keep up their
morale. I was to be in charge. It was a new experience for the
library and was never repeated. I served as referee and
general factotum with the aid of Harry Grumpelt, who had
been the Amateur Athletic Union high-jump champion a
few years earlier and was at that time financial officer of the
circulation department. The meet went off well for one that

had not been organized in advance. Without the aid of a megaphone, I pretty well "yelled my head off," and by the time the meet was finished, I was very tired and had a sore throat which I blamed on the overuse of my voice. By the time I got back to the library I realized that I was not only tired but sick, and I turned the stack over to Harry Lips and took the subway home. Our apartment was up quite a hill from the Jerome Avenue subway station and I was not sure that I would be able to get up the hill and the stairs to our second-floor apartment. I felt completely done in. I knew I had a high fever. Mart got out the medical thermometer and we never knew whether she washed it with hot water in her haste, but at any rate after a time under my tongue it read 106°. Mart telephoned our doctor and was given directions on how to bring down my temperature with cold packs. This was done with Nelson's help. The doctor came as soon as he could and found that my temperature then was 103½°. I was a very sick young man with one of the early American cases of the Spanish flu, as we called it. It was already raging throughout much of the rest of the world.

With good care I recovered quickly, except for a slight heart murmur which disappeared after a few months and did not return until 32 years later, when I was 60. I went back to work, probably too soon for my own good, and for the next few months looked a little ghostly and weighed less than I had in my high school days. My great fear, of course, was for Mart and the baby, who was due to arrive in a few weeks. Our son, William Gerrish Metcalf (Gerry), was born practically bald during the hottest August week that I experienced in my years in New York. He developed a heat rash on his bald head, scratched it with his sharp little fingernails, and rubbed them in his eyes and infected them. Dover, the nurse, was persuaded to stay an extra week with orders from the doctor not to let Gerry cry because that would complicate the infection. She was successful—no mean feat with a week-old-child—but, of course, he was completely spoiled in the meantime so that when she left he naturally cried unless he was held. After two weeks of this we decided one night to let him cry it out, which he proceeded to do so vigorously that he ruptured himself and for many months thereafter had to wear a minute truss which did not make him easy to care for.

I might add at this point that I was nearly 50 years ahead of my time; I stayed with Mart and helped as much as I could during the delivery. The birth was not an easy one and some immediate repair work was necessary. A fallen uterus complicated the situation and, with a two-year-old daughter and a new baby son (he's now over 60, stands 6 feet 6 and has had a very heavy head of hair which is getting thin again although he's far from as bald as he was when he was born), Mart still was afflicted with frequent severe migraine headaches.

During the fall the Hasse incident came to a head and the extra work that it involved was not easy. Then, when I heard of my two new assignments, beginning with January 1919, which are dealt with later, I realized that I would be beyond my depth. I asked my niece, Marion (Polly Root), who was going back to Oberlin for the Christmas holidays, to take Mart and the children with her and turn them over to Mart's parents to care for until the spring, when I would be able to bring them back and Mart would be ready for the major operation that she required.

I was left completely alone in my apartment. Soon after January 1 1919, several young New York Public Library staff members who had shared an apartment had to find new quarters. One of them was Donald (Don) Cameron, the first professional librarian I had employed at the NYPL. He had previously spent some time with Franklin Poole, librarian of the Association of the Bar of the City of New York. In 1918 Don had completed his library school work. He was looking for new quarters and I invited him to use my apartment until he found them. He was with me for a couple of months. We got our own breakfasts and had our other meals near the library. I speak of him primarily because I was helped a great deal by a single sentence that Don ventured to say to me. After six difficult months, plus the two new assignments that had begun on January 1, I was for the first time in years in poor shape nervously. Donald said to me one day, "You may not realize it, but you shake your head sideways with a nervous twitch from time to time." I cannot say that "a word to the wise is sufficient," but this word from a friendly young man to an associate who was under nervous strain proved to be just what I needed. I realized what had happened and fortunately was able to overcome my affliction and in the more than 60 years that have followed have had no similar trouble, although I have gone through other periods of stress and strain.

Don Cameron came from Haverhill, Massachusetts, and his widowed mother was still living there. In due course he went back to Haverhill as head of the public library. We kept in touch. He sent me his annual reports and they were among the few library reports I have read that had true literary flavor, were not just a bundle of statistics and plain statements. I am glad to take this opportunity to speak with feeling and pleasure of one of the finest librarians whom I have known. He was small and far from handsome but a good librarian and a credit to his profession.

Mart came home in the spring with the children, bringing a sister with her to help while she had a successful operation, but the migraine headaches continued. My work during the months from January through June 1919 is dealt with in the next chapter.

Chapter 5
New Assignments in 1919

The Director's Office

In January 1919 I began work as an assistant in the director's office and acting chief of the Reference Department's Order Division. As assistant in the director's office, I had no title assigned to me for the first of the nine years that I was there. I was not even called assistant. I asked Mr. Lydenberg for some kind of designation so that the library staff, with whom I was to deal in various capacities, would understand what I was doing. I realized that, without a title, my name would not appear in the annual report of the library, as it had during the preceding years when I was chief of stacks. I suggested that I be called executive assistant, which had been my title during my stay at Oberlin in 1912. But Mr. Lydenberg did not think that a title was important and so I spent the year without a title or, for that matter, any definite assignment, except for the temporary one in the order division. Since I was to be there only six months, I was called the acting chief until my successor, Carl Cannon, took over in July. The 1919 report gave no evidence of my existence but I do not believe that this did me or anyone else any harm.

The following year Mr. Lydenberg decided to call me executive assistant and I kept that title through 1927. A year or two later I had a rather amusing experience when the chief clerk of the Library of Congress, Allen Boyd, called on me one day and asked what were my duties, and I told him that I did what I could to help Mr. Lydenberg and Mr. Anderson and was called executive assistant. He said that was a very nice title. I learned later that he went back to Washington and asked for and received the title of executive assistant to the Librarian of Congress instead of chief clerk. I am not sure that it did him any good because in later years, during which I spent a good deal of time in Washington, I found that the chief clerks in the government seemed to be the persons who had more influence than anyone else in making the wheels go around and actually, in many cases, determining policies.

Theoretically my new assignments did not begin until January 2 because offices were closed on New Year's Day. But as my family had gone to Oberlin and I was at loose ends I went to the order department on New Year's morning and spent the day at my roll-top desk, the first that I had ever used, examining everything that Mr. Hopper had left and going over in my mind the things that Mr. Hopper had told me about on an afternoon a few days earlier, which had been my only opportunity to talk with him about the work.

My assignments as chief of the stacks and acting in charge of the documents and economics division had kept me unusually busy during the preceding weeks. But I was looking forward with pleasure and a little apprehension to my new assignments. The one break in the day on January 1 was a long visit from Victor Hugo Paltsits, the chief of the recently created manuscript division, which had been combined with the American History room under his direction. I remember I felt very much honored that he was ready to spend so much time with me. I had barely met him before but I found him much easier to talk with than I had anticipated; to my young mind, his appearance was formidable but this proved to be an inaccurate judgment when we became acquainted.

The next day, January 2, I occupied for the first time a small flat-top desk nearer the door than any of the four other desks in the director's outer office, which served as a reception room and also was used by the office secretaries. Mrs. Kitzinger, the director's secretary, was one of the most capable and agreeable persons whom I have ever known. She had charge of the filing for the whole office, which she did so well that we seldom had any difficulty finding old correspondence. She was very kind and helpful to me. Mr. Lydenberg had a number of secretaries during the years that followed and they were all good ones. The third secretary was Miss Leffingwell, who had been Dr. Billings' secretary. She had charge of the staff records and, as changes were made in personnel or salaries, sent a note of them to the bursar's office. She also had charge of the old-fashioned copying machine on which all outgoing letters were copied for the library's file. A fourth secretary helped out the first two when the work was especially heavy, took my dictation, which was generally negligible in quantity, and spent the rest of her time writing form "beg" letters. These originated with Mr. Lydenberg, who searched papers and periodicals for items which could be obtained on request.

Every morning before 9 a.m. when the building opened to the public, a messenger from the shipping room brought up the office mail; letters directed to Mr. Lydenberg went to his

desk and the rest came to me. I sorted them, giving Mr.
Anderson's to Mrs. Kitzinger and opening the remainder
myself and then sending them along to the proper person.
When Mr. Lydenberg was away on library business or vacation, I opened his mail and sent reference letters to the
various division chiefs who dealt with them.

At the end of each day, the acknowledgements for gifts
came to the office after being prepared by the gift section of
the order division. Mr. Anderson had authorized me to sign
them with his name, with a little "m" at the end to indicate
that I had signed for him. This often took me as much as 15
minutes between 4:30 and 5 and finally reached a point
where it was almost easier to sign his name than my own.

My desk was close to the office entrance and I greeted
visitors as they came in. I turned them over to Mrs. Kitzinger
if they wanted to see Mr. Anderson. Mr. Lydenberg's visitors
went directly to his office; his door was always open and he
could be seen sitting at his desk. Much of my work was
dealing with job applicants. I would interview them briefly
and then, if it seemed worthwhile, would ask them to fill out
a printed application form on which was space for what we
now call a "resume", a term that was not then in general use.
I soon decided that the application form was not satisfactory
and, with the approval of E.H.A. and H. M. L., it was
changed.

It was not long before Mr. Anderson began to ask me to
draft letters for him dealing with matters he thought were
within my capacity. This has been dealt with in the section
on Mr. Anderson. When it came time for the annual budget
to be made out, I was asked to make suggestions in connection with increases in salary for all except my two superiors,
the division chiefs, and the building and binding staffs.
Hence, I found it desirable to become acquainted with the
staff as a whole, which I did to the best of my ability. I had
made a good start already while in the bookstacks. I put the
detailed budget together after E.H.A. and H.M.L. approved
each item. Mr. Anderson then dictated the budget letter to
the trustees, making sure to keep the total within the esti-

mated income that had come from the treasurer. He asked me to go over the letter with him and make sure that he had made no mistakes in the figures, and I brought out any special features, additional positions, or changes from the preceding year.

Because of the amount of work in the director's office, it was difficult to spend enough time in the order division to keep things going smoothly there. It was a very busy six months before Carl Cannon returned to take over as chief of the order division. After his return Mr. Lydenberg continued to talk with me about special order division problems, particularly those relating to the selection policy and the book budget. I realized that he was wrapped up in this work, was doing it remarkably well, and was convinced of its importance. I might add that I learned enough about it so that I gradually took over most of this phase of the library's work between 1928 and 1934; then all of it except for very expensive items, and was able to "get away with it" in spite of my language deficiencies and lack of scholarly training. As I look back on it, I have often wondered why the library's reputation as well as my own did not seem to suffer.

But before the year 1919 was over I was involved in two other things beyond the routine mentioned above. All of my assignments were interesting. E.H.A. and H.M.L. were friendly and, while I was careful not to make suggestions continually, when I did make them they were welcomed and often were followed. Although it was definitely out of my field, I ventured to make proposals about three senior members of the staff. I suggested that Mr. Helbig, the capable head of the American History division with whom I had worked a few days during my library school practice work eight years earlier, should be shifted to classification work and be replaced by W. B. A. Taylor, who had been the chief of the accessions division since the opening of the library in 1911. I knew that Taylor had made Mr. Lydenberg unhappy by arranging without his approval for a new classification for the classics, using four letters instead of the customary two or three. Mr. Taylor and his wife had been in college at Oberlin at the same time my librarian sister was there. He was a fine, quiet, capable man who had come to the library from the Cincinnati Mercantile Library, which I had the pleasure of surveying more than 25 years later.

As already related, Mr. Taylor had been constantly "picked on" by Miss Hasse because she felt that he had not arranged for the right lettering on the binding of public document volumes. He was glad to escape from the accessions division and was well fitted for the American History position. Mr. Helbig spoke with a very heavy German accent, which irritated many readers in the American History division who had decided to have nothing more to do with Germans. He proved to be a satisfactory classifier. Then I proposed that Paul North Rice, who was just returning from military service, be made chief of the accessions division, which had charge of accessioning and classification. I already have recorded how he took my place in the bookstack when I went to Oberlin in the autumn of 1916 and then left to join the Plattsburgh group, which resulted in my coming back to take over the stack again two months before I had expected to and before my year was up in Oberlin. A place had to be found for him, and it was realized that he was ready for promotion from his earlier work at the reference desk under Mr. Waite.

My suggestions were accepted; they solved three problems and apparently caused no resentment. Aside from this shift, we had very few new appointments to the staff in 1919 because men returning from the service took the place of those who resigned. This was fortunate for me because it gave me an opportunity to break into personnel work gradually.

Rob Henderson, who had shifted from the information desk to my old position in the stack, was still having trouble keeping up with the work on Sundays. At my suggestion, Mr. Anderson agreed that those who worked in the stack on Sunday should receive extra pay at the regular work-day rate, not time and a half, and I began again to take every third Sunday in charge of the stacks with a small amount of very welcome extra pay. This also made it possible for me to keep well acquainted with the stack and reading room staffs.

Acting Chief of the Order Division

The part of Franklin F. Hopper's work that I took over in January 1919 dealt with the reference department only. He had been in charge of the work for both departments, reference and circulation. He left a staff of 32, all but three of whom had been in the library no more than a few years, none of them as far as I know going back to before the opening of the new library in 1911 except the three section heads. Mr. Coombs, who had been senior assistant and kept track of the finances, was a rather feeble old man with gray hair and beard and was to retire in a few weeks. But he helped me to get acquainted with many sides of my problems and I had no difficulty in taking on his work when he left, as one of my chief responsibilities.

The second assistant was Miss Gertrude Hill, who had been in charge of the serial section of the Division since the consolidation in 1895. She was very capable, a perfectionist, and had built up such a detailed and complicated system that when 'she was faced with the loss of almost any one of her assistants she was in despair. Her first assistant left only a few weeks after I took over, and she said it would take at least six months to break in a successor, and her whole operation would collapse in the meantime. What could she do? I brought the problem to Mr. Lydenberg. He solved it very quickly and smoothly. He had known Miss Hill for more than 20 years. He talked with her quietly and without upsetting her. They came to the conclusion that it was time for her to retire, which she did without tears or other complications. Mr. Lydenberg told me that she could well afford it, although we had no pension system to make her retirement easier. Mr. Lydenberg put it up to me to find her successor. I immediately arranged to bring Florence Muzzy from her position as head of the inventory staff, which had completed the first and was now starting in on a second inventory. Miss Cannon, her assistant, took her place. Miss Muzzy proved to be an ideal person for the assignment, and quickly simplified the procedures in her section so that a new person could handle the vacant position in a couple of weeks with complete satisfaction. And Keyes Metcalf had another demonstration of the desirability of avoiding complicated procedures; like so many other lessons that he learned during his first 20 years in library work, this proved very useful to him during the years that followed.

The third order department section head, Miss Maria Leavitt, also went back to the early days of the library's consolidation. She had charge of checking the receipts of books and their bills and preparing for their payment. She presented no special problems and was always easy to work with. She also had automatically taken on the responsibility for being the leader of the older women on the staff and worked well with Mr. Lydenberg. Her cheerful ways had much to do with keeping the women of the reference department staff happy and contented.

Besides keeping the regular work going smoothly in the order department, I had four other problems in the short six months that I spent there:

1. The space problem—32 persons and their equipment had only 1,000 square feet available to them. This presented an almost impossible situation. A long, narrow aisle with two turns in it made it difficult to reach my desk, and the staff was so crowded together that their work was seriously hampered. We shifted the opening of the mail and the writing of "beg" letters to the space available in the ends of both the broad corridors adjacent to the order department, placed staff desks on both sides of all aisles in the room, and finally moved all the new material that had to be held for more than

a few days on to the book shelves surrounding the narrow gallery which had only room for a passageway and the shelving. This gave me my first practical lesson in crowding more persons and their equipment into an inadequate amount of space, for 33 gross square feet per person is obviously not adequate while 75 square feet can be managed temporarily and an average of 100-plus is what I call standard today. It was not until years later that the library was able to add to the order department area what had been the trustees' committee room.

2. The war had come to an end only seven weeks before I took charge of the order department and it was one of my chief immediate tasks to renew connections with our dealers in Germany, Belgium, England and Holland. The elderly head of Stevens & Brown, who was in his 70's, came over to New York and I became acquainted with him. I had unpacked books shipped from his firm to Oberlin 17 years earlier and I saw him again 19 years later as a very old but alert gentleman at his office in London. My connection with the firm and Mr. Brown's successors has continued for two more generations or 75 years altogether. Walter Nijhoff then came over from The Netherlands and we became good friends; I saw him regularly from then on in this country and also in Europe in 1950, when he was selected to be the Farmington Plan agent for The Netherlands. We had been using the Stechert Hafner firm for many of our European books and serials but, perhaps unfortunately for all concerned, I soon disagreed with Alfred Hafner, feeling that he was taking advantage of the library in connection with the rapidly falling value of the German mark. He insisted on going to see Mr. Anderson to tell him that I was taking advantage of him. Mr. Anderson took my side and we shifted to Mr. Stechert's son, who had started up by himself but who unfortunately was unable to carry on. In time we shifted most of our German and some of our other European orders to Otto Harrassowitz in Leipzig. During the 1920's he provided us with serials and books from Germany, which con-

sisted at that time of about 23% of all our acquisitions, and we also bought some French and Swiss material from him. These were my first direct contacts with foreign dealers.

I did very little book selection myself. That was supervised by Mr. Lydenberg, who saw all current book lists, book trade catalogues such as the *Publishers Weekly* and *Publishers Circular,* reviews in the *New York Times* and the London *Times Literary Supplement,* and the corresponding publications for all the Roman alphabet countries, as well as the second-hand catalogues from all countries. He passed on to the people in charge of the 14 special reference divisions in the library the catalogues relating to their specialties. He checked the current trade lists himself and when they contained items which he thought one of the division chiefs should decide upon he sent them on to the person concerned. They all came back to me and once a day I went to Mr. Lydenberg in regard to any titles, especially expensive ones, which I questioned. I soon became reasonably knowledgeable about the library's acquisition policies and later, after Carl Cannon took over and Mr. Lydenberg went on his regular October vacations during which he "put his garden to bed," Carl came to me and, except for the most expensive and questionable items, we made the final decisions, holding over comparatively few for Mr. Lydenberg's return.

I still remember how inadequate I felt during my six months in the order division but gradually I gained confidence. As has been indicated, I was already fairly well acquainted with the division chiefs in their special reference rooms. But this gave me an opportunity to talk to them about their book-selection problems. I shall write later in another chapter on my experience during the following 18 years with decisions on selection of books.

Chapter 6
Special Assignments in the Early 1920's

Soon after my first year in the director's office special assignments began to come my way. Some of those that were of particular interest and provided valuable experience for me are described in this chapter.

Shifting the Collections

As stated in Chapter 2, sizable sections of the second and third levels of the bookstacks were not full when I became chief of stacks. But by the end of 1919, one year after I left, some rearrangement of the collections throughout the building had become necessary to take care of the uneven growth in the main stack and the special reading room collections. The science and technology divisions had grown rapidly and were becoming very much overcrowded, as was the economics and documents division. Altogether, there were at least half a million books that needed to be moved, and Mr. Anderson and Mr. Lydenberg asked me for a plan of action. After studying the problem, I made a proposal which it was agreed would bring about satisfactory results. My superiors naturally were very much worried about the cost involved and how the work could be managed without disturbing regular service to readers. I proposed that the part of the work that would involve the public areas be done on Sundays before the library opened at 1 p.m., and that all the work be done by volunteer help on Sunday mornings and in the evenings. I estimated that it could be done for $1,000.

When this proposal was approved I was asked to take charge. I was glad to accept because my regular salary was inadequate to provide for an ailing wife and two children. It was agreed that the pay scale would be at the regular rate, not at time and a half, and I had no difficulty in finding the required help on that basis. I selected Sylvester Vigilanti and a few others, including some of the better young men and pages who could be trusted and had volunteered for the work. I personally handled almost all of the 500,000 volumes involved in the move. Since the general science collection, which had been on the second floor, had to be transferred to the first floor, it was necessary to use one of the public elevators, which was available only on Sunday mornings between 9 a.m. and 1 p.m. No regular elevator man was on duty, and it seemed best for me to take responsibility for operating the elevator myself. It had no leveling device and, being inexperienced, I had great difficulty in stopping it at the exact level of each of the floors, with the result that the four-foot-long book trucks, three four-foot shelves on each side filled with 24 running feet of heavy books, were pushed or pulled up or down one or two inches nearly every time they went in or out of the elevator. This was hard on the wheels and joints, and before the move was finished some 20 different trucks were in poor condition if not past repair.

This added to my previous knowledge of book trucks (or trolleys as they are called in other parts of the English speaking world). I had used the standard, three-foot-long book trucks at Oberlin and also three-foot-long steel trucks with only two shelves on each side, hung on a central post at each end, the uprights being similar to those in book stacks. These were made by the Art Metal Company. A shelf-full of books could be placed on a shelf in the stack if one were strong enough to handle it without dropping. I felt that I had become a specialist in truck construction by the end of the big shift at the NYPL. From then on I was able to arrange to have the library trucks, which were all made by our own very competent building staff, constructed with wheels made in Elyria, Ohio (the town where I was born) by the Colson Company, which still, if I am not mistaken, provides book truck wheels as good as any in the country. Angle irons were attached to all the corners on each side. We placed the four wheels in new positions, with two in the center as far apart as was possible without interfering with personnel or passing trucks, and a pivot wheel on each end, so placed that you would not trip on it. We found that in this way we could swing a fully loaded truck around and around with one finger without changing its position on the floor. During the years that followed I gave annual lectures about book trucks and other specialized library furniture to our library school and, after it shifted to Columbia, to the library's training class.

My interest in library equipment and building planning grew out of this situation. I might add for the benefit of other librarians that these trucks cost far less than those purchased from library equipment houses but were fully as sturdy. The greater part of the cost was for the Colson wheels. I also made a blunder in this connection by arranging to have new trucks supplied to anyone on the staff who asked for one, and soon found that most of the senior members of the staff had acquired trucks and were placing them beside their desks and using them as stationary bookcases. We gave up making any new book trucks before my later years at the New York Public Library.

But to go back to the big shifts of books: The library's great collection of patents for the United States, the United Kingdom, France, and other countries (more about the German patents later) was shifted from the area under the document room to the third stack level and was replaced by the main technology collection. This housed the combined science and technology collections on the same building level. The move also provided a separate room for the chemistry collection and more suitable space, where the science collection had been, for Dr. Williamson's headquarters and his newly started public affairs information service staff. In addition, a good many of the main stack books were moved. I was fortunate enough to have made a good estimate of the time required for the work, and the cost as I remember it was just under the $1,000 estimated. Those who took part in the move were almost as pleased as were Mr. Anderson and Mr. Lydenberg. I never knew what they thought about the extensive damage done to the book trucks.

Book Census

Each year the library's annual report gave statistics on the number of volumes, pamphlets, and manila-rope bundles in the reference department. These statistics were made up by adding the number of new acquisitions during the past year to the figure used the year before. I came to realize that subtractions had never been made for books lost or discarded, and also decided that we should have no faith in the statistics that

had come from the Astor, Lenox, and Tilden Foundations
when the library was consolidated. Consequently the total
number of volumes was probably greatly exaggerated. Mr.
Anderson and Mr. Lydenberg decided that it was time to
make a definite count of the collections. This was in February
1921. It should be remembered that no books left the building
but there were always books in use in the reading room or held
at the circulation desk for readers who used them one day and
expected to come back to use them the next day. There were
also books at the bindery or in process of recataloguing, etc.

We made the 14 subject reading room chiefs responsible
for counting their own material and I took charge of the
main bookstack assignment. It contained a large percentage
of the total, since many additional volumes had been moved
into it from the economics, documents, technology, and science divisions. We had enough cards printed to provide one
for each side of each stack range in the main bookstack. Each
range had its own number, which I wrote in on the cards.
There were 10 sections on each side of the center aisle, so the
cards were printed with a line for each section. We called
for volunteers to come in on a Sunday morning and nearly
60 came. Each one was given a group of cards with range
numbers and they were asked to record the number of volumes in each section assigned to them. I had two tasks left to
do myself, which I succeeded in carrying out during the
following weeks. Each volunteer had signed his name to the
cards that he turned in. I then counted very carefully several
sections at random for each person and found to my amaze-
ment that in practically every case from 1% to 3% of the
volumes had been missed, largely because of thin pamphlets
in binders or because of carelessness. I then checked the total
for all the cards on an adding machine, rechecking the
figures for each range, having realized from my surveying
experience 14 years earlier that the best of mathematicians
make mistakes unless they add their columns from both
directions. I also added the figures for the books temporarily
elsewhere and the 2% which I decided had been missed by

the volunteers, and reached a total which was used for the library's next annual report. It was 50,000 less than we had been reporting. This was embarrassing but Mr. Lydenberg and Mr. Anderson believed that the task had been worth doing. The count was repeated 10 years later, in 1931, and we found, after adding new accessions and subtracting discards, that we came very close to the total expected. I do not think a similar count has been made since but I believe that books discarded or lost since 1920 have been subtracted from the total reported.

Technical Services

As was stated in the introduction of Part II, the New York Public Library card catalogue had a strange beginning. One way to speak of it would be to state that like "Topsy" in *Uncle Tom's Cabin,* it "just growed." Another is to be a bit irreverent by recording that in the first chapter of Genesis God said, "Let there be light and there was light." Dr. Billings said, "Let there be a catalogue" and there was a catalogue. It was made by clipping entries from the printed catalogues of the Astor Library (the Cogswell and the Nelson), the various special collection catalogues that had been prepared by the Lenox Library, and other lists supplementing those just mentioned and pasting them onto three-by-five-inch cards. To these were added entries for new acquisitions prepared according to the Charles Ammi Cutter rules. It was a dictionary catalogue with author, title, and subject entries interfiled. A second copy of the main-entry cards made up the official catalogue in the catalogue room; some of these copies, printed in blue ink, were on copying paper. The second copy was necessary because the catalogue room was on the floor below the public catalogue, a long walk away with no convenient elevator. This building arrangement was not unusual at that time and I found the same situation at Harvard's Widener building in 1937.

In 1911 the library began to print its own cards in its newly-established printing office, except for those that it could obtain from the Library of Congress, which currently amounted to less than 25% of the total. This office was headed by a man who had been in charge of the printing office in the Carnegie Library in Pittsburgh when Mr. Anderson was there. He was assisted by Mr. Thurman, the very competent head of the bindery which did the reference department binding (the circulation department binding went to commercial binderies) and by John Archer, a good friend and a remarkably capable mechanic who later became the head of the whole division. Archer assisted Mr. Lydenberg in writing their well-known volume *The Care and Repair of Books* and was also one of the finest printers in the country. He designed over the years a number of books which were included in the Graphic Arts Fifty Books of the Year. Mr. Archer often amazed me when trouble arose in the printing and bindery apparatus by his ability to take it apart, find what was causing the difficulty, and put it together again. He bought a new Ford every few years and rebuilt the engine in a way that increased very considerably the mileage he obtained from each gallon of gasoline.

But to go back to the catalogue: It was a hodge-podge, to put it mildly, inconsistent in many ways because of its complex history but very useful. In 1914 it was already showing wear and tear resulting from its tremendous use. Sometimes there were 150 persons consulting it at the same time. Some of the cards were printed or typed on stock that was not as durable as that used by the Library of Congress or the New York Public Library after 1911. Mr. Lydenberg had taken great interest in paper preservation and bought the finest card stock available in the country from the manufacturer, not from library supply houses. Among other things, he experimented with a washable card stock for the cards dealing with sex and other subjects often consulted by persons who had unusually dirty hands

My first special interest in the library catalogue came from difficulty arising from its inconsistency when I was in charge of the bookstack and Mr. Waite called my attention to the improvement in the quality of the cataloguing that Miss Minnie Sears was trying to bring about after her appointment as assistant to the chief cataloguer. The chief cataloguer, Axel Moth, was of Danish origin, quiet, serious, and a perfect gentleman. He knew practically all the European languages and saw to it that no linguistic mistakes were made by his staff, which he had inherited from a German predecessor recruited by Dr. Billings in the early days of consolidation.

Miss Sears, who was a close friend of Isadore Mudge, Columbia's great reference librarian and the author of the *Standard Guide to Reference Books,* felt that good reference work called for cataloguing more detailed and uniform than the New York Public Library's had been. Miss Sears was reasonably aggressive, as she had to be to change things in the catalogue division. With Mr. Anderson's approval, she went to work to improve the quality of her staff. Within six years she had established an author authority file, built up more consistent subject headings, and assembled the finest group of perfectionist cataloguers that this country has ever seen. But in the meantime the production per cataloguer dropped by nearly one-half because of the work involved in making absolutely correct entries in the authority file and of Miss Sears' insistence on accuracy in following the rules. Each cataloguer typed her own cards, after which they were revised by a senior cataloguer and then again by Miss Sears and Mr. Moth. By 1920 the library was in a desperate situation financially.

After coming to the office I reported regularly to my superiors that inadequate salaries made it difficult to keep the fine cataloguing staff that Miss Sears had recruited. Mr. Anderson and Mr. Lydenberg were at their wits' end trying to find a way out of the dilemma. They appointed a committee to make suggestions for a solution of the cost problems in connection with acquisitions. Mr. Moth and Miss Sears were, of course, appointed to it, as were Carl Cannon of the order division, Paul North Rice and Charles C. Williamson, an expert economist. No chairman was appointed but I was asked to serve as secretary and to call and preside over the meetings and prepare a report for the director. We met irregularly but generally twice a week for some six months and carefully went through all the details of the work involved in adding books to the library.

The committee made no recommendation about the methods of paying bills, except to change the name of the order division to acquisition division because it included seeking and recording gifts of all kinds. The remainder of the work, which had been divided between the catalogue and accessions divisions, was to become the preparation division under Mr. Moth, with Miss Sears in the catalogue section and Mr. Rice for the classification and accessions and final processing work. The accession book was to be given up but each volume was to be given an accession number which continued numerically from the accession numbers in the accession book. I am afraid that I have to claim responsibility for the names Acquisition and Preparation which are now widely used.

We all regretted some of the rules recommended but they seemed necessary in order to speed up the cataloguing process and reduce its cost. One of them stated that no cataloguer could spend more than 20 minutes in establishing an author's "authority card" before appealing to Mr. Moth or Miss Sears for suggestions for other places to look. There were other points along similar lines. The most important suggestion came from Dr. Williamson. Like the rest of us, he had worried about the great mass of uncatalogued pamphlets that the library and its predecessors had acquired during the previous half-century and stored, untouched, in various places - the basement, the lower levels of the stack and in the special subject divisions. Large-scale additions were coming from the current gifts of approximately 125,000 items each year. It was evident that not all of the material was worth cataloguing, but it was also evident that it should be dealt with in some way. Some of it related to fields that Dr. Williamson's division covered and was being used as a basis for the *Public Affairs Information Service*. (The PAIS publication was continued, after Dr. Williamson left the library for the second time to become director of the Columbia University library and dean of its Library School, by Alice Jewett and then by Rollin K. Sawyer and John Fall for more than 50 years, and has provided information on a tremendous amount of heavily used but previously hard to locate material.)

With the problem of uncatalogued, chiefly pamphlet, material in mind, Dr. Williamson proposed that our great accumulation of it, which amounted (if you include receipts during the next 17 years before I left the library) to some 3,000,000 pieces, be dealt with as soon as possible and kept that way. Many items not worth keeping should be discarded. Many more, as will be explained later, were stored again and over a half-million which were not worth full cataloguing were sorted by the classifiers and dealt with as recorded in Chapter 12.

The report of the committee was finally completed, printed by the library (I cannot find my copy of it), and distributed to the cataloguing staff. As a result Miss Sears, a woman of great administrative and other abilities who did not approve of all of our recommendations, took the first opportunity to leave and joined the staff of the H. W. Wilson Company, where she did great work on that company's publications and prepared her well-known list of subject headings. Not much later, Mr. Moth, one of the finest gentlemen I have ever known, died suddenly, and Paul North Rice took over his position and became responsible for all the work of adding material to the library after it had been received, paid for or acknowledged as a gift. He carried on the work with great success; the staff produced as much work as it had before Miss Sears came to the library, and the quality of the work continued at a high level, although not as high as it had been under Miss Sears. Paul resigned to become head of the Dayton Public Library in 1927.

In spite of my efforts to find a satisfactory successor, it was more than 18 months (during which I took over the task myself) before Rudolph Gjelsness was trained for the work and became chief of the preparation division. During more than half of that period I served also as chief of the reference department and, as you can imagine, had a busy time of it. While I was there each cataloguer talked over with me his or her work during the preceding month, and the special problems experienced, and the number of items catalogued. They varied greatly, of course, in the number, depending on the languages in which the material was printed, the date of publication, and the difficulty experienced in finding suitable classmarks and subject headings. I was not a cataloguer but I did learn a good deal about the problems cataloguers face, and my interest in the subject proved useful when I became chairman of the American Library Association's Cooperative Cataloguing Committee two years later.

Beardsley Ruml

In the early spring of 1920 the library was in a rather desperate financial situation. As a result of inflation its endowment income was no longer sufficient to support a staff capable of providing first-class service. Mr. Anderson called me into his office one day in April and introduced me to a rather short, elderly gentleman, whom he called simply "Mr. Gates". Mr. Gates then said that he would send a younger man to the library to talk about our problems. There was no hint as to who he was or what he had in mind but a few days later another call came from Mr. Anderson and I was introduced to a giant of a man who towered over my 6'1" and was considerably overweight as well. His name was Beardsley Ruml; there was no indication of his purpose, except that he had some connection with Mr. Gates. Mr. Anderson said that

Mr. Ruml was to use the trustees' committee room as his office, and that I was to be at his disposal and should answer freely any questions that he put to me about the library, its physical condition, its organization and services, its staff and its finances, or anything else. My background for the assignment was by this time as good as anyone's except Mr. Lydenberg's.

I took Mr. Ruml through the building from top to bottom and told him what I could about the professional staff members, the duties they performed, the salaries they received, and when and how much they had been advanced in salary in recent years. I spoke of the trouble we were having in keeping together an adequate clerical and page staff. We examined the collections and I explained the different subject fields with which we tried to keep up and how new books were selected, purchased and catalogued. I showed him the catalogue and explained as best I could its many idiosyncraeies. He seemed particularly interested in the various art collections on the top floor and asked why we did not sell them and use the space they occupied for other purposes. His questions seemed endless and for six weeks I had to neglect my other duties to a considerable extent. I found Mr. Ruml completely inscrutable. He gave no hint of the purpose of his questions nor what he would do with the answers. I was surprised and amazed by one thing about him. He would often sit in his office writing, and several times when I came in to see him, as I did regularly, I would find him telephoning. He would signal me not to leave and would go on with his conversation, which I realized was with his Wall Street broker, to whom he would give directions about buying and selling stocks and bonds. I had, of course, read about Wall Street but this was a new experience.

One day Mr. Ruml announced that he was through and that he would not be back again. I was as puzzled as ever. This was in May 1920. In February 1921, as I was reading the New York Times on a Monday morning on my daily trip to Forty-Second Street, I came across headlines saying that the

New York Public Library had received a gift for its endowment of $6,000,000: three million from John D. Rockefeller, Jr., two million from one of the trustees, and one million from another. I later learned that Mr. Gates was the right hand man of John D. Rockefeller, Jr., and that Mr. Ruml was working for him and had been asked to find out what he could about the library's financial needs. I might add that at the beginning of the library's next financial year most of the members of the staff, including me, received larger increases in salary than we had had for a considerable time and my own financial situation, which had been a precarious one, improved.

I saw Mr. Ruml again only once, when I passed him while going to my train in the Grand Central Station. He did not see me. I did hear about him from time to time. He became the director of the Spellman Rockefeller Memorial Fund and was a trustee of that fund for many years. He served as dean of the Social Science Division and Professor of Education at the University of Chicago for two years under "Bob" Hutchins, whom I had known as a boy in Oberlin, where his father was a professor of theology whose Bible class papers were corrected for many years by my sister, Marion, who brought me up. Mr. Ruml was treasurer of R. H. Macy Company, Inc., of New York for 11 years and chairman of its board for four years after that. He was chairman of the Federal Reserve Bank, economic advisor to the government, and a trustee of Fisk University, the Museum of Modern Art, and Dartmouth College, among other things. In 1959 he wrote a volume entitled *Memo to a College Trustee,* which informed academic trustees that if they would reduce the number of subjects taught and have larger classes they could increase faculty salaries and still balance their budgets. I am afraid little happened as a result of this volume, although it made good sense to me. His final and perhaps most important accomplishment was that he was primarily responsible for the withholding tax plan. After I came to Harvard I found that Mr. Ruml's sister, Frances Ruml, who married W. Kitchener Jordan, was a dean at Radcliffe College; Mr. Jordan later became president of Radcliffe.

The Winter of 1923-24

When Dr. Billings was planning for the use of the new library building and began to arrange for special reading rooms he decided in 1897 to establish a Jewish division under Dr. A. S. Freidus, one of the country's foremost scholars in the field of Semitic and Hebrew literature and history. The Oriental division was headed by Dr. Richard Gottheil of Columbia University, and two years later, in 1899, a Slavonic department was begun under Dr. Herman Rosenthal. This was one of the earliest attempts in an American library to build up a Slavonic collection. By 1917, when we went into World War I, it amounted to some 25,000 volumes, the great majority of them in Russian.

Dr. Rosenthal, a scholar who had written widely in his field and in the field of Jewish literature, had come to this country many years earlier and helped found a Jewish agricultural colony in the south. He made it clear that Slavic studies should be developed in the library. I remember well Azariah Root telling me how much he enjoyed making Dr. Rosenthal's acquaintance in the autumn of 1916 when he was acting as principal of the library school. But Dr. Rosenthal died early in 1917 and was succeeded by a Serbian who was not successful and then in 1918 by Avrahm Yarmolinsky, whose son, Adam, was on the freshman library committee at Harvard with me and who has made a distinguished record.

After World War I Dr. Yarmolinsky and Harry Lydenberg, realizing how important a role Russia and Slavonic language, literature and history were to play in the future of the world, made plans for an expedition to Russia. They were able to go early in the winter of 1923-24, armed with a shelf list of the Slavonic division so as to avoid acquiring duplicates. If I am not mistaken, they were the first Americans who were able to

get into Russia after the war on what might be known as a
business trip. Everything went well with them. Mr. Lydenberg, who had not been abroad before, made the most of the
opportunity by going to theaters, museums and concerts as
well as buying books. He carried his portable typewriter with
him and wrote letters to Mrs. Lydenberg and occasionally to
me telling something of his progress. He and Dr. Yarmolinsky were able to purchase some 20,000 or more volumes of pre-war material and made a start on the war publications. This brought the collection up to more than 40,000
volumes and made it one of the best Slavonic collections in
the country. Another major collection was acquired by Archibald Cary Coolidge, director of the Harvard library and
the founder of the magazine *Foreign Affairs*. The largest was
the Yudin collection at the Library of Congress, which had
been purchased at the end of the 19th century; unfortunately, however, it was not catalogued until after World War
II.

Inevitably, the large collection that H.M.L. and Dr. Yarmolinsky brought back to the United States included quite a
number of duplicates of volumes already in the library,
because some of their acquisitions were block purchases.
This gave H.M.L. an opportunity to compare volumes which
had been in the NYPL for a generation—suffering from
pollution, too much heat and dampness in the summer and
dryness in the winter—with those which had stayed in little-
heated places in Russia. The comparison was probably the
first real proof of the damage that was being done to books in
American libraries, and made Mr. Lydenberg even more
worried than he had been before about the unfortunate
results.

During H.M.L.'s absence I took on much of his work and
the final decision as to purchases, analyzed periodical articles
for cards in the public catalogue, carried on the reference
correspondence, etc. I think I managed reasonably well but
two special problems came up. One morning soon after my
arrival at the office a telephone call came from the police

department saying that someone had fallen dead in the street late at night and was unidentified except for a card indicating that he had a connection with the New York Public Library, and asking me to come to identify the body. I did so and found that it was that of Dr. Freidus, chief of the Jewish division, who had been walking to his residence after a late dinner with friends. He was unmarried.

A little later one of our senior staff members who had been in the library since 1897 went to the bank where his brother was working and begged to be permitted to go into the vault because he was being pursued and was fearful for his life. I called Mr. Gaillard and we went to the bank and took the poor man to a doctor certified as an "Examiner in Lunacy". He told us that our man was schizophrenic and hopelessly insane and should be sent to a state institution. We knew that he had been involved in identifying and reporting to us a number of men who had tried to steal books from his section of the library and had been spending a good deal of time watching for persons of this kind; he had worried about this so much that he finally decided that at least one of the persons he had identified was going to murder him.

I was unwilling to accept the doctor's recommendation and telephoned the New York Hospital whose president was our treasurer, Edward Sheldon. I asked if we could bring the man to one of the hospital specialists in mental difficulties. The New York Hospital doctor discussed the matter with all three of us and persuaded the man who was in difficulty that he needed a rest. It was winter, but in talking with him we found that he had regularly taken his summer vacation in an out-of-the-way village in the Catskill Mountains that took in summer boarders. I telephoned the proprietor, who said he was ready to take the case over, which he did. We reassured our employee that his position was safe and would be held for him, that he should avoid any of the problems that he had been dealing with. After a few months he did come back and continued for some 20 additional years as a useful member of the library staff.

By this time I found that I was having difficulty in running up Battle Hill to my home at night, as I had often done in the past, and even was finding it difficult to keep up with my neighbors who had come out from New York on the same train and walked briskly up the hill. Six or eight of us often walked in the road rather than on the sidewalk. I called my doctor and asked him to give me a checkup. This was the first time I had gone to a doctor in nearly six years, that is, since my bout with the Spanish flu in the summer of 1918. He checked me over and found that my blood pressure was 165 over 100, or something of the sort, and that I must have been under too much of a strain. He gave me medication to take once a week and a month later I was back to normal and, as far as blood pressure is concerned, have been so ever since. By late February Mr. Lydenberg and Dr. Yarmolinsky returned, my workload had been reduced, and Mr. Lydenberg had resumed his regular schedule.

Interesting Visitors

During my years in the administrative suite of the library, between 1919 and 1937, we had many interesting visitors. Most of them came to see Mr. Anderson or Mr. Lydenberg, but I became involved in some way with many of them and I write of them simply to give you some idea of how a junior librarian may meet interesting people.

I've already related my experience with Beardsley Ruml and Frederick Gates when they were working for the Rockefellers.

Soon after I went into the office, Colonel Henry Metcalfe came to call on E.H.A., who without introducing me to the colonel asked me to take him around the library. After the tour and before he left I ventured to say rather hesitantly that he and I happened to have the same family name. He stopped in his tracks, stood facing me, and said, "Do you have an *E* on the end of your name?" I said, "No." Without another word or even saying goodbye he turned around and marched out of the building. I remembered then that there were two families of Metcalfes who came from England before 1640. The Virginia branch, like those who remained in England, kept the *E,* while the Massachusetts branch, to which I belonged, had lost it. Colonel Metcalfe had suddenly realized that I was one of the "damned Yankee" clan.

It was several years later that a gentleman came to arrange for photostats of some patent drawings and specifications which he said proved that he had been the first to invent a useful gasoline engine for automobiles in this country, preceding Henry Ford. He came in again and again to tell me how he had not received his just rewards for his discovery, his name was Charles E. Duryea.

Next came perhaps the first of our famous radio news analysts, H. V. Kaltenborn. He came in often to see Mr. Anderson and I remember well the time when he brought with him Willa Cather, who gave us a manuscript which she had prepared for publication but which could not be published without alterations. She wished to have the original preserved and we put it in the vault.

S. S. McClure was the founder and very successful editor of *McClure's Magazine,* a magazine that my father subscribed to in the 1890's and in which I read stories by Rudyard Kipling. Later, however, it was kept out of my hands because of stories - subsequently published in the volume called *Stalky and Co.* - which dealt with badly behaved boys whom I was not allowed to read about until I was considerably older. I might add that this was also the case with Robert Louis Stevenson's *Kidnapped* and Mark Twain's *Huckleberry Finn* and *Tom Sawyer.* I was not allowed to read them until I was twelve. Mr. McClure, as an elderly man in his seventies, used to come to my office when he wanted some information from the library (this was after I had an office and a roll-top desk). Instead of sitting down in a chair, he would stand behind this desk with his elbows on the top and reminisce about his publishing exploits.

George Kennan, Sr., the uncle of the well-known diplomat, was a distinguished reporter, particularly on Siberia, which he visited a number of times. He gave the library a wonderful collection of photographs, books, pamphlets and manuscripts that he gathered together in his many trips in the pre-revolutionary days going back to the 1870's. He always had interesting stories to tell, for he was probably the first American to become acquainted with the Siberian exile situation and to write about it. He was a fascinating person.

To get ahead of myself, years later I had the pleasure of sitting beside the junior George Kennan while he joined a group from the American Academy of Arts and Sciences which was working on what became a volume of *Daedalus* to which he had been invited to contribute as an outside expert. Later I sat beside him at lunch at the time of the dedication of the Swarthmore library that I had helped plan and at which he spoke in no uncertain terms about the undesirable violent activities of college students then prevalent throughout the country. As we left the hall he seemed to be in real danger of being assaulted by a radical group whose members did not hesitate to speak their minds about Kennan. His dedication speech was published later in the Sunday magazine section of the *New York Times*.

An interesting person whom I took around the library at Mr. Anderson's request was Josiah Wedgewood, the head of the British china company bearing his name. At that time he was prominent in British politics.

The man who later became Cardinal Tisserant was another. I met him at the 1926 ALA Conference in Atlantic City when he was librarian of the Vatican. He stopped at the library that same year and I had the honor of showing him around. To get ahead of myself, I later saw him at the dedication of the University of Notre Dame library building where he received an honorary degree. He was then in his 80's and had flown over the night before, arriving at Notre Dame about 1:00 a.m. after a 30-hour day because of the change in time zones. I saw him at breakfast the next morning at 7:00 a.m. looking completely exhausted. At 9:00 he acted as honorary chairman of a philosophical discussion. Tisserant sat on the platform and quite understandably went to sleep. He also snored from time to time. At the end of the discussion he was asked to comment on it. Without hesitation, he said, "I had a long day yesterday and am not sure that I took in all of the discussion" and he then proceeded to talk on the subject in a brilliant manner. I saw him later in the library at the Vatican after he had been made a cardinal and one of the Pope's chief advisors.

As reported earlier, the library from time to time entertained royal visitors from abroad and I remember when Queen Marie of Rumania came after World War I seeking financial help for her suffering country. The library was not closed for her, as it had been for King Albert of Belgium. She was taken with her entourage on a tour of the building. I had the task of leading the procession around the reading room as well as through exhibition rooms and the work-rooms.

I had a somewhat similar task not long before coming to Harvard. A call came from a leading Japanese businessman whose office was in downtown New York. He told me that the crew of a Japanese naval training ship wished to be taken through the library. If I remember correctly, the ship was an old-fashioned four-master, and the several hundred young men on it were students at what corresponded to our Annapolis Naval Academy. I went down to his office and made the arrangements and I led a long procession of Japanese cadets through the library, including a trip around the big reading room where, I am afraid, research work was slowed up at least temporarily.

Another interesting experience came when John D. Rockefeller, Jr., acquired from London what was known as the British Headquarters papers dealing with the British in New York during the American Revolution. The library was asked to photostat and arrange them. Mr. Lydenberg and Mr. Paltsits were, of course, very much interested. The papers were kept in the vault, except when in the photostat room, and I worked with them daily for several weeks. We hoped that the originals would come to the library but they were sent to Williamsburg.

My final story for this chapter deals with a German, Doctor Otto Vollbehr. He had begun, immediately after World War I when the German book trade and German owners of private book collections were in a desperate financial situation, to collect incunabula—that is, books printed before 1501. He had amassed for an amazingly small sum of money the largest collection of incunabula ever in private hands. In the early 1930's he sold what was supposedly his complete collection to the Library of Congress, after a Mississippi Congressman named Ross had persuaded Congress to appropriate something like a million dollars for the collection, which included a copy of the Gutenberg Bible. Sometime later it turned out that Vollbehr had a second collection, which he sold to the Huntington Library in California for another large sum of money. Then, toward the end of my time in New York, it turned out that Vollbehr had still a third collection and that he was trying desperately to sell it. He persuaded an American businessman named Emerson to become his agent and Emerson knew a step-son of one of my brothers in Kansas, a Mr. Woodward. Woodward was a book collector but not on the scale of Vollbehr's third incunabula collection. As it turned out later, the asking price was $750,000. Mr. Woodward suggested to Mr. Emerson that there was a man at the New York Public Library, named Metcalf, and that this library might be interested in the collection. Vollbehr's agent came to me. I turned him over to Mr. Lydenberg, who went over the list of books with Mr. Paltsits. They decided that the collection, while an interesting one, was nothing that the New York Public Library was prepared to buy. But this is far from the end of the story, which will be completed in the account of my Harvard years. A reader interested in this part of Vollbehr's story can obtain further information about it in a *Saturday Review* article entitled *The Library of Congress Has a Book*.

Chapter 7
Personnel Officer

Some of Those Whom the New York Public Library Tried
To Recruit but Failed to Employ More Than Temporarily

After I took charge of the library's personnel work in 1919, I was urged every day by Mr. Anderson to employ as many good men and women as possible, selected from new library school graduates. I will note in this section some of those whom we tried to employ but failed to keep for any length of time. Most of them came for a brief period, perhaps only during Christmas and summer vacations or between the two library school years which were then necessary to obtain a master's degree. I list generally the men rather than the women, as in the 1920's and 30's the library was making a special effort to bring men into research library work, and many capable women preferred the library's Circulation Department.

To go back historically in this connection, Charles Folsom, who was Elinor Gregory Metcalf's fifth predecessor as librarian of the Boston Athenaeum, wrote in an annual report in the 1850's that such a large percentage of the literature of that period was not fit reading for members of the female sex that they should be excluded from the stacks in the Athenaeum. It might be noted that the determination of Hannah Adams before that time had broken the rule which, of course, is no longer in existence. But the lack of available men because of the Civil War brought women into the library profession in large numbers for the first time.

By the year 1876, when the American Library Association was founded, some 17 women were in attendance at the first ALA conference. But their admission, I understand, was with the definite understanding that they would not take part in any discussions. During later years the picture changed quite rapidly. Melville Dewey admitted women to the library school at Columbia and was fired two years later when his trustees found out about it. He had broken the university's all-male institution rules. Mr. Dewey again admitted women in his library school at the New York State Library in Albany. Less than 25 years later, in the library school of the New York Public Library, I was the only member of my sex in the first class of nearly 40. Mr. Anderson was interested in attracting women as well as men to library work. He brought Miss Plummer to head the New York Public Library's library school. He employed Margaret Mann and Alice Tyler in Pittsburgh, and Minnie Sears, Jenny Flexner, Elizabeth Butcher, Pauline Fullerton, Esther Johnson, Carolyn Ulrich, Florence Overton, Rebecca Rankin, Gladys Leslie, Mrs. Paul Bucher, Marion Root, Margaret Stillwell and many other top-grade women in the library in New York.

Lucile Morsch was one of the first-class women whom we

were able to keep for a short time only in the reference department. She later became a senior member of the Library of Congress staff and president of the ALA. We had a similar experience with Ralph Ulveling, who was with us between library school years but was sure that he wanted to go into public library work and became assistant director and later director of the Detroit Public Library and in due course president of the ALA.

Ralph Munn was another. He worked in the NYPL during the summer of 1920, between his two Albany years. In 1921, in spite of my efforts to persuade him to come back to New York after graduation, he became assistant librarian under Judson Jennings in the Seattle Public Library and then went on to head the Carnegie Library in Pittsburgh and its library school and to become president of the ALA. He stayed in my apartment in the Bronx in the summer of 1920 while my family was in Oberlin.

After a summer with us Herman Fussler was persuaded by Llewellyn Raney to go to the University of Chicago to take charge of its photographic reproduction work. He later succeeded his chief. For a short time we had Benjamin Powell, who later became librarian at the University of Missouri and then went to Duke and while there was president of the American Library Association. We wanted to employ Carl White, but he went to Fiske instead in 1934 and then later to the University of North Carolina, to Illinois, and finally to Columbia. Jack Moriarty, who spent most of his career at Purdue, was another man whom we were unable to employ.

Ralph Shaw worked for us while in library school but left after graduating to become assistant librarian at the Engineering Societies Library and later to Gary, Indiana, as librarian of the public library while he obtained his doctorate from Chicago. Still later he went to Rutgers as professor and finally dean, and then to similar positions at the University of Hawaii. His work for and against automation will not be forgotten. He also founded the successful Scarecrow Press, which has contributed so much to the publication of library and library-related literature. He was president of the ALA during an exciting re-organization.

Donald Coney accepted a position at the NYPL but was released when he was offered the librarianship at the University of Delaware. Subsequently he became librarian of the University of Texas and then went to Berkeley to head the University of California library; later he also was vice-president for development there. J. Periam Danton was with the library while at library school. Since then he has spent most of his career as dean or professor at the University of California library school at Berkeley. David Haykin was with us for a summer and then went to other positions before going to the Library of Congress where, among other things, he directed the subject heading work very successfully. Rutherford Rogers, now Yale's librarian, came to us for work while in library school, did not remain after graduation, but returned later.

In 1937 I offered Homer Halvorson a reference position at the NYPL, which he turned down; he came to Harvard to work for me there in 1938 and in 1941 went to the University of Illinois as assistant librarian. Later he was in charge of the Johns Hopkins University library until he retired.

Among others who fell in the same category were Herbert Anstaett, whom I very much wanted to keep following his library school year; he worked with us through the summer but was persuaded to go to Franklin and Marshall as librarian, and stayed there throughout his career. Harold Brigham, who had had wide experience at the Trenton Public Library, Princeton and Rutgers, talked with me before deciding to come to the NYPL library school but could not be persuaded to stay with us. He became librarian at New Brunswick, the Nashville Public Library and the Louisville Library before becoming director of the Indiana State Library. Leo Etzkorn, after a summer at the NYPL, followed by experience as librarian of the Cambridge and Fall River Public Libraries, finally went to Paterson, New Jersey. We had a similar experience with Elmer Grieder, who left us for the Detroit Public Library. I brought him to Harvard in 1938; he later became librarian of the University of West Virginia and then associate librarian at Stanford University. Albert Gerould, the son of James Thayer Gerould of Princeton, was not ready to stay at the New York Public Library after a short period with us and worked in various other places before his extended term on the staff of the Philadelphia Free Library. Joseph Rounds, after a short period at the NYPL, went to the Grosvenor Library in Buffalo and then became librarian of the Erie County-Buffalo System.

After this account of persons who turned out very well after we had failed to keep them, it is pleasant to go on to some of the persons who came to the New York Public Library for longer periods. Most of them stayed until we could not provide them with the advancement for which they were ready. Then we helped and encouraged them to find more suitable and better-paying assignments in other libraries. We theoretically had no scheme of service and were in a position to adjust salaries if we wanted to keep someone. But after consultation with Mr. Anderson and Mr. Lydenberg, we carefully avoided giving raises to individuals whom we wanted to keep if it put them out of scale with colleagues having equal experience and ability. In many cases we realized that those we lost were going to positions for which they were particularly fitted and where their future prospects were much better than we could hope to offer. We did not try to keep a librarian if we felt he was better suited for a position elsewhere. We did always make efforts to shift a man from one position to another in a different division of the library when it would be a promotion. This will be brought out in more detail in the next section.

Some of Those Who Came to The New York Public Library

I have a list of 75 persons, all first-class librarians, who joined the reference department of the New York Public Library while I was in charge of personnel work. Some of them stayed with the library for the rest of their careers, while others went on to serve in important positions elsewhere.

I cannot attempt to mention them all here but will select some in order to give an idea of what the NYPL was trying to do under the direction of Edwin Hatfield Anderson, who made a great contribution to library development by urging the importance of improving personnel. I will not include those mentioned earlier in this chapter whom we tried and failed to persuade to stay with us, or (with a few exceptions) those who are mentioned in more detail elsewhere in this volume because of my special involvement with them at the New York Public Library or elsewhere. I hope that those whose names are not included will not feel hurt but will realize that I appreciate and understand the importance of the work that they have done as the years have gone by.

Charles M. Adams, from North Dakota and Amherst College, worked at the library's information desk for four years. This was followed by assignments at Columbia, the Women's College of North Carolina in Greensboro, and the University of Hawaii. Paul Ballance, from North Carolina State College and Columbia, was at the library's information desk for seven years and went to positions in Texas and North Carolina. Karl Brown from Kansas and the next-to-last class of the New York State Library School at Albany worked for 15 years as a general assistant in the New York Public Library and then for six years in bibliographical work, where he was responsible for and completed the publication of the first edition of a guide to the library's reference collections. I had worked on this for several years before going to Harvard but had been unable to complete it. He made it one of the best publications of its kind and a far better one than I would have produced. Later Brown was on the staff of other libraries and did important work for the *Library Journal*.

Ralph Carruthers, from Manitoba, Queens University, and the Columbia Library School, after one year in the science and technology division and some time at the information

desk, spent many years in charge of the NYPL's Photographic Service, which he developed into an important part
of the reference department's service to the public and the
library world.

Donald Clark from Seattle, the University of California at
Berkeley, and the Columbia Library School, came to the
library in 1935. After five years in the main reading room,
the information desk and the economics division, he went to
the Harvard Graduate School of Business Administration in
1940 as assistant librarian, became associate librarian in 1948
and librarian in 1957. He was the only person whom I took
from the New York Public Library to Harvard. From 1962 to
1972 he was the first librarian of the University of California
at Santa Cruz, where I had the pleasure of serving as consultant in connection with the new library building.

David Clift, from Kentucky and the University of Kentucky, followed by the Library School at Columbia, came to
the New York Public Library in 1931 to serve at the information desk. We had never recruited anyone from the University of Kentucky and were a little afraid that a young man
from a small town and a then little-known university might
not be of New York Public Library calibre. But he turned out
to be one of our finest reference workers until he became
assistant to the director at Columbia in 1937. He later served
with the Office of Strategic Services and as a member of the
Library of Congress Mission in Europe at the close of World
War II before becoming associate librarian at Yale and then
executive secretary of the American Library Association until
his untimely death.

Benjamin Custer from Lima, Ohio, graduated from Oberlin College and the Western Reserve University Library
School. He came with David Wahl, a classmate of his at
Oberlin who was then in library school, on a week-end excursion to New York from Cleveland. I took them to my house
in White Plains and decided to employ them. Custer worked
as a cataloguer and classifier for seven years and then, after
experience in various other libraries, became editor in

Dewey Decimal classification work at the Library of Congress and the development of the Dewey Classification. Wahl went into the NYPL's printing office, after doing cataloguing, as we needed an experienced cataloguer to compose our printed cards. More recently he has done library work in Israel.

Archibald DeWeese from Kentucky graduated from Harvard and the Columbia Library School and then, after a year in the music division in 1928, became an assistant at the information desk before becoming chief of that division until his retirement.

Robert B. Downs needs no introduction. He was a very successful reference assistant at the information desk for three years, during which he completed the second of his two years at Columbia. He then preceded Joseph Ibbotson, J. Periam Danton and Orwin Rush, all of whom worked at the New York Public Library following Columbia, as librarian at Colby College in Maine. This was followed by work at the University of North Carolina, as director of the New York University libraries (when I persuaded Paul North Rice to leave that position to succeed me when I went to Harvard), and director of the University of Illinois Library and dean of its library school. He was president of the American Library Association and his noteworthy publications on library work and related subjects, which are still continuing after his retirement, place him in the top rank of librarians in this country.

Leslie Dunlap, from Portland, the University of Oregon, and Columbia, was a reference assistant for five years in the reading room, stacks, photostat and economics division; following wide experience in a number of other libraries he became director of the University of Iowa Libraries.

John Fall came to the New York Public Library in 1936 and made such an impression that I persuaded him to do the field work when I was asked to study the desirability of what became the Midwest Interlibrary Center. This was at a time when I felt it undesirable for me to leave Harvard for the period required to visit a dozen or more Midwest universities and research libraries. Results of this study will be recorded elsewhere. After World War II he carried out for me the task of visiting Western European book dealers which made possible the first arrangements for the Farmington Plan. At the New York Public Library, John worked in various positions and finally became chief of the economics and document division and editor of the Public Affairs Information Service, which had been started by Charles C. Williamson and which still plays an important part in reference work in broad fields.

George Freedley, from Richmond with a Yale master's and fine arts degree but not one from a library school, made a name for himself in the New York Public Library as head of its great theatre collection.

Edward G. Freehafer from Pennsylvania had graduated from Brown and the Columbia School of Library Service and started, as did so many of his colleagues, as reference assistant at the information desk in 1932. This was followed by similar work in the economics division. He took Quincy Mumford's place as general assistant in the office of the New York Public Library in 1936 and later was in charge of the acquisitions division. In 1944 I tried just a few hours too late to persuade him to take charge of acquisitions work at Harvard; he already had agreed to go to Brown University as assistant librarian. He returned to the New York Public Library as executive assistant and then chief of the personnel office, chief of the reference department, and finally director from 1954 until his retirement. While not as well known as he might have been, considering the positions that he held, he has been one of our soundest and most likable librarians.

Rudolph Gjelsness was born in a small town in North Dakota. He received an A.B. from the state university there and a Master of Library Science from Illinois, followed by experience in Norway, France, Oregon, California and Michigan. He came to the preparation division of the New York Public Library in 1928 and took charge a year later, after I had filled that position for a year and a half while also acting as chief of the reference department. In order to find him, I had checked all the way through the list of ALA members and selected him as the best possible candidate for the position. He stayed for four years before becoming librarian and professor of bibliography at the University of Arizona and then joining the staff of the University of Michigan library school, where he later became dean. He took a year off from Michigan to succeed Harry Lydenberg at the Benjamin Franklin Library in Mexico City. After his retirement from Michigan he went to teach in Puerto Rico, where he was killed in a traffic accident.

Charles F. Gosnell, who was born in Rochester, N.Y., received his bachelor's degree at Rochester and his library service degrees at Columbia. He specialized in Latin American studies and his interest in that field has continued. He was at the New York Public Library as reference assistant for five years; thereafter he was librarian of Queens College in New York, and then librarian of the New York State Library, where he was also assistant commissioner of education for libraries. At his request I studied his library situation there with Andrew Osborn. Later Charles became librarian and professor of library administration at New York University, where he encountered difficult problems in connection with the planning and financing of the present New York University library building in Washington Square.

The men whose names begin with *H* included Richard Hensley who came to New York from the Library of Congress and left for the Boston Public Library, where he became chief librarian for reference and research; Robert Hill, an historian, not a library school graduate, who after some years in the New York Public Library became chief of its manuscript division; and Oliver Wendell Holmes, an American history specialist, also not a librarian, who, after two years in the library's American History room, went to Washington and became one of our best known archivists.

The Ibbotson brothers, Joseph and Louis, whose father

was librarian at Hamilton College, graduated from library school, Louis from the next-to-the-last class at Albany and Joseph from Columbia. Each came to the New York Public Library information desk for a few years. Joseph went on to Colby, spent nearly a decade in the Rosenberg Library in Galveston, then went to Fort Worth and finally to Tacoma. Louis went to assistant positions at Duke and Rochester and then to the University of Maine. I had the pleasure of visiting Louis at his library in Orono, Maine, while I was studying the possibility of cooperation between the Maine academic and research libraries.

Alfred Keator, from the New York State Library School and the University of North Dakota library, came to the New York Public Library after arrangements for a year abroad went awry and we later suggested him for the Reading, Pennsylvania, Public Library, from which he went to the Pennsylvania State Library as librarian. Robert Kingery, who had worked with Paul North Rice in Dayton, came to us without library school training just before I left for Harvard and later obtained a library degree from Columbia; after wide experience in the library and elsewhere, he became chief of the New York Public Library's preparation division.

Harold Lancour from Duluth, Minnesota, the University of Washington in Seattle, and Columbia Library School, worked in the genealogy and local history division for two years, after which he went to Cooper Union, to the University of Illinois Library School as assistant director, professor and editor of *Library Trends,* before becoming dean and professor of library science at the University of Pittsburgh Graduate School of Library and Information Sciences. He has done a great deal of consultation work in Latin America and Africa.

William D. Lewis graduated from Oberlin and the NYPL and, after some years at the information desk and in the economics division, became librarian of the University of Delaware. Guy Lyle, a Canadian, had two years with us in the stacks and the reading room before going to Antioch, the

Women's College of North Carolina, the University of
Louisiana at Baton Rouge, and finally Emory University.

Gerald McDonald remained in the New York Public Library for some 35 years beginning in 1930, in important
specialized work in the research book room, the American
History and the map rooms. Marvin Miller spent four years
in the book stacks and the information desk. After leaving
the NYPL, he went to the University of New Hampshire and
the University of Arkansas, where I helped him plan a new
building. Robert A. Miller joined us as a classifier for two
years before going to the University of Nebraska and later
helped make the Indiana University library one of our great
libraries. Russell Munn, with experience in British Columbia,
came to us for four years before going on to other work and
then to the Akron Public Library.

L. Quincy Mumford came to the New York Public Library
right out of library school at Columbia, which followed years
at the library at Trinity College, now Duke University, in
North Carolina. His wide experience in the NYPL has been
exceeded only by that of Harry Lydenberg, Ed Freehafer
and my own during the past 80 years. He served as reference
assistant at the information desk and became executive assistant in the office, a position that I had previously held, and
was at other times in charge of the preparation division (as I
had been) and chief of the readers division, which then
included the information (reference) desk and the main
reading room and stacks.

Andrew Osborn, an Australian, who had charge of moving
the Australian National Library from Melbourne to Can-
berra, followed his family to the United States. As a result of
a chance meeting of his father with a Cornell professor who
had been an Oberlin classmate of mine, he applied to me for
a position in 1928. While with us he earned a Ph.D. in
philosophy at Columbia. Later he completed the two-year
library course at Michigan in one year, organized the library
school at the University of Southern California at Los
Angeles, and taught a year at the University of Michigan

Library School before coming to Harvard in 1938. More will be written about him later.

Wyman Parker, after library school and one year at the New York Public Library, became librarian at Middlebury, survived a broken neck in Australia during the war, and was then librarian at Kenyon College, the University of Cincinnati, and finally Wesleyan in Middletown, Connecticut, until his retirement. I had the pleasure of serving with him on the Bowdoin College Library Council for several years. Walter Pilkington, in addition to working for 10 years at the information desk, edited the *American Notes and Queries* for a decade and then spent most of his career as librarian of Hamilton College, where I was the consultant on his new building.

Orwin Rush was a native of Oklahoma; after college in Kansas and library school at Columbia, he worked at the New York Public Library information desk for four years before going to Colby, Clark University, the University of Wyoming, and finally Florida State University. John R. Russell, one of three John Russells with whom I have worked, came from the University of Michigan Library School to the New York Public Library as a classifier. After four years we recommended him to the General Education Board for one of its first Library Fellowships in Europe. Unfortunately he never returned to New York because he was offered the position of chief cataloguer of the National Archives when that organization was established. He succeeded me as chairman of the American Library Association's Cooperative Cataloguing Committee while continuing his work in the Archives. One morning at Widener I had a telephone call from the president of the University of Rochester. I had suggested two candidates for the position of librarian there and he now demanded that I tell him which of the two should be offered the position. Taken by surprise, I did something that I did not like to do, because both men were suitable for the position, and said, "John." He stayed at Rochester until his retirement. I consulted with him on his difficult library building situation and I saw him last in Lausanne, Switzerland, when the library building planning group of the International Federation of Library Associations (IFLA) was meeting there earlier in this decade and he was spending his retirement teaching in an American school not far away.

Francis St. John, who worked through his college course in the library at Amherst College, and Wyllis Wright, who was student assistant at Williams, came down to the New York Public Library to question us about the desirability of attending library school. Both were persuaded to enroll at Columbia and then come to the New York Public Library. Both rose to senior positions in the library. St. John was general assistant in the preparation division and the director's office for five years, after serving in the stacks and the main reading room for three years. He wrote for me one of the first articles proposing library internship as a "trial balloon" while I was chairman of the board of education for librarianship. Then, after two years as assistant librarian of the Enoch Pratt Library in Baltimore, he returned to NYPL as chief of the circulation department before becoming chief librarian of the Brooklyn Public Library. Wyllis Wright was with the NYPL for 18 years, from 1927 on, as a cataloguer, then chief classifier, and finally chief cataloguer. St. John and Wright each had a period as librarian of the Army Medical Library in Washington, while I was serving as consultant there; the former as an Army officer during the war and the other just after the war. Wyllis became librarian of Williams College in spite of the fact that he had not been selected for the position there two years earlier because he did not have a Ph.D. I might add that this was the same year that I came to Harvard in spite of not having any degree beyond my bachelor's from Oberlin because the New York Public Library library school did not give degrees, and that Wyllis was one of the most scholarly librarians whom I have known.

Louis Shores, after some years in libraries in Toledo, Ohio, worked at the New York Public Library for two years while going to library school at Columbia. He then served as libra-

rian at Fiske University, the George Peabody School for
Teachers in Nashville, Tennessee, and later became dean of
the library school at Florida State University, where he made
a name for himself for his publications. Wayne Shirley,
whose mother was a librarian, graduated from Dartmouth
and the Pratt Institute Library School, was at the New York
Public Library doing reference work for a year in the 20's
and several years in the 30's before returning to Pratt, where
he served as librarian and dean of the library school for
many years. This was followed by service at Finch College in
New York and Wentworth Institute in Boston. His interest in
library history and the A.L.A. library history roundtable will
be long remembered. Lewis Stark from the University of
New Hampshire spent after library school a lifetime at the
New York Public Library, much of it in charge of the library's
rare book collection.

R. W. G. (Glen) Vail, from upstate New York, graduated
from Cornell and the NYPL Library School, had five years at
the information desk and then, after being librarian of the
Minnesota Historical Society and the Theodore Roosevelt
Memorial Library, where he built up the Theodore
Roosevelt Memorial Association collections (the books and
manuscripts from which are now at Harvard), came back to
the New York Public Library to help us on our acquisition
program. This was followed by his being librarian at the
American Antiquarian Society, the New York State Library
at Albany, and then the New York Historical Society in New
York City. Constantine Vesselowsky, who was born in Russia,
where he received a law degree, came to the United States
after the Revolution and went to library school at Michigan.
He worked for 25 years as a classifier in the NYPL and I last
saw him when I was doing consulting work at the University
of Notre Dame, where he was in charge of classification.

Ellsworth Young came from Nebraska, took his college
degree at Iowa and, after library school, had five years in the
New York Public Library in the book order section, the stacks
and reference. I tried to get him to come to Harvard but he

preferred to stay in his family's book store just off Harvard Square.

The above will give some idea of the width and depth of the New York Public Library staff selection during the years when I was in charge of reference department personnel work, directly or indirectly. It must be repeated that we tried to attract these men to the New York Public Library because of the emphasis placed by Mr. Anderson on the importance of building up and improving the quality of librarians. We believed that the library was a good place to gain experience following library school. These men represent only a fraction of the male librarians to whom the New York Public Library gave a good start between 1920 and 1937. While finding good men was considered of first importance because of their limited numbers in the profession at that time, I can assure you that many women who have done well also were employed. A number of them were recorded earlier.

This chapter can be closed by stating that I was never called personnel officer. This work just fell into my hands and I kept it there until going to Harvard in 1937, except that the routine part of it was carried on by the executive assistants who succeeded me after I became chief of the reference department in 1928. I enjoyed this part of my work tremendously and have taken great pleasure over the years in my association with these men and women while they were in New York and my contacts with them wherever they were after I went to Harvard in 1937 and during my retirement since 1955. I want to make clear that during the early years of my work with personnel, Frank Waite helped me greatly with the selection and during the later years I relied on advice from Quincy Mumford, whose judgment was superb; as I grew older I was convinced it was better than mine for persons under twenty-five.

Chapter 8
The New York Public Library Building Staff

John Fedeler

It was not long after I came to the New York Public Library in September 1911 that I "ran into" (and I use the words advisedly) the library's first and, during my 26 years there, only building superintendent, John Fedeler. He was of mixed German and Swedish descent and his wife was a fine, upstanding Irish woman. They then had two young boys, John, Jr., and Edward. I remember Fedeler (we all called him by his last name) often bragged that the combination of races found in his family provided the best possible results genetically.

How he happened to come to his position I never heard, but Fedeler once showed me a group picture taken many years earlier in which he and Harry Lydenberg both appeared, and I judge that it was taken in their student days, when H.M.L. was at Harvard and Fedeler at M.I.T. in the middle 1890's. Fedeler had some ability in all of the fields which his position involved: wiring, lighting, carpentering, cabinet making, janitorial work, heating and ventilating, and other building maintenance. He was of medium height, somewhat heavy, and was often very excitable when something went wrong. If he was reporting to Mr. Lydenberg about an untoward incident, he would wave his arms violently. Mr. Lydenberg, who was always calm and kept his voice low, would control Fedeler by saying, "Please sit on your hands." As I have indicated in the chapter about Mr. Lydenberg, I had difficulty in dealing with Fedeler to start with but in time we came to terms. After I was appointed executive assistant to Mr. Anderson and Mr. Lydenberg, all went smoothly.

Fedeler had an apartment on the mezzanine level of the library's first floor, that is, one and a half floors above the 40th Street entrance, with windows facing the east and south sides of the 80-foot-square south court. He was available and in many ways responsible for the building 24 hours a day, although there were always night watchmen.

Two stories about Fedeler are worth recounting. In late spring of 1917, while I was at Oberlin as acting librarian, the library was asked by the city for the first time (as far as I can remember there was only one other such occasion between 1911 and 1937) to close for the afternoon so as to make possible an official reception for Viviani, the French Premier, and Marshal Joffre. They had come over after we had entered the war with Germany to seek aid for France and the reception was to take place in the library (the library contract with the city, which owned the building, provided that it would lose its rent-free status if it were not open to the public between 9 a.m. and 10 p.m. Monday through Saturday and 1 to 10 p.m. on Sunday every day of the year except Christmas and the 4th of July). That day Mrs. Fedeler gave birth to a daughter who, in honor of the occasion, was named Viviani Joffret Fedeler.

The second occasion for the closing of the library came later when King Albert of Belgium and his Queen Elizabeth came to this country on a somewhat similar mission and also to say "thank you" for what the Hoover Commission had done for their country. They were accompanied by their young son, Prince Leopold, later Leopold the Second, still in his teens, who was quietly dressed, unlike his parents, who were in royal regalia. Leopold naturally kept fairly close to his father and mother in the crowded exhibition room where the reception took place. Mr. Fedeler felt very responsible for the safety of the king and queen. When he saw this young man edging closer and closer to the royal couple, Fedeler became suspicious, grabbed Leopold by the shoulder and demanded he identify himself, which he did quietly. All went well except that it took a long time for Fedeler to recover his equanimity.

Fedeler had a good crew under him; I had comparatively little contact with them except for Tom Mahoney and John Benson, the head janitor, about both of whom I will write later in this chapter, and Tony Esposito, a small, quiet young man who became chief electrician during my years in New York. Tony was pleasant, reliable, and capable of working in what became, as time went on, an increasingly difficult assignment. The library then was using d.c. current, which resulted in complications. The light intensity seemed adequate at the time with a good supply of table lights and large, very high windows in the Main Reading Room but actually was far below present-day minimum standards. I remember, after going to Harvard, meeting the engineer who had designed the lighting for the New York Public Library and for Harvard's Widener building, neither of

which then was considered satisfactory. He bragged to me
about how good the lighting was in both libraries and also told
me that it was physically impossible to light a room satisfactorily if it had a ceiling less than 10 feet high. The NYPL
building was not air-conditioned and the lighting and ventilation systems were complicated. However, ventilation was
aided to some extent by the fact that the main reading room,
with its 768 seats, had such a high ceiling. At that time the
library produced its own light and heat from furnaces in a
sub-basement on the 40th Street side of the building. This
location had been chosen because preliminary borings
showed that there was less likelihood of finding rock ledges
there than on the 42nd Street side. But during construction
it proved to be a wrong diagnosis; rock was found. In the
long run this was fortunate because on the 42nd Street side
at a later time the subway was put in. If ledge rock had been
found there, it would have required a great deal of disturbing blasting which would have been very serious for the
library, in spite of the fact that the basement walls in that area
were 14 feet thick.

The ventilation for the library was not satisfactory, although there was a forced-air system and fresh air was
brought in through ventilators in the open south court and
pushed through oil and water filters. These theoretically at
least removed the dust but were difficult to clean or repair.
After I went to Harvard the NYPL purchased its steam and
power and found that on the whole it saved money by making
the change.

Tom Mahoney

During my first ten years in the Library, the head carpenter
and man-of-all-work was a good natured, tall, slender
Irishman named Thomas Mahoney. I remembered John
Fedeler saying one day, before Tom left to go into business
for himself, "I taught Tom everything that he knows until

now he knows more than I do." Mahoney left the library in
the spring of 1921 and three months later, when I was
looking for a man to build a house for me, I selected him,
and I think the results were unusually satisfactory for both of
us. I knew that I would have a very difficult time financing
the operation. Mart had recently had a serious, major operation which was expensive, we had two children, and my
salary was small, though a few months before it had been
increased by a small part of the six-million-dollar gift that the
library had received the preceding winter. I had no savings
but a small bank account on which I dared not draw. I knew I
could not borrow money for construction unless I owned the
land on which the house was to be built.

After carefully covering Westchester from Mount Vernon
as far north as Larchmont, White Plains and Tarrytown, and
considering various houses already built, we settled on two
lots, each 50 x 100 feet, making it 100 feet square, which
would cost $1200. It was a little beyond the top of the slope
which was called Battle Hill, after the Battle of White Plains
in 1776, one mile southwest of the White Plains railroad
station. The site looked out onto the great Warburg Estates
on the next hill to the northwest, with two of the Warburg
houses showing through the trees and with Pocantico Hills
farther to the north, less than eight miles away. Pocantico
Hills is where the John D. Rockefeller clan had built their
houses some years before and where they still are.

I turned to my sister, Marion, to whom Father had left the
sparse family funds with the request that they be used to
make sure the younger members of the family completed
their education, which was now a thing of the past. She had
supported me through my first year in college and I had
provided my own funds which I had earned before and after
that myself. She lent me the required $1200 at the standard
interest rate of 6%, as she had done for my brothers in
similar situations and as she continued to do during the 32
years until her death in 1930.

With this transaction completed, I then went to look for

mortgage money. As already reported, Harry Lydenberg
had very generously offered to let me use securities that he
had as collateral but I felt it unwise to accept the offer and be
indebted, financially at least, to my employer. You may understand how glad I was that I had not taken advantage of
his offer when later I turned down three other positions, all
paying much higher salaries, without a debt to him influenc-
ing my decision. Money still was scarce after the 1920 depression but I finally received encouragement from the Franklin
Society for Savings and I asked for a $6500 mortgage, the
amount that Mahoney estimated would be the cost for the
house that he and I had been planning. The Franklin Society
was interested but, after checking, reported to my horror
that its charter provided for mortgages only for buildings on
land within 25 miles of its office, which was two miles south
of Grand Central Station. The White Plains station was recorded on the time-table as 24 miles from Grand Central. I
was nonplussed at first but hastened to the library's map
room and, on checking the United States Topographical
Survey section for the area, found that my lot was, as the
crow flies, less than 24 miles from the Franklin Society office.
All concerned were happy and the agreement was signed.
With the exception of the $400 that I paid for my first
automobile—after I was 40 years old, money borrowed from
another sister and repaid within a few months—this was the
only money I ever borrowed except for the mortgage on my
Belmont house near Harvard, which was paid off in five
years.

   Tom and I looked into "ready-built" pre-fabricated
houses, several of which recently had been constructed in the
White Plains area. But Tom found that he would be in
trouble with the labor unions if he started work of that kind
and said that he could not attempt it. We then developed a
plan closely resembling one of the many made by a pre-fab
company. I discussed the plans with the architect who had
planned Mr. Lydenberg's home nearly 10 years earlier and
took advantage of all his suggestions except one and paid

him $50. I later found that he was right in the unaccepted suggestion, although I had disagreed with him at the time.

Tom went to work in June, we were able to move in during September, and the total cost was more than $100 under his estimate. Our first child, Margaret, who was six, was able to start school at the beginning of the term at the local Battle Hill Elementary School. Across the street she found a very satisfactory playmate her own age who had a very large dog which loved to wander with them through the nearly square mile of vacant land beginning less than 100 yards from our house.

The seven-room house with one bathroom had a fairly large sitting room. The house faced south, was 26 x 28 feet overall, or 1,400 square feet for its two floors. It was placed close enough to the lot line on the east side so that there was just room for a stone wall less than three feet high on the lot line to make up for the greater height of the neighbor's 50-foot-wide lot and leave space for a driveway and garage. I put in the driveway later, built on a foundation of stones gathered from our garden. With my own hands and the aid of a bushel basket and a spade, I built up the grade to meet the side porch steps. The space under the porch was five feet high at the rear, lowering to a foot in front, and was used for a toolshed. After we had the mortgage paid six years later, I bought my first car.

I planted my own grass and bought shrubs to surround the house. I planted an asparagus bed and a raspberry patch, built a compost box, and put in a hedge on the line of the lot below us. With the stone wall separating us from the house above us, which was close to our border on the side but away from the area where we spent most of our time, we were very much in the country. I then built a successful grape arbor, with four varieties of grapes, and bought five varieties of currants. In the woods less than a mile away we found a small tulip tree with a very long tap root which we managed to transplant and place to the southwest of the house. For 16 years it grew more than an inch in diameter yearly and became a large tree. After we left White Plains, its top blew off and it was no longer the well-shaped tree of yore. But in the more than 50 years since its transplanting it has become by far the largest tree in diameter in the area.

I enjoyed the walk down the hill in the morning to catch a train to Grand Central and the walk up Battle Hill at night. I left Grand Central at 5:05 and reached home by 6 o'clock. On Saturday afternoons I would leave the library ten minutes early and catch a non-stop train at 4:56 which, on the Saturday afternoon closest to Washington's birthday (February 22, old style), would enable me, if I ran up the hill, to see the sunset over the Warburg Estates for the first time each year.

In addition to the trees, shrubs, and lawn, I left room for a flower garden and some 2,500 square feet for a vegetable garden in which I grew about every vegetable that could be grown in Westchester County. I found we were just enough inland so that the length of the growing season was virtually the same as northern Ohio, which was affected by its proximity to Lake Erie (I might add that our garden in Belmont, Mass., because the ocean is not far east, has almost exactly the same climate as Oberlin, Elyria, and White Plains).

We had 16 very happy years in the house in White Plains. The children, who for the first few years of their lives had been cooped up in an apartment house area in the Bronx with few friendly neighbors, blossomed out. But we were somewhat disappointed in the schools. I served as president of the Battle Hill School P.T.A. one year and the children both graduated from White Plains High School and had gone to college at Oberlin before we moved to Massachusetts. The schools seemed to be filled with children from families more interested in money and social life than we were. Mart, who was far from well, underwent two major operations during these years but made friends with the neighbors and in the Ridgeview Congregational Church, with which I still keep a rather tenuous connection. The walks up and down the hill, with the exercise in the garden, suited me. Robert W.

Henderson of the library, who had gone to work there a little before I did and had succeeded me when I left the bookstack, moved out to a house built for him behind our second lot but in a place where it did not seriously cut off our view of the Warburg Estate or Pocantico Hills. These were good years for us. Yet we never felt as much at home during our 16 years in White Plains as we did in Belmont within six weeks after we moved there.

John Benson

Back to the New York Public Library building staff: during the construction of the 42nd Street and Fifth Avenue building, one of the construction foremen was John Benson. He stayed in the library when the Astor and Lenox Libraries and the Tilden Trust collections were moved into the building. Obviously he was a capable man who could handle workers, and John Fedeler, who had been appointed building superintendent, employed Benson as head janitor. Benson ruled his staff with an iron hand and perhaps knew better than anyone else what was going on in the very large library building. He was not always easy to get along with and he could properly be called hard as nails. We had numerous uniformed men on the staff who controlled the entrance doors, manned the elevators and had charge of the various elaborate closing duties for the building at 10 o'clock at night and in addition checked the behavior of the 10,000 people who, during my 25 years in the library, often entered its door in a day. They numbered in all some 75,000,000 between September 1911 when I came and August 1937 when I left to go to Harvard.

Benson had an uncanny faculty of catching up with coat thieves, by whom we were beset every winter. Many readers, instead of leaving their overcoats at the checkrooms near the two main public entrances, would take them upstairs and place them on the backs of the large, comfortable reading-room chairs, sometimes sitting on their coattails for safety and sometimes just hanging them over the backs of chairs. In the late fall or early winter every year, readers would report leaving their coats on their chairs while looking in the reference books on the reading room walls, going to the public catalogue to select another book, to the charging desk to pick up books that had been sent for, or to the washroom. Benson was notified immediately when a coat disappeared and would spend a good deal of time watching for the thief as inconspicuously as possible, from somewhere in the reading room, reasoning that the man, having successfully obtained one coat and probably having pawned it, would think it so easy a game that he would come back and try again. Benson usually caught the thief after several coats had been lost, then would turn him over to the special officer (of whom more later) or to the police. They would search the culprit and frequently find a number of pawn tickets in his pockets; many if not all of the stolen coats would be recovered. This sometimes happened several times a year, although as far as I know we never found a repeater.

Another problem for Benson, one which arises all too often in public buildings with no publicity resulting, was an infestation from time to time of what we called "public exposure artists". This would go on for some time because the unfortunate women involved would hesitate to lodge complaints. But sooner or later someone in the library would hear about it and it would be reported to Benson, who would be on the watch and in time would discover the malefactor. Benson either would catch up with him and tell him to come with him, or the man would realize that he had been identified and would bolt for an exit. Benson was quick on his feet and would catch up with his victim and would do what we could not condone but what was very effective: give the man one very hard blow on the chin and either knock him completely unconscious or at least hurt him so much that he would not try to repeat his offense in the library. I did not learn about this procedure until it had happened at least three times and I realized that I must see to it that it did not occur again.

Poor Benson finally succumbed to cancer. While he was able to return to work briefly after an operation, he finally faded away and the library lost one of the toughest and most useful men I have known.

But I must end the Benson story by going back to his days as a foreman in construction of the library building, long before I knew him. One day an elderly man asked permission to look through the building and Benson courteously gave him a complete tour. The man left with a "thank you." But that is not the end of the story: the man was William Augustus Spencer, son of a well-known New York lawyer who had spent most of his life abroad, collecting finely illustrated and finely bound books. Spencer was one of the victims of the Titanic disaster in April 1912. In his will, dated some time after his visit to the library, he left approximately $1,000,000 and his entire collection to the New York Public Library, as well as half of his residual estate, subject only to his wife's interest during her lifetime. She died a year and a half later. The books numbered 272 and had been illustrated by more than 200 artists and bound by 26 of the best modern binders. The directions in the will stated that the money was to be used for the acquisition of handsomely illustrated books which came in handsome bindings or, if not in satisfactory bindings when purchased, should be bound by the best available binders. The books could come from any country and in any language and were to represent the work of the world's best book binders. The collection was to be kept as a unit. The first curator put in charge as specialist in the field did not come until 1929. He was Phillip Hofer, a Harvard graduate of 1921, who entered business after his graduation but had started collecting the Spencer type of books during his college days at Harvard under the direction and with the aid of Paul Sachs and George Parker Winship. With the Spencer income and with later 1920 and 1930 prices, the collection grew rapidly. In the more than 60 years since Mrs. Spencer's death it has developed into one of the great collections in its field and is still growing. Mr. Hofer left the library after four years' service to become associate director of the

Morgan Library and there will be more about him in a later chapter. But to go back to John Benson, few could have realized the results that an act of courtesy on the part of this rough, capable man would have for a great library.

Chapter 9
Special Investigators

Edwin White Gaillard

Soon after I entered the service of the New York Public Library, I met Edwin White Gaillard, who was the library's special investigator, and as problems arose that required the use of a detective, I was told to get in touch with him. This was a new phase of library work to me.

Mr. Gaillard was born in Louisville, Kentucky, in 1872. He was a member of an old and distinguished South Carolina family. He had a relative (also named Gaillard) who for years was a senior officer at the Library of Congress under Herbert Putnam. Mr. Gaillard was educated by tutors, at Trinity, and in New York night schools. Beginning at 16 in 1888 and continuing until 1895, he was engaged in literary and scientific (coal tar preparations) pursuits. He travelled extensively in Nova Scotia, the western United States, Mexico, the West Indies, and the islands of the South Pacific, and was special correspondent from Tahiti and the Marquesas for *Harpers Weekly,* the *Independent* and the *New York Evening Post.* In 1897, at age 25, he became librarian of a new library on New York's East Side, called the Webster Free Circulating Library. He continued in this position until January 1906. In the meantime his library had been taken over by the circulation department of the New York Public Library. Mr. Gaillard had then shifted to the central office of the circulation department as supervisor of its public education work, a position in which he remained until 1913. At that time the library was becoming worried about the loss of books, particularly in the circulation department, and he was appointed special investigator (he might have been called "detective") for the library, a position that he occupied until his death in 1928 at the age of 56.

Mr. Gaillard was an unusual man in many ways with considerable ability in various fields. I was inclined to dislike his somewhat flamboyant and aggressive manner and particularly the way he treated suspects from whom he was trying to obtain information. But he did important work for the library and was perhaps the first man in a full-time position of this kind in any library in the country. He liked nothing better than to talk about his exploits. He used to brag that he was greatly stimulated in the winter by putting on his bathing suit and going out and rolling in the snow in his yard. He was very fond of highly flavored Mexican and other exotic foods and was properly proud of the giant dahlias his garden produced.

Most of Gaillard's work was with the circulation department; we had little trouble with the loss of books from the reference department during his regime because most of these books were on closed shelves and had to be signed for before they were given out and there was always a check at the doors through which everyone had to pass. Briefcases had to be left in the checkrooms near the exit doors so it was difficult to hide a book.

My first official dealings with Mr. Gaillard came in connection with young boys (pages) on the reference department staff when I was in the bookstack and later when I was executive assistant. In the bookstack, as has already been related, I was in charge of up to 50 boys (many of them part-time), from 1913 through 1918 with the exception of the year when I was at Oberlin. After 1918 I had some responsibility for all of the boys in the building (they numbered close to 100 in all), as well as being "trouble man" for the reference department, and it is not surprising that over the years there were instances of trouble. Much of it could be blamed on me, at least indirectly, because I had selected many of the boys.

The first case that I can remember in which Mr. Gaillard was involved was with one of my stack boys, a tall, lanky young man who, strangely enough, was named Robert Louis Stevenson. He was suspected of taking books out of the building without authorization. Mr. Gaillard went to his house but failed to find printed material of any kind in it, much to his disgust.

The second case was that of a young boy who had dropped out of high school to help his widowed mother support her younger children. Mr. Gaillard, for some reason which I do not remember, suspected this boy of having stolen a book from the stack and in my presence accused him of the theft in what I thought was an undesirable manner. He then told the boy that if he would invite Gaillard to his apartment on the lower East Side, it would give him an opportunity to prove that he was innocent. The young man accepted the challenge readily and I insisted on going with them to the apartment. Fortunately, the mother was working and the younger children were in school, which saved embarrassment for all of us. The apartment was a six-room, top-floor, cold-water flat and the boy's room—and the flat as a whole—was entirely bookless. His room had no window or outside light except for a small skylight in the ceiling. I was naturally pleased, although I felt that Mr. Gaillard was unhappy about his failure.

The upshot of the visit was that the young man, whose name was Nathaniel Schwartz, was called to my special attention. The photostat room was under my jurisdiction at the time and needed a young helper, and I arranged to have Schwartz assigned to it. He soon became a skilled photostat operator and in time a good photographer. Eventually he became the head of our whole photographic enterprise with receipts of $250,000 a year. I remember his coming to tell me that he was to be married and ask if it would be wise for him to buy a small town house that had just been built in Queens. I had not so many years before been through a similar experience. He had reached a stage where he was receiving what in those days was a good salary, so I encouraged him and I am glad to report that all went well. The year before I left the New York Public Library we had him take individual pictures of all the reference department staff members for our records. I still have a copy of mine which, considering it was done hastily as one of a series of several hundred individuals, was a good likeness.

More of the New York Public Library's photography story is told in another chapter. But to go back to Edwin White Gaillard, he died after a fairly short illness while he was still comparatively young, in October 1928. Finding someone to take his place was up to me.

G. William Bergquist

My acquaintance in New York was not very wide, except for librarians. It did not seem to me that the task of special investigator called for a professional librarian, and I could think of no one on the library building or mechanical staff or anyone else who would fit it. But I had just enough sense to telephone Ernest Reece, then at the Columbia University School of Library Service, who had been principal of the New York Public Library Library School from 1917 to 1926 and for whose judgment I had the greatest respect.

Professor Reece replied immediately, "What about Bill Bergquist? He has a long acquaintance with all kinds of persons and with human nature in general as well as being a trained librarian and if he would take the position, he would be the ideal man for the place." I agreed.

Seven years before this, in January 1921, and two years after personnel work in the reference department had become one of my principal assignments, a heavy-set man in his 40th year, several inches shorter than I and weighing about 100 pounds more than I did at the time (he was not fat but massive), appeared at my desk and, before I had an opportunity to ask him to sit down, said, "My name is Bergquist. I want to become a librarian." He did not fit my picture of a librarian and, somewhat taken aback, I made what was perhaps a natural reply, "Where did you go to school?" His answer was, "I had a year in high school at Groton, Massachusetts, where my father was groundskeeper at the Academy. My mother had died and my father married again and I ran away at 14 because I disliked my stepmother and did not have a chance to go to school again." Then he repeated, "I want to be a librarian." We talked further. I found that he had been manager of a chain grocery store in Chicago, and then a travelling salesman for two years; after service in the First World War in France, where he became a lieutenant in the Army Engineers, he had been manager of the Yale Towne Cooperatives, Inc., in Stamford, Connecticut. He had a wife and child to support. I did not question him about what he had done during the years between 1896 (when he ran away) and 1912. While he hesitated to talk about himself during the years that followed, I was able to piece together some of what he had done during that period. His first job after running away was as a jockey. I confess that this was hard for me to believe when I saw this 275-pound man but I could readily believe that he soon outgrew the job. Apparently his employers liked him well enough to keep him on; he became a horse trainer who was good enough to take race horses abroad, at least to England, France, and Germany. I found that he was acquainted with each of these countries and with other parts of Europe about which I did not know enough to question him.

After giving up horse training, he had tried a number of other positions, none of which could be called professional. At one time he tried prize fighting but admitted that he was not very successful at it. He had been a barkeeper. Indeed, it was hard for me to think of any type of work that he had not done at one time or another and it was hard to think of a place in the United States that he had not visited. I have travelled rather extensively but I rarely, if ever, while talking with him and casually mentioning an American or European city, found that he had not been there. When his work for the library took him to Philadelphia, Boston, New Haven and Cincinnati, it was evident that he was intimately acquainted with each city.

Why did Mr. Reece recommend Bergquist for the position of special investigator at the New York Public Library and how had I become acquainted with him? Let me go back to my bafflement with the man who sat at my desk in January, 1921, and insisted that he wanted to be a librarian. I had been sufficiently impressed by a brief talk with him so that, with some hesitation, I went into the office of my chief, Mr. Anderson, who I knew was very much interested in library personnel and in drawing the right people into library work. I told him that I had an unusual situation on my hands, that there was a man at my desk with whom I would like to have him talk. Mr. Anderson talked with Bergquist for perhaps 20 minutes and then called me and said, "I think we should give Mr. Bergquist our library school examinations." I gasped to myself but followed through. These examinations were still on the same basis as those that I had taken 10 years earlier for entrance to the Pratt Institute Library School and were still five in number: General Literature, General History, General Information, and a reading knowledge of French and German. We gave them to this middle-aged man who had dropped out of school 26 years earlier at the age of 14—and certainly to my surprise, if not to Mr. Anderson's, he passed them all.

We asked Bergquist if he would be ready to take an evening and Sunday assignment and go to library school part-time, as the second semester of our library school was about to begin, and take two years to obtain his certificate. He agreed and we put him to work as soon as he could leave his old position, appointing him supervisor of the main bookstack from 5 to 10 p.m., six weekday nights and from 1 to 10 p.m. on Sundays. This was the same schedule that I had had in the spring of 1913 while going through library school full time, but when I was considerably younger and unusually active. I had found that my task was too heavy before the end of the term. In the bookstack, Bergquist had more than a dozen boys on duty each evening and double that number on Sunday, scattered over six levels, and his work as supervisor took him up and down the seven levels, including the main reading room, without the aid of an elevator, walking almost continuously on the marble stack floors and stairs. He did his work exceptionally welll in both the bookstack and at the library school. But as I remember it, it was some 6 to 9 months later that he appeared at my desk a little shamefacedly and said, "I like my work very much and I want to continue in the library. I am getting acquainted with a tremendous number of books that are used each day. But while I hate to admit it, as a result of my weight, the hard floors and the constant walking, I find that my arches are breaking down. Is there some other assignment you could give me?"

We were fortunate enough to have an evening vacancy at the reference desk of the Economics and Document Division at that time. With some hesitation on my part, Bergquist was appointed to it. Again all went well and by the time he was ready to graduate and receive his library school certificate, two years after he first came to us, he was prepared for a regular full-time assignment.

The library belatedly had decided to install an "Inquiry Desk" in the large entrance hall at the 5th Avenue entrance because so many first-time visitors were completely nonplussed when they entered the doors and saw no sign of books. We had found that some of them wondered if they had come into Grand Central Station by mistake and they asked where to go to get the trains, or, if they knew this was the library, where they should go to find what they wanted. Bergquist was assigned the task of selecting the location for the desk and helped design it. It was built in the library's carpenter shop. He also decided what he wanted to put in it. All of this was as well done as his previous assignments had been and the desk proved useful as a "first aid point" with a limited number of quick reference books at hand, copies of library publications for sale and postcards of library material.

Another year passed by. Vacancies on the staff in the higher positions were few at the time and there seemed to be no satisfactory promotion for Bergquist, who definitely had earned one. The library could not afford to pay him as much in this position as we knew he should receive. I assumed the task, as happened very often through that decade and the next, of helping a staff member to find another position that would pay more, broaden his experience, and move him up a step in his chosen profession. We did not have to wait long before Bergquist was asked to take charge of the library at the United States Naval Station in San Diego, California. He accepted this and was in San Diego five years later when Ernest Reece suggested that he would be the ideal person for the special investigator assignment. I wrote to him offering him the position and he immediately wired back his acceptance. I do not remember the salary we offered him. But whatever it was, he was well worth it. He reported for work in

March 1929. It was not much later that the reference department had to call upon him to investigate its first serious book loss.

The Reserve Book Room, the name given to the library's rare book collection, which required special protection, was housed on the top floor. It was made up of four comparatively small rooms with locked shelving in each of them, one of them being the reading room to which the readers were restricted. While the library staff at this time was comparatively small, in theory two staff members were always on duty in the reading room, one of them staying in the room while the other might leave to find and bring books to readers. But on Saturdays, in order to give one member of the staff Saturday afternoon off before another returned from lunch, there was only one person on duty from 1 to 1:30 p.m.

I was accustomed to work on Saturday afternoons except during the football season, when I refereed games. One Saturday at about 1:30 p.m. my telephone rang. Mr. Elliot, an elderly, rather heavy-set man who had spent some 40 years in all in the NYPL or the Lenox Library before that and who was one of the regular attendants in the Reserve Book Room, reported excitedly that while he had left the reading area to get a book from the adjoining room for a reader, the reader had left with three books that he had called for earlier and had been using. Elliot, knowing that he could not leave the room and pursue the thief on foot, had called both public exits by telephone to ask them to close the doors but had found both lines busy and then had called me. I rushed to the entrances but it was too late, the reader had gone. It seemed pointless to call the police, and early the following Monday morning Bergquist, Mr. Lydenberg and I conferred. H.M.L. called Arthur Swann, then head of the largest book auction house in the city and a man whom we knew and trusted, and one or two of the other senior men in the book trade concerning whom we had no doubts, and told them our story. The stolen books were a copy of Melville's *Moby*

Dick, a first edition of Hawthorne's *Scarlet Letter* and, of much more importance, Edgar Allan Poe's first book, *Tamerlane,* which was very scarce and probably irreplaceable. We estimated its value then at $10,000; I think that if a copy came on the market at present it would bring at least six figures. We then settled down to wait.

Our first lead, which could not properly be called a break, came that afternoon when a second-hand dealer named Harry Gold, whom I had known slightly and distrusted, appeared at my desk and announced that he understood that we had lost a copy of *Moby Dick.* He would not tell me where he had obtained the information but went on to say that he had a copy which was made up of an imperfect duplicate that the library had sold him some time ago which he had combined with another imperfect copy to make a perfect one. He said he didn't want us to think that this copy that he had for sale was the one that was stolen. I kept as blank a face as I could and let him go. I had known that R. W. G. Vail, who had worked for us and had become librarian of the American Antiquarian Society in Worcester, had told me that an imperfect copy of *Moby Dick* had been sold to Gold, since we had more than one of the perfect ones. I did not admit that we had lost a copy but by the time Gold left I was convinced that he had been directly or indirectly involved in what had happened two days earlier.

Several months passed with no leads and then, about 4:30 one afternoon. Arthur Swann telephoned me in a state of great excitement. He told me that he was serving on a murder jury and could speak only briefly but that Harry Stone, a dealer in rare books on 57th Street, had just shown him a copy of *Tamerlane* and asked if it was genuine, and he thought it might be ours. I said, "Please hold Mr. Stone and the book and I'll be with you in 10 minutes." He replied that he was sorry that he could not wait and that he had given the book back to Stone, who already had left. Instead of telephoning, I rushed up to Stone's establishment on foot. Stone told me calmly (I confess I was a bit excited) that he had gone to Arthur Swann but that immediately after leaving Swann he had returned the *Tamerlane* to another dealer who had given it to him. This dealer was on 59th Street, only a few blocks away (I confess that after 50 years I have forgotten the name of this dealer, someone whom I had known). I rushed to his shop. His assistant said that the owner of the shop had gone, he supposed to eat supper, and that he would be back in a few minutes. I waited impatiently for more than a few minutes and then was told that the dealer regularly ate in a small restaurant only a few steps away. I went there but found that the man I was looking for had been there and gone. I returned to the store and the assistant told me that he doubted if the owner would come back that night but that he would be in the store at 9 the next morning. So I went home to White Plains and called Bergquist at his home in Stamford.

We agreed to meet at the 59th Street store at 9 the next morning. The owner did not arrive until an hour later. When we asked him about the volume that Harry Stone had returned to him the evening before, he replied that Harry Gold had given it back to him and asked him to check on it. Bergquist went promptly to Harry Gold's shop on the Bowery and was told that the story was correct: Gold had had a copy of *Tamerlane* but was convinced that it was a fake. He therefore had returned it to the man who had brought it to him, whom he knew only as "Jim" and whose address he did not know. He would, he said, "be glad to give us further information if he received it." We were foiled again with nothing further to go on.

But apparently not all was lost. It was some months later that a young man looking somewhat distraught came to my desk. After considerable hesitation he told me he understood that the library had lost some books and that perhaps he could help us to find them. I drew him out enough so that I was convinced that he did know something about it and that it would be wise to take him to Bergquist. Bergquist, who also was sure the young man knew something definite about our lost books, did not try to push him vigorously and possibly frighten him before he had given us any really valuable information (our visitor had a rather full face and we learned later that he was known as "Babyface" by his friends, and that is the name I will use for him in telling this story). It gradually came out during the next few months, in the course of which Babyface made several calls on us, that he and a man with whom he had worked whose name was Clarke had been engaged in stealing valuable books from libraries and book stores, working under the direction of second-hand book dealers. To obtain this information we promised him immunity if it would help us. One dealer, who was named Harris, specialized in pornography and was the proprietor of a second-hand store dealing in a variety of printed material. The second was Charles (or "Charlie" as he was called) Rowe, who dealt primarily in English and American history and literature, and the third was Harry Gold, with whom we had had the previous experience.

In due course, arrangements were made for Babyface to have dinner and spend an evening with Harry Lydenberg, Arthur Swann, Dr. A. S. W. Rosenbach, Byrne Hackett of the Brick Row Book Shop, Bergquist and myself. We learned two things that evening (in addition to seeing Dr. Rosenbach drink a large bottle of whisky without any apparent effect on him, something he was unable to repeat a few years later). One was that Babyface, after working closely with Clarke, had quarreled with him because, as Babyface put it, Clarke had stolen his girl. The second fact was that Clarke, Babyface and Rowe (one of the dealers named above) had gone to Cambridge one day to visit Harvard's Widener Library. At this time the Widener stacks were almost wide open to anyone who wanted to enter. Rowe had gone to the early American history section and turned down on the shelves the books that he could sell to advantage. Then his two assistants spent the day collecting them and taking them out to Rowe's waiting car. Babyface estimated that they might have taken more than 100 volumes in all. Some years later, when I became librarian at Widener, I checked the records and found that Babyface was right and that Harvard listed about 100 volumes in the American history section as having disappeared. Theoretically, all rare books had been transferred to the rare book room. But the bookstack had not been examined for a considerable length of time for books that could be considered valuable now and which had not been so considered when assigned there many years earlier.

Babyface told us that he remembered one of the volumes that had been taken and what happened to it. It was a volume printed in the 18th century about Fort Ticonderoga during the American Revolution and included maps and charts. He said that Rowe had sold it to a New York second-hand dealer named Schulte, who specialized, I had supposed, in theology rather than American history. Schulte in turn had sold the book to the New York Historical Society for $1,200, which was a bargain price.

With this rather definite information, I wrote to Alfred C. Potter, who was then the Harvard librarian, and asked if he had the Ticonderoga volume and if it had a secret mark that I understood was used. Mr. Potter replied promptly that Harvard had had this volume but that a recent inventory indicated it was missing. He also gave me the secret mark that it should have. Bergquist and I then went to the New York Historical Society and asked to see the volume. The librarian, Mr. Wall, brought it to us and reported that he had recently bought it from Schulte for $1,200. We then asked him to turn to the place where the secret mark should be and there it was. The volume was returned to Harvard. Schulte returned the $1,200 to the Historical Society and we let him make such arrangements as he could with the man from whom he purchased it. This was my first experience with the Harvard library.

About this time a letter came from the Lancaster, Massachusetts, Public Library, saying that a recently completed inventory indicated that their first editions of standard 19th century New England authors such as Emerson, Hawthorne,

Thoreau, Whittier, Alcott, etc., had disappeared. Could we help them? Bergquist talked with Babyface, who told him that this seemed like Clarke's work; his ex-friend had been going through New England public libraries and removing the first editions of New England authors. Later we found that this had indeed occurred in a number of libraries. Babyface added that he understood that Clarke was now at the Essex Hotel in Boston. Bergquist called on Clarke there and found a quantity of books from various libraries as well as the tools that Clarke was using to remove the signs of ownership. He had Clarke arrested. He was tried and convicted but the judge, finding that he was a Canadian citizen, ordered his deportation with the understanding that he would not return to the United States. The result was that Clarke set up a second-hand book shop in Canada and began to issue catalogues with covers inscribed in large type, "25 YEARS OF HONEST DEALING IN CANADA." Some of the readers of this volume may have seen these catalogues; I found when I came to Harvard that it had dealt directly or indirectly with Clarke and I stopped the practice.

Babyface's next disclosure told of the well-known Columbia professor, Brander Matthews, who not long before his death in 1929 had given to the New York Public Library (I had the pleasure of going to his apartment and taking the books off his shelves) his collection of material on prestidigitation or "sleight of hand" because we had the best collection in the country in that field. His books made a fine addition to it. At the same time Professor Matthews had given to the Columbia University library his fine collection of English and American literature. Columbia, by way of saying thank you, printed a list of the books. Charlie Rowe, the dealer mentioned earlier, then wrote to the Columbia library, according to Babyface, saying that he had been a good friend of Matthews and had obtained many of the books for him and asking Columbia to give him a copy of the catalogue, which it did. Rowe then marked his copy, indicating the items that he thought he could sell to advantage, and gave the list to

Babyface and Clarke; they went up and brought the books back to Rowe. Babyface then said he knew just where some of these books were shelved in Rowe's store. To shorten my story, I will simply say that by this time Babyface had told us that Harry Gold had the three New York Public Library volumes which had been stolen and that Harris had volumes that could be identified easily as stolen from other libraries.

As the next step, Bergquist, Heinle, his assistant, and I decided that the time had come to raid the three stores simultaneously. All were within a few blocks of each other, two of them on and one just off the Bowery. The three of us took the subway together down to 14th Street early one evening when we knew the three stores would be open and the crowds would have thinned out on the streets. Bergquist had arranged to have a policeman within call of each store. As we stood on the corner some 15 minutes before the time we had set for the raids, I noticed a young man who had worked in the New York Public Library some years earlier, whom we had been glad to let go in spite of his obvious ability, pass us and then hurry on. When the appointed time came, we separated, Bergquist going to Harry Gold's, Heinle to Harris' and I to Charlie Rowe's. Bergquist found nothing and was convinced that our former library assistant had got there first and that anything Gold had that we might be looking for was in the vault, which Bergquist could not get into without a search warrant.

Heinle had adequate proof to show that material he found had been stolen, and he had Harris arrested. I found one of Brander Matthews' books with his marks in it and made a personal arrest on the spot and turned Mr. Rowe over to a policeman who was waiting nearby. We were pleased, of course, by the two successes but upset that we had been unsuccessful with Gold, who we were convinced was the culprit so far as the New York Public Library losses were concerned. Rowe and Harris were tried and convicted. Rowe went to jail for a fairly long term. He had to give up his store and after a year or so we learned that he had become seriously ill, was released, and allowed to go home to die soon thereafter.

After another few months had passed, Bergquist and I were called on by Harris' brother and it was agreed that I would go over to what was then known as Welfare Island, reached by an elevator and stairs from the Queensborough Bridge, and see Harris in the city penitentiary there. I had a long talk with Harris, who said that he missed his wife and children as well as his work and suggested that the library would have enough influence on the court so that if he did us a favor we could obtain his release. He then went on to say that it was well known in the trade that Harry Gold had, as we suspected, the copy of Poe's *Tamerlane,* knew it was "hot," and was anxious to get rid of it at a very low price; Harris' brother, with whom we had talked, could buy it for $400, on condition that Harris be released from jail. Bergquist took the matter up with the District Attorney and received his approval for the scheme.

Early one evening Bergquist and I stood near an agreed-upon street corner on the Bowery and saw Harris' brother turn over $400 in marked bills to Gold in return for our copy of Poe's *Tamerlane.* Bergquist quickly stepped up and arrested Gold and turned him over to a nearby policeman. The trial came off fairly promptly. I testified about the loss of the volume and the story of its being traced to four dealers, then my niece, Marion Metcalf Root (Azariah's daughter, who was in charge of rare book cataloguing at the New York Public Library), identified the volume by its secret mark, and Bergquist told the story of how he got the book back, to say nothing of the $400. We left thinking that the case finally had come to a satisfactory end. But the next day we learned that the judge, who we were told was a personal friend of Harry Gold, had thrown the case out of court on a technicality, and we were back where we started, except that we had regained the most valuable of the three lost volumes.

But the story of *Tamerlane* and book theft was far from over. Through additional information obtained from

Babyface, Bergquist had at least three more interesting adventures. Babyface had known not only Clarke but others in his profession and he casually remarked one day that two other men who were "professionals" in what had been his line were going to raid Byrne Hackett's Brick Row Book Shop in New Haven on a certain day. Bergquist warned Hackett and drove to New Haven that morning and, with the information that he had received, saw the prospective book thieves go into the Brick Row Book Shop. He parked behind them (it was fairly easy to find a parking space in those days). In due course, he saw his prey appear loaded down with books and, before they had an opportunity to drive off, he turned them over to the New Haven police. Bergquist then went to the shop and asked why the clerks had not noticed what was going on. They had a hard time believing it when they were shown the loot. The two men had been there and had been watched but apparently one of them would divert the attention of the clerks just long enough for the other to take a book and put it into his coat.

Babyface told us another story about these two men, who worked together. He said they set up a competition to see which one could steal the largest book from a library and that one of them took from the Avery Architecture Library at Columbia a mammoth volume which weighed 54 pounds.

These two men were, as far as I can remember, the only book thieves that Bergquist caught, had tried, convicted and jailed. He was looking for larger quarry, the "fences"—that is, the second-hand dealers—who in most cases were directing the thefts and whom he considered the really guilty parties. But the men who were caught in New Haven seemed to be free-lancers who worked independently from any one dealer and disposed of their booty as best they could.

Another of Bergquist's victims was a well-known Philadelphia dealer with a representative who was one of Babyface's friends. The thief was caught but turned state's evidence, which led to the trial of the dealer. While there was no question of his guilt, the case was tried before a judge who simply refused to sentence and disgrace him. The actual thief, in this case, some years later, wrote an article for the magazine "Commentary" entitled something like "How I Stole a Million Dollars Worth of Books."

An equally sad case occurred with a Cincinnati second-hand book dealer who had a fine reputation. He was brought into court by Bergquist as a receiver of stolen property but again was released by a friendly judge.

In this connection, it should be recorded that Edwin W. Gaillard had, as a triumph of which he was particularly proud, gotten through the state legislature in New York a law that I am not sure would have stood up before the U.S. Supreme Court. Contrary to the general rule that any man is innocent until he is proved guilty, it provided that, if found in possession of stolen property, a second-hand dealer automatically was to be considered guilty unless able to prove his innocence.

All in all, in a period of perhaps three years beginning in 1930, Bergquist had put into jail three of the "fences" and there were three other cases where the thieves were arrested and used as witnesses. At any rate, his work broke up a gang of professional book thieves, frightened the dealers who directed them, and discouraged them for a considerable period of time. But of course this did not end book thefts from libraries and secondhand book stores.

One more and especially interesting episode completed the story of *Tamerlane*. A fine looking, nicely dressed man in his 30's appeared in my office and showed his badge as a New York city probation officer. He said he had a strange and rather sad case on his hands which he thought would interest me. I immediately took him to Bergquist's office and he told his story to us. A young man who had been turned over to him in his position as probation officer had told this story. He was having a difficult time making a living in his native North Carolina and had come to New York hoping to better himself. He was apparently interested in books although he had had little formal education and one day had dropped into

Harry Gold's book shop. Gold asked him if he wanted a job. Of course he did and it turned out that Gold suggested that he go to the Reserve Book Room in the New York Public Library, "case" the place, and find out what were the chances of getting books from it.

The young fellow followed instructions and came to the library's Reserve Book Room every day for a week, calling for various American literature volumes. He convinced the staff that he was a serious student in the field. Then, on Saturday, using the same false name and address that he had used all the week on his call slips, he called for the three volumes which started this story. He read or pretended to read them for some time and then, when he knew that Mr. Elliot was alone, asked him for another book which was out of the room. As soon as Elliot left the room he took the three books, fled and delivered them to Harry Gold. Gold came to see me to learn what we knew about the case and later, to avoid any possibility of being involved, had let his "assistant" go. The young man, who had done his best to survive in the big city, had been in trouble on another matter, was convicted and jailed and finally had been released under the supervision of the probation officer.

We were, of course, delighted. The young man was sent back to jail in protective custody and we brought the case into court again, with a different judge this time. Bergquist now knew his way about in court and had become acquainted with the District Attorney. While the case was waiting for its turn, the probation officer came in several times to talk about his probationer, in whom he seemed to be very much interested. One day he said the young man had told him he was completely out of underwear and asked if we would buy him some. We felt it was not improper to give the probation officer $15 to buy the underclothes and a few weeks later, when Bergquist visited the poor fellow in jail to talk over the case, we found that the probation officer simply had pocketed the money. The case finally ended on a happy note. The probation officer lost his job and was convicted of petty larceny. A little later Harry Gold was tried again, and this time convicted and sent to Sing Sing for a long grand-larceny term. He was compelled to sell his business and, so far as I know, when he finally was released he did not go back into the field.

More about book thefts will appear in later chapters but this one should not be closed without saying that Babyface, on Bergquist's and my recommendations, was engaged by one of our large public libraries, not in New York State, as a special officer and was successful in catching and convicting at least one man who was stealing books on a large scale, to say nothing of a number of other minor cases. This fact was confirmed to me recently by an old friend who was at that time employed in the library where Babyface worked and remembered the excitement that resulted.

I came to Harvard in 1937 and left Bergquist still doing well in his work. I should confess that while he was breaking up the book-thief ring, I occasionally became provoked because he did not become more excited and move faster. But as time went on I came to realize that his lack of speed was due to his desire to be sure that he had the cases completely in hand, as a defeat might be dangerous. He was particularly unhappy about his failure in the out-of-state jobs in Philadelphia and Cincinnati but I am sure that they were in no way his fault.

Mr. Strippel, who was in charge of our local history room, called to our attention a genealogy printed during the first half of the 19th century from which a large number of blank pages had been skillfully cut out. Bergquist kept the matter in mind and when Mr. Paltsits, who was in charge of our manuscripts, was offered a letter signed by Lincoln which he suspected was a forgery, he talked with Bergquist about it and the latter found that it was written on paper with the same watermark as that which had been removed from the genealogy. Paltsits told him the name and address of the man who had offered the letter. Bergquist called on him and discovered in his room more of the same paper, old quill pens, and specimens of writing not only by Lincoln but by Edgar Allen Poe and other noteworthy persons in the 40's, 50's and 60's of the last century. He found that the man, who went by the name of Cosey, had been copying letters, poems, etc., by various notables and then taking them to libraries and booksellers and offering them for sale at very reasonable prices. When he was questioned about their origin, he said that he had found them but he could not guarantee that they were genuine. We had nothing on which Cosey could be convicted. But Bergquist called the matter to the attention of the dealers who would be likely to be offered such material and to libraries throughout the country. He also kept track of Cosey as time went on.

The rest of Bergquist's career should not be forgotten. The library's compulsory retirement age then was 65, which would have required him to retire in 1947. A few years before this he went to Paul North Rice, my successor as chief of the reference department, as shamefacedly as he had come to me earlier when his arches gave out on the stack marble floors and stairs, and stated that he felt that he could no longer be as active as his job required. It was getting too much for him and he would like to be transferred to less strenuous physical work. Paul understood the situation and without hesitation appointed him, to the surprise of many I expect, chief of the library's Preparation Division, a position which both Paul and I had filled earlier, and one which I still believe was at that time the most difficult cataloguing assignment in the United States except for the one at the Library of Congress. In this position he succeeded Quincy Mumford, who later became Librarian of Congress. Bergquist again performed satisfactorily. I remember visiting him at the time and finding, as I expected, that he was on top of his work.

Bergquist retired from the Library in 1947 but his career was not ended. Albert Boni, realizing that he needed help at Readex from someone who knew librarians throughout the country, asked Bergquist to join his company, which he did with great success, thoroughly enjoying his work as he had done ever since he decided to become a librarian. G. William Bergquist was most assuredly one of the most unusual and useful men in the library profession whom I have known during the past 75 years.

Chapter 10
Scientific Aids to Learning

Photostats and Microforms

As has been recorded in Chapter 2, Mr. Lydenberg asked me to superintend the business end of our photostat work soon after I began my work as chief of stacks. A few months later I also took charge of a shelf list to be made from photostated cards, supplemented by those already available that had been made by other methods. But it was a year later before I fully comprehended Mr. Lydenberg's great interest in what we much later called scientific aids to learning. He realized by 1914 that the New York City newspapers, for which he felt we had special responsibility, had been printed on wood pulp paper since the 1870's and were deteriorating. They were so brittle that in the newspaper room the janitor had to sweep up what we called "Post Toasties" twice a day. It was evident that if something were not done promptly we no longer would have a useful newspaper collection.

With his customary energy and sagacity, H.M.L. went to work on the problem. There were others, of course, who were interested, including William Warner Bishop, who had shifted from the position of superintendent of the main reading room at the Library of Congress to become librarian at the University of Michigan at Ann Arbor in 1915. But it was Mr. Lydenberg who first did something beyond worrying and talking. Within a couple of years he tested 22 methods by which paper could be preserved and a summary of the results was printed in the library's *Bulletin.* All the methods were expensive and the one that seemed most useful was adopted. This was pasting, with a rice paste, a sheet of tissue-like Japanese rice paper on both sides of each sheet of newspaper. It was a difficult task. But with the aid of Mr. Thurman, who was in charge of the bindery, a way of mechanizing the procedure was found so that the pasting could be done quickly and comparatively inexpensively. The results promised well. Mr. Lydenberg persuaded five New York City newspapers to pay for the work, which came at that time to about $10,000 a year. This was continued for more than 15 years. But in the early 1930's it was realized that, while the disintegration had been delayed and the life of the paper extended, the pages again were disintegrating.

H.M.L. was in despair. Fortunately at just this time the Recordak Corporation, a subsidiary of the Eastman Company in Rochester, had found that microfilm was a suitable method of reproducing, in reduced size and bulk, life-insurance policies, bank checks and other business records.

One of its salesmen came to the newspaper room at the library to ask if there were some way that microfilm could be of use to the library. Louis Fox, chief of the newspaper division, sent the salesman up to me. I was just bright enough to realize that this might be the solution to our newspaper problem and, with Mr. Lydenberg's enthusiastic approval, we purchased a Recordak reading machine and began to send our newspapers to the Recordak Company. They were reproduced on 35 mm microfilm and made available to our readers. This was, if I am not mistaken, the beginning of the direct use of micro-reproductions for readers in libraries, although it should be recorded that the Library of Congress had reproduced American archival material that its European agent, Worthington Chauncey Ford, had found and microfilmed. But when it was required by readers this material was "blown up" on to paper because the Library of Congress had not yet acquired reading machines.

We soon learned that it was easy to use the microfilm, if one knew the date and could turn to it readily and was not doing research which required going back and forth over a considerable period of time. It occurred to me, when I learned in the early 30's that reduced-size offset reproductions could be made, just large enough so that they were legible without a magnifying glass, that it would be possible to reproduce newspapers on a good quality paper in a volume 11" high, 8" wide and an inch thick for two weeks of the *New York Times,* occupying less than one fourth as much shelf space as the original form and one-eighth as much as with the rice paper. With Mr. Lydenberg's approval, I had a sample volume made by the best offset printers we could find in New York. It would be financially feasible if enough libraries would subscribe so that a fairly large edition could be printed. After studying the proposal, Charles M. Puckette, the business manager of the *New York Times,* reported that if we could obtain subscriptions for 135 copies at $175 per year they would adopt the method. This was less than the cost of the space saved by the use of the film plus the cost of binding the original file. I took some sample numbers of the *Times* prepared by the offset printer to a meeting of the Eastern College Librarians at Columbia the Saturday after Thanksgiving in 1934. I was encouraged by the reception. I then solicited subscriptions at $175 a year from all the libraries in the United States which were listed in the Bowker Library Directory with annual book appropriations of over $10,000. This was in the depths of the Depression. After months of struggle, I was able to obtain only 100 subscriptions and had to report to the *New York Times* that I had failed. This was a bitter blow and I realized I was a poor salesman.

Several years later, after I shifted to Harvard, Mr. Puckette wrote to me and said: "Since economic conditions have improved, would it be wise to try again for subscriptions?" After careful consideration and consultation with Mr. Lydenberg and others, I decided that if this were done it might discourage libraries from going ahead with microfilm for other newspapers, something that they now were doing rapidly, and it would be unwise to "upset the apple cart" with a new method for the one paper that could sell enough copies to make it practicable. As I look back on the situation, I feel that this was a serious mistake on my part. The cost for the offset reproduction would match that for the microfilm. It would be easier to find one's place with the offset form and a magnifying glass would help those with defective vision. Experience now shows that reduced-size offset reproductions for many types of material are satisfactory. I still have a copy of the offset volume for two weeks of the *New York Times*.

Mr. Lydenberg proposed several other studies that had to do with the preservation of paper and binding. The first had its origin in our finding that the bindings of heavy, much-used volumes, such as the H. W. Wilson Company Indexes and lists, were breaking because of their weight and the difficulty in turning the pages. We tried rebinding them in two or more volumes to see if that would help the situation. This led to a study of the question of whether leather binding, which we always had considered stronger than buckram, was desirable. We compared the best leather and buckram binding for this type of reference volume and found that leather was stronger; if the best quality were used, it was desirable for heavily-used reference books because the oil from the hands of the user helped preserve the leather. If the volumes were little used, buckram was better because even the best leather tended to deteriorate in a non-humidified atmosphere if not used or oiled regularly.

I then came up with another proposal which HML approved and for which he obtained a grant from the Carnegie Corporation. It was to test the use of microfilm for reference books and other types of material where one frequently had to refer to an index and then shift back and forth through the volume. We found that microfilm was not desirable for encyclopedias, genealogical volumes and dictionaries, where the reader often would want to turn anywhere from "A" to "Z"; the time that it took to turn back and forth would be long and the film might be damaged in the reading machine. On the other hand, it could be used to advantage for many books and particularly for those printed on poor paper which wore out quickly with heavy use. It was not until after I went to England in 1938 and had seen what was being done with microfiche that the latter came into the picture. It will be referred to in Part III.

We were fortunate enough to become acquainted with Albert Boni in the middle 30's and work with him on micro-reproductions, first in the hope of being able to replace the public catalogue with microfilm, using the class mark on the upper right-hand corner of the catalogue card as a stroboscopic device by which one could find his place easily. Unfortunately we were unable to work this out satisfactorily. But Mr. Boni did not give up. He continued with his struggle to find uses for reduced-size reproductions, and finally came up with Microprint. This has enabled him to make available to libraries, in inexpensive reduced format, tremendous amounts of research material which they could not obtain otherwise. Much work was done also by Eugene Power and others during the Second World War in copying onto microfilm American archival records and irreplaceable manuscripts in Europe. This enriched American libraries tremendously. I was fortunate enough to be chairman of the committee in charge of those arrangements.

The New York Public Library, except for its efforts to find subscriptions for the *New York Times* in reduced-size offset, did comparatively little to publicize its work with microfilm and the preservation of wood-pulp paper. But Mr. Lydenberg was convinced that wood-pulp paper, properly washed to remove acid chemicals, could be made so that it would last as long as much of the rag paper that had been used almost exclusively before the 1870's and which, we have found to our disgust since then, often was as fragile as wood pulp paper. His interest in the problem provided much of the inspiration that many years later resulted in the "permanent" paper now used by many university presses.

HML also took the lead as a member of a committee that arranged for the British Museum's attempt to print its catalogue again in book form and tried to persuade the Library of Congress to do likewise with its own catalogue and its *Union Catalogue,* both of which ultimately were carried out by Edwards Brothers of Ann Arbor.

The New York Public Library began to segregate books with disintegrating bindings or such poor paper that corners of the pages were breaking off, and then tried to control their use and store them until the situation could be corrected when suitable ways of doing so were found. In this connection, we found that some sections of the Oxford English Dictionary, the British Roll Series and Sessional Papers and parts of the Early English Text Society publications among others, were printed on paper that was much inferior to other parts and that some volumes were inferior to others. My interest in the problem became great and I decided that the deterioration of paper is perhaps the most serious problem that research libraries faced then. This still is true today.

As a result, as time went on and we studied other phases of the paper preservation problem, we were amused and in some ways irritated when at the 1936 conference of the American Library Association Llewellyn Raney, librarian of the University of Chicago, took command of the situation and gave the impression that he had been responsible for the whole development of micro-reproductions. In the meantime, Mr. Lydenberg and I kept in touch with Robert Binkley, as is reported in the next section. When Watson Davis organized the American Documentation Institute we worked closely with him and were involved in the Carnegie Corporation's interest in the appointment of Mr. Davis' top assistant, whom the corporation recommended and for whom it paid the salary. Eventually, in fact, I became president of the Documentation Institute, although I confess as I write this I do not remember the year and had forgotten all about it until the present secretary of the Institute (it is now called ASIS) sent me a letter asking for a photograph to go into the archives with those of other past presidents.

This section will close with a repetition of my statement that the preservation of printed material published in the last 100 years on poor paper that has not been properly processed (this includes a large percentage of publications printed since the 1870's) is the most serious problem that libraries face today, in spite of the importance of audio-visual work, automation and inter-library cooperation.

Robert Binkley

Too few librarians realize that Robert C. Binkley gave methods of reproducing print their greatest boost between the invention of the Photostat, which was first used in libraries in 1912, and the Xerox (a trade name, as is Photostat), which came into use many years after his death.

Dr. Binkley was born in 1897. He received his Ph.D. from Stanford in 1927, having served as reference librarian at the

Hoover Library before doing his graduate work. He then taught history at New York University, Smith College and Western Reserve until his untimely death in 1940 at the age of 42.

My first experience with Bob was not a happy one. It was during the academic year 1928-29 when he was a history instructor at New York University. He sent his freshman English history class to the New York Public Library, where I had recently become chief of the reference department, asking his students to list all the source material that they could find dealing with the year of the Spanish Armada, 1588. Many of them found their way to the local history division and got their hands on the "British Roll Series." Unfortunately a large number of its volumes were printed on poor paper and, because of the heavy handling they received from inexperienced young people, more than a thousand dollars' worth of items were ruined on one day. Henry Strippel, the division chief, reported this the next morning and told me that the New York University instructor who was responsible for the invasion was named Robert Binkley. I was able to get in touch with Binkley and asked him to come to my office, which he did promptly. He was an attractive young man, just over 30. I told him what had happened to the expensive, hard-to-replace volumes and said that we would have to refuse to serve his or any other undergraduate students on similar assignments. He came back at me strongly, saying I was an old-fashioned librarian who was more interested in the preservation of his collections than in their use by budding young scholars. We went at each other hot and heavy and were disgusted with one another and very unhappy about the situation. I reported the encounter to Mr. Lydenberg, who agreed that I had done what was necessary.

Our readers had increased in numbers rather steadily, and I then began to study them more carefully than before to learn where they came from. We found that a rapidly growing percentage were students from local colleges or universities which had inadequate collections to cover their curriculums and very often lacked duplicate copies for required reading. As a result, a large group of the more imaginative, energetic students were finding the reference department as well as the branches of the New York Public Library convenient and useful. The problem became greater for us during the year 1929 and climaxed that autumn when the great Depression resulted in unemployment on a large scale and many of the unemployed quite naturally came to the library looking for reading material that they thought might help them to obtain new positions.

Our regular research readers were complaining about the crowded conditions in the reading rooms and also about the noise that came from the students talking and whispering together, particularly on Saturday afternoons and even more so on Sundays, at the only hours when many serious older persons could find time to come to the library to work on their legitimate reference problems. In an effort to deal with the situation, I came in on a Sunday afternoon and patrolled the main reading room. When I was convinced that one or more students were disturbing others, I asked the culprits as quietly as possible to come with me to the entrance where a conversation would not distract others and told them that they would have to leave, as I had done in the Oberlin library in 1913. Before the day was over I ejected more than 75 persons. Two of them suggested that I come out to Bryant Park in back of the library and settle the problem physically. But I declined and got away without trouble, something that I probably could not have done in the late 1960's.

I realized that my afternoon had not solved the problem. There were no members of the reading room staff whom I could ask to do what I had done that Sunday, and I did not think it wise to assign the task to uniformed guards. Another solution had to be found. It should be added that this noisy and disturbing group that I had dealt with was using comparatively inexpensive and easily replaceable books which should have been available elsewhere.

I knew that the Christmas holidays were always the busiest

time of the year because many advanced scholars came from all over the country to use the library for material they could not find in their own libraries. So in December of 1930 I decided to check attendance in the two main reading rooms during the 10 days from before Christmas until after New Year's, every hour on the hour. At that time the two reading rooms had 768 seats between them. The average attendance during this whole period was around 1,050, which meant that for much of the time more than 300 persons were waiting for books at the circulation desk, examining the reference books shelved around the walls of the reading rooms, sitting on the floor, or wandering about the room looking for vacant chairs. The number of readers served with from one to a half-dozen books was at times 150 every 20 minutes, which meant that the indicators which told readers that their books were ready for them sometimes would be over-lapped if the service slowed up, since there were only 150 numbers. The rooms were so over-crowded that the scene could be called without hesitation a nightmare or a bedlam.

With these statistics in hand, I went to Mr. Lydenberg and Mr. Anderson and recommended that we refuse to admit to the reading rooms or accept call slips from any young persons who had not graduated from college, unless they carried letters from their college or university librarians asking us to help them because their libraries lacked desired material. E.H.A. and H.M.L. took the problem to the trustees and they approved. The library staff then was told that if a student objected when he was turned away, he should be advised to come to my office at any time between 9 and 5. As a result, during the following five months until the academic year ended, I did comparatively little except explain the situation and make it a point to talk with each student who came to me until he seemed to understand and almost invariably said as he left, "Thank you."

This experience may have had two direct or indirect results. At any rate we found that the total use of the library was reduced immediately in spite of the Depression: more of this Chapter 14. An indirect result was that after talking almost seven hours a day, five days a week, for five months, I have been inclined to be hoarse ever since and as I have gotten older the hoarseness has increased. My doctor tells me that my throat muscles have worn out.

One of the persons refused admission because of her undergraduate status was a daughter of Robert Moses. Mr. Moses, probably because of his conviction that all park areas should be kept sacrosanct rather than because of this incident, did everything he could—which was all that was needed—to prevent the library from having an addition built at the rear, in Bryant Park, this in spite of the fact that the library's charter stated that the building, which was paid for by the city, could be placed anywhere in Bryant Park. It also resulted indirectly in the library's acquisition long after I left New York of the Arnold Constable department store building, on the southeast corner of 5th Avenue and 40th Street. A collection primarily for college students' use was placed there. For most undergraduate purposes it is more convenient than the main library building, although students now can use either one.

My decision to reduce undergraduate use of the reference department was one of the most difficult ones I ever had to face; it went against the grain but I still think it was the right decision at the time. I believe that it resulted in better library collections and longer hours of service in the schools throughout the metropolitan area, which helped solve the New York Public Library's very serious overcrowding problem.

But to go back to Robert Binkley: he left New York University for Smith College in the summer of 1929 and a year later became a history professor at Western Reserve University in Cleveland, where he continued through the last 10 years of his life. I temporarily forgot all about him except for the bad taste in my mouth that resulted from my unhappy experience with him. But Binkley took his side of the matter even more seriously than I did and went to work to find a solution. He had come to realize the necessity of preserving scarce and expensive research material and decided it would help if inexpensive methods of reproducing the printed page were found. His *Manual on Methods of Reproducing Research Materials* was published in 1931. In 1932 I learned that he had been appointed chairman of the Joint Committee on Materials for Research sponsored by the American Council of Learned Societies and the Social Science Research Council, and that Mr. Lydenberg was a member of the committee. H.M.L. was president of the American Library Association for the year 1932-33 and as a result was unable from time to time to attend some of the meetings of Bob's committee and asked me to go in his place. So Binkley and I met again. We had forgiven each other and I was delighted by what his committee was doing. Bob and I began to call each other by our first names and soon became good friends. In other chapters, in the New York Public Library and in the Harvard parts of my story, I relate other experiences in connection with scientific aids to learning and methods of reproducing research material. I saw Bob Binkley from time to time during the remainder of his life and we worked together closely in his special field from 1932 to 1940, in New York or Washington, in connection with his work and that of the American Documentation Institute. I keep near my desk a copy of his masterpiece, *Manual on Methods of Reproducing Research Materials,* published by the ACLS and SSRC, and still make use of it.

It would be hard to exaggerate the great influence that Binkley had in his too short life on what we now often speak of as scientific aids to learning and I treasure my experiences with him and am much happier with them than I was in 1928 after our first encounter. Only a few weeks before his death, we had lunch together on the Arlington side of the Potomac and he ordered a very Mexican-hot "hot tamale," which he said felt good on his throat. He said nothing of the fact that he realized he was dying of throat cancer.

Chapter 11
Troubleshooter

During my nine years as executive assistant in the New York library from 1919 to 1927, and as chief of the reference department under Mr. Anderson and Mr. Lydenberg from 1928 to 1934 and later (after Mr. Anderson's retirement) under Mr. Lydenberg only until August 1937, I might be said to have served as an administrator of sorts and also as an ombudsman, personnel officer and troubleshooter. These tasks involved work for the library administration in its dealings with the staff, including the division chiefs, except that with the latter E.H.A. and H.M.L. handled the selection and policy decisions. I dealt with the day-by-day operation and with staff and readers. Staff members came to me with their questions and their division chiefs approved my recommendations for staff promotions and salaries. I talked with all professional assistants at least once a year about their future prospects and helped them find other positions when we could not promote them in the New York Public Library. I had the responsibility of dealing with the readers and visitors who were troublesome because of their behavior or were troubled by the treatment that they received in the library. This chapter will cover some of the special problems that came up with the three groups. The visitors were more numerous than the readers in those days because of the library's location at 42nd Street and Fifth Avenue, the heart of the city, and because it was a showplace among the city's buildings. We were fortunate that the plans of Carrere and Hastings and Dr. Billings had provided broad corridors with walls which could be used for exhibits.

If we include staff members who came in through the 40th Street entrance, the number of staff, readers, and visitors who came into the library between 1911 and 1937 amounted to considerably more than 75,000,000, and during the time that I was "troubleshooter" well over 50,000,000. The special problems that I faced can be divided into three groups:

(1) Disorderly readers (I do not include here the book thieves who are dealt with in Chapter 9 or the problems relating to the over-crowded Reading Room which also are related elsewhere).

(2) Staff problems not included in the sections under other topics.

(3) Liability insurance problems, for staff and public.

Disorderly Readers

Among our millions of readers, it had to be expected that some would be disorderly. Libraries seem to attract eccentrics.

There were many cases in all, but three special ones seem worth reporting here.

One of our regular readers was a tall, overly heavy man of Greek origin who was writing a book on the history of prostitution. He had made friends with some of the staff members, particularly one who was in charge of the public catalogue filing unit, to whom he used to give Greek candy, one specimen of which once was passed on to me. I first heard of him in that connection.

Late one afternoon my telephone rang and I was told that there was a terrible disturbance at the main reading room desk. I rushed up to the desk, an enclosure some 20 feet wide and 70 feet long where the circulation desk had its headquarters. At the far end of the area, at the top of the stairs leading down to the bookstack, the circulation staff was gathered along with a considerable number of readers who had come into the enclosure and perhaps 200 more who had been attracted by the noise and crowded outside the enclosure. In the midst of the group at the top of the stairs was our Greek reader, yelling at the top of his voice and using words which are not used customarily in polite society. I was able to work my way through the crowd to the staff member who was trying to deal with the situation. I asked the reader to quiet down so we could talk over the matter, something he refused to do.

He had reserved a book at the desk which he had been using day after day. This should have enabled him to obtain it without asking the library staff to search for it in the bookstack and send it up to him and would have saved him and the staff five or ten minutes. But the book could not be found on the reserve shelf and he blamed the staff and was letting them know what he thought of them. When I found that I could not quiet him, and the watching group was becoming larger, in desperation I pushed him—you might even say I threw him— down the stack stairs (he had been standing at the top of them). I should have found some other way of dealing with the problem. But I was fortunate. My victim fell down the stairs and landed at the bottom without breaking a bone or hitting his head. In fact, the man was so surprised at not being hurt that I was able to push him without difficulty out of the storm enclosure at the bottom of the stairs which had been installed to keep down the inevitable draft from the stack to the reading room in cold weather. He quieted down, became quite reasonable and we were able to talk over the problem. After considering all the circumstances, I decided it would be unwise to exclude him from the building in the future, as I was tempted to do, and we let it go at that. We had no further trouble with him. I never learned whether he completed his study and had it printed.

The second episode started in somewhat the same fashion. A man with a clerical collar became noisy inside the desk, yelling and shouting. I rushed up to the desk and apparently made enough impression on him so that, when I took him by the arm, he quieted down. I led him out of the desk, through the public catalogue room and down the long corridor toward the elevator. He was lame and carried a cane so I did not attempt to take him down the stairs. By the time we reached the elevator the onlookers had gone back to their work. As we waited for the elevator we stood about six feet apart, facing each other. Suddenly he raised his cane over his head and, staring at me, said, "The wrath of God is descending upon you." I was petrified for I didn't know what to do. I didn't think I should take his cane and attack him, which I might have done. I simply stood there and stared at him. Fortunately for all concerned, the cane was lowered, the elevator came, we got into it and rode down together, and I pointed him out to the doorman and told him that this man should not be allowed to come into the building again. He never came back. But on investigation we found that he was a Baptist minister who had been defrocked and undoubtedly was unbalanced.

The third case took about 10 years to come to a conclusion. It began in 1935 or 1936 when a man of perhaps 30, flushed and angry, came into my office to report that he had been treated rudely by the staff in various parts of the building. He could not understand it, he said. He went on to relate how he had used all the great libraries of the world—the British Museum, the Bibliothèque Nationale, the Library of Congress and the Harvard University library—and that at each of them he had been treated civilly and had no difficulty whatever. But whenever he came to the New York Public Library, he claimed, he was mistreated and unable to get any help. Naturally I did my best to calm him down. I tried to obtain some definite information as to just what had happened but was unable to do so. He finally went away and I thought the affair was concluded.

The scene now shifts to the Widener Library at Harvard and, while this is getting ahead of my story, it seems best to relate it here rather than in the next part of this volume. We had on the staff of the Harvard library a man of about my age named John Shea, who had gone to work there at the age of 14, as you could in those days, and already had been there for 40 years. During this time he had worked up to the post of building superintendent and, you might say, "general factotum." I will tell more about him later. But I can say here that he kept track of what was happening throughout the library involving both readers and staff and if there was any difficulty he knew about it. He came rushing down to my desk one day and said there was a man upstairs in the main reading room who had been quarreling with several different readers and talking loudly and disturbing others. I asked him to bring the man down to my office, which he did. I saw that this was the same man who had complained to me so bitterly in New York 10 years earlier. But he did not recognize me. I asked him what his problem was and he said, "The staff and the readers are just impossible. I don't understand the situation. I have used all the great libraries of the world without any trouble. I have been to the British Museum, the Bibliothèque Nationale, the Library of Congress, and the New York Public Library and now I come to Harvard and everyone is stupid and abusive." I then broke in and told him that I had heard that story from him before in the New York Public Library but there he had said that he had had no trouble at Harvard. I told him that he would have to leave the building and not come back. Mr. Shea took him to the front door, pointed him out to the doorman, and left him there.

It was not more than 20 minutes later when John came in again and said, "The man we just put out of the building is standing on the stoop outside the front door and as the readers with whom he had quarreled come out he spits on them." I asked John to bring the man to my office again. He sat down in a chair close to mine and I told him that we could not permit this behavior, that he not only would leave the building but that if he came into the Harvard Yard again we would have him arrested. He paid no attention to what I was saying, drew his chair closer to me and said, almost in a whisper, "I am the person who discovered nuclear fission which has resulted in the atomic bombs which went off in Japan earlier this month. The United States Government stole my invention from me and I am suing them for a billion dollars." I was so flabbergasted—I cannot think of another word to describe my feelings—that I simply told Mr. Shea to take him outside the Yard and tell him, as I had done, that he was never to come in again, which John Shea proceeded to do. I suppose I should have taken him to the policeman who always could be found at Harvard Square even if I had to make a personal arrest. It was not more than a few minutes later that John appeared at the office again, this time to tell me that after he left our troublesome visitor at Harvard Square the man had gone up to the policeman, picked a fight with him and had been arrested. What happened after that I never knew.

Staff Problems

Problems with pages were related in another chapter. Of course, older staff members also caused trouble. We had four cases where staff members of the reference department became mentally unbalanced and, at least temporarily, had to be confined in institutions. One of them is reported in the chapter dealing with events during Mr. Lydenberg's absence in Russia in the winter of 1923-24. Another occurred outside the library and we learned of it only through the newspapers. The third involved one of our best assistants, who had mental difficulty from time to time and had to have sessions in an institution on several occasions but who came back and continued to do first-class work at the library. The fourth and saddest case involved a very capable young man who had worked his way through his university in its library, in the meantime taking care of his widowed mother so that it took him a good many years to graduate. He had been in this university library at the same time that two of our senior staff members were there before they came to the NYPL and they had encouraged us to take him on. He proved to be an excellent reference worker and, while working with us, managed to get through our library school. Since his mother was no longer living, he found himself for the first time in many years with no financial problems. But he suddenly reached the conclusion that he had committed "the unpardonable sin." He would not tell what it was but he was sure of it; he talked to us frankly and said he would be found out and would be pursued and was in danger of his life. He wanted to be put into protective custody.

With the approval of our treasurer, who was president of the New York Hospital, I took him to a mental specialist who arranged for him to go to the Bloomingdale Hospital in White Plains. This was on a Saturday and I was to take him to the hospital at 3 o'clock in the afternoon. We went to White Plains by train and walked up the hill to my house, where we had lunch with my wife and two children. During the meal a noisy truck came past the house and he shook with fear and said, "They are coming for me, they are coming for me." The truck passed and I was able to calm him down and then took him to Bloomingdale and turned him over to the authorities. His sigh of relief as he realized that he had been accepted and was out of danger was hard to believe. One of our staff members with whom he had worked volunteered to serve as his guardian; when Paul North Rice, who knew the troubled man well, came back to the library to succeed me as chief of the reference department, he took over the guardianship and continued to visit him from time to time until his death, after he had been shifted to Islip State Hospital on Long Island as a hopeless case. One time when Paul went to see him he said that the source of his difficulty was that he was the illegitimate son of Queen Victoria. This was one of the saddest cases that I have known, and it had no happy ending.

In the course of my years at the New York Public Library we did have other cases of at least partial mental breakdown. For several of them I always have felt some responsibility because I failed to realize that many people have a lower limit of strength and ability to face a sometimes difficult public for long hours than Paul North Rice, Frank Waite and I had. We worked our public service staff at the information and main reading room desks very much harder than we should have and it was late in my New York Public Library years that I realized this. I should have learned this during my library school practice work in several of the branch circulating libraries, where the staff did not work more than two hours at a stretch under pressure from the public. Individuals were then shifted to other work behind the scenes. But at the information desk, the main reading room desk, and in the special reading rooms, attendants often faced the difficult public for as much as four or even five hours at a stretch. As I now realize, many found it too much of a strain. This situation was unfair to the librarian and often the public suffered from it also, because the librarian became routine in his answers and perhaps unreasonable in dealing with complaints.

I remember a man who was employed at the main reading room circulation desk who had been a literary agent. Because of the depression he was working at the library in a position that did not require library training but was important in connection with the impression the library made on the public. Because of great pressure and inadequate staff, or because books had been misplaced, it sometimes took 20 minutes or more before a book was delivered or a report could be made to the reader that it could not be found. The reader was inclined to complain bitterly. This poor desk assistant, whom we had found satisfactory as an attendant, came to me one day and said he just could not take it any more; that one reader after another had insulted and abused him, and that the next time this happened he was going to jump out the circulation desk window and beat up the complainant. I suggested that, while I did not like to say so, it might be better if he resigned. He did resign. I am sure he was a good worker. But he simply could not stand the pressure that we asked him to face.

Three fine trained librarians at the reference desk, two of them women, gave up. One we shifted to a less trying position but the other two resigned because the pressure had become too great and they were afraid they would suffer nervous breakdowns. Two others were shifted to other positions before they reached the breaking point.

I have studied the situation in other academic and research libraries and have known of more than one case where a circulation desk attendant became so calloused that it seemed as though he delighted in being able to say "No" to the reader, blaming him instead of his library. It is one of the great regrets of my career that I did not learn my lesson earlier.

Liability Insurance Problems

The New York Public Library, as is the case with most libraries, carried two kinds of liability insurance, one for employees and one for the public. They are separate because the penalties under the law differ. A person entering an eleemosynary institution, such as a non-profit free library,

does so at his own risk. If he has an accident, even if the
institution is indirectly responsible for it through negligence,
he cannot recover damages. This, of course, is not the case
with staff members who come to the library to work and for
whom the library is responsible if injuries result and it can be
shown that the library is at fault. Two cases from each group,
the public and the staff, are related here.

A young woman was in the public catalogue room one day.
There is a one-step platform around the room on which one
stands when pulling out drawers of catalogue cards. As she
was shifting from one catalogue drawer to another and going
down the step because another reader was in the way and
prevented her going along the platform to the drawer she
wanted, she tripped on a vacuum-cleaner plug which proj-
ected on the face of the step, fell and broke her leg. We
reported it to the insurance company to which we paid several thousand dollars a year for taking care of problems of
this kind. The company refused to pay damages and said
that its sole responsibility was to fight the case if it came to
court. The library felt responsible and wanted to pay the
woman's medical expenses involved. But the insurance company said we must not do so and we had to leave the matter
in this way although we did feel responsible.

The second case took a very different turn. If you come to
the library from Fifth Avenue, you go up a few steps between
the library lions to a wide platform before reaching the
monumental main front steps to the library entrance. In the
winter, snow and ice accumulated on this platform made it
difficult to enter the library. The building staff constructed
storm steps on the stairs and across the platform. One day a
woman was walking across the platform, going from 42nd
Street to 40th Street, and, not noticing that you had to go up
an inch or so as you crossed the storm boardwalk, tripped
and fell and broke her leg. Since she was not going to the
library and the accident had happened on Park Department
property and the library had not obtained permission from
the Park Department to install the boardwalk, the library was

found guilty when the case was taken to court and had to pay damages, while the insurance company declared the matter was outside its jurisdiction. The law can be difficult to understand.

Two cases involving staff members presented different problems. A young man under 16 years of age who had his working papers was employed as a page at the circulation desk. There was a service elevator inside the desk on which books on book trucks were returned to the bookstack. This young man decided he would like to ride in the elevator, although he had not been directed to do so. It was illegal for a person under 16 to operate an elevator. He went up and down in the elevator, which had a Bostwick gate with an open grating. He stuck one toe of his shoe through the grating to see what would happen and, as he came past the landing on a stack floor, the toe caught between the landing and the floor of the lift and one of his toes was broken. The library was declared negligent in letting him use the elevator and had to pay Workmen's Compensation for him.

The other case came out differently but made me very unhappy. In the 1920's the library installed a cafeteria for the staff on the ground floor. It was able to find an experienced woman to take charge of the enterprise. She employed a young man to handle the serving table and then to wash the dishes. He was pleasant, worked well and seemed to be completely satisfactory. One day he was sent up to me because he had complained that he was made to use such strong detergents that his hands were damaged and were breaking out. He said he would have to give up the work or have the dishwashing procedure changed. If this were not done, he would sue us. The manager said she did not think the detergent used was sharp enough to cause any difficulty. When the problem was taken to court, the library insisted on a doctor's examination of the young man. The doctor reported that the difficulty with the hands did not stem from the detergent but from syphilis. My heart went to my throat, you might say, but at any rate the suit was cancelled and the library never learned of any problem in connection with the staff's use of the cafeteria.

These problems have been related for two reasons: First, to show the problems a librarian in a large institution may have to face; second, in the hope that those who read them will be able to avoid some of the mistakes for which I was at least partly responsible.

A Communist Cell!

In the depths of the great depression of the 1930's a number of the young male pages on the staff (many of them working in the main bookstack where I had been in charge from 1913 to 1918) stayed on after graduating from high school or college because they were unable to find better positions elsewhere. They had been warned when they began work in the library that there probably would be no advancement for them in salary or position. But, understandably to those of us now living through the unhappy crisis of unemployment for young people in the 1970's, these young men (they were all young men, no women), some of whom had married and had one or more offspring, were becoming desperate. One of them, perhaps the most attractive youngster in the group and one of whom I had been quite proud, was a natural leader. He became interested in Communism, as did a good many of the superior young people of that generation. He never admitted it to me but I have no question about it. His group began to hold meetings and it became evident that something was about to break.

I decided to "take the bull by the horns" and asked the group to meet with me in the library auditorium office at 5 o'clock one afternoon as they went off duty. We spent a long period discussing the situation. I told them that the library understood their predicament and reminded them that they had been told that few if any of them had any future in the library but that the library was using all of its income and that there was nothing more that it could do for them. I said that we felt we must continue to give service to our readers, many of whom needed it in connection with their work and also were in serious financial straits. I let them talk and was sympathetic. But the meeting ended with my speaking firmly, saying there was nothing that the library could do for them but to let us know if they thought of any way in which we could help. To my pleasure and surprise, they accepted the situation and we heard nothing more from them. I was relieved but far from happy. It was another incident which I look back on without pleasure.

Chapter 12
Libraries Have Books
As Well As Readers,
A Catalogue and Staff

Book Acquisition

I have always been interested in books and book selection. Because I wanted to be a reference librarian and help persons find information they wanted, I went into library work without fully realizing the importance of building up a library collection. I suppose I did know, before I went into the director's office in January 1919 and at the same time became acting chief of the order department, that book selection and satisfactory cataloguing were very important parts of library work. But it was not until then that I began to realize (it probably came to me gradually) that, if you take the long-term view, the most important thing that a librarian can pass on to his successors is a well-rounded collection on the subjects that his library covers, together with the services required to make the collection readily available. Of course, these services must include a satisfactory catalogue.

It was from Mr. Anderson that I learned the importance of building up the staff for all of these purposes and from Mr. Lydenberg the importance of book selection and all the things involved in it. From each of them I learned the importance of the catalogue, although I had known something about all three of them from my years of work under the direction of Azariah Root in Oberlin.

Beginning in January 1919, my assignments brought me into regular touch with Mr. Lydenberg, particularly with everything related to book acquisition. Every day I took the division chiefs' recommendations for acquisitions to him for his approval and for his additional suggestions. I saw how much time he spent on this work himself.

After Carl Cannon came to the order division in July 1919, and I was in the director's office full time, I continued to sign the acknowledgments for gifts. Some of these came in without solicitation; some were of comparatively little importance; some were large collections; a great many came as a result of "beg" letters sent out by Mr. Lydenberg and, after he returned to the library in January 1919, by Dr. Williamson for material indexed in the *Public Affairs Information Service* which he founded and edited. The gift acknowledgments were on special printed forms, except for the more important ones, for which individual letters were written. The total number of pieces in the gifts (not the number of acknowledgments) averaged about 125,000 a year.

After acknowledgment the gifts were turned over to the catalogue department and, as Mr. Moth or Miss Sears found time, they selected items for cataloguing and put the remain-

der to one side. Mr. Lydenberg had learned that there was
some dissatisfaction with this arrangement and in 1920, after
the report of the committee on the technical processes which is
dealt with in Chapter 6 of Part II of this volume, I was asked to
take charge of the distribution and disposal of the gifts. Any
book or pamphlet which fell within fields that the library
attempted to cover was sent on for cataloguing if it was
deemed to be of research importance. I soon found that there
was a considerable mass of material that in the past had not
been catalogued but had been set aside, often for many years,
for a later decision.

During the 1920 technical services survey, Dr. Williamson
suggested that there was much of this gift material which was
not important enough for cataloguing but could be arranged
by specific subject and made useful. In time enough material
on a subject would accumulate to make what he suggested
should be called "n.c." (not catalogued volume). We had
previously collected and sent to the stacks many thousands of
volumes made up of pamphlets too small to bind separately
(even in "Gaylord binders") which we called "p.v." (pamphlet
volumes). Each pamphlet received full cataloguing, generally
with a handwritten title page with a number, author and title
for each item at the beginning of the volume. The pamphlets
in the "n.c." volumes which dealt with a specific subject were
catalogued with a single card that had printed on it (beginning
on the second line), "The Library has a collection of pamphlets dealing with_____ ." Then the
subject selected was placed there and again on the top or main
entry line and used for filing in the catalogue.

Here are some samples of the different types of subjects for
these volumes: Grain Dust Explosions, Bicycle Trade
Catalogues, George Washington, Spanish American War. I
arranged these pamphlets after taking the responsibility of
selecting them for the "n.c." volumes, at the south end of the
sixth stack adjacent to the catalogue room, alphabetically by
subjects with the shelves labeled with the subjects selected.
There they would accumulate until enough for a volume

became available. Of course some subjects were selected for which there never was a large enough collection to bind. But by the time I left the library in 1937 to go to Harvard there were 14,054 "n.c." volumes that had been bound and catalogued with a single card for each volume and containing 175,638 individual items. This number by 1970 had increased to 24,405 "n.c." volumes. They have not increased in number as rapidly in the last 40 years as earlier because of the large accumulations of material that were at hand when the plan was adopted and which I worked through between 1920 and 1937.

The backlog of these pamphlets that I had to face in 1920 included:

1) 2,000 bundles tied up in brown paper, each some two feet high, numbering more than 150,000 pamphlets in all. They were part of a collection gathered by Gordon Lester Ford and given to the library in 1899 by his sons, Paul Leicester Ford, the historical novelist, and Worthington Chauncey Ford, the librarian of the Massachusetts Historical Society and later the head of the manuscript division of the Library of Congress and the Library of Congress representative abroad who brought or sent back microfilm copies of archives relating to the United States from various European countries. Mr. Lydenberg had been through this collection soon after its receipt by the library and had arranged for the cataloguing of many of the pamphlets and all the books unless they were duplicates. The collection consisted of what might be called American social history. The only comparable collection in this field made by an individual scholar was the Peter Force collection at the Library of Congress.

Mr. Lydenberg had examined the pamphlets but at that time he and Dr. Billings did not feel that the library could afford to catalogue all of the pamphlets that were worth keeping and he placed most of them in storage. It took me considerably more than a year, using such time as I could spare for it, to go through the lot. I picked out many thousands of pamphlets to be fully catalogued in "p.v.'s". The catalogue department had doubled its production without increasing the size of the staff after the 1920 catalogue study, and it was able to deal with this material. The number of pamphlets selected to go into "n.c." volumes also was very large. But the greatest surprise was finding more than a thousand items that the reserve book room (as we called the rare book collection) wanted. Twenty-five years had made a great deal of difference in what was considered "rare" material. I discarded a great many items which I was convinced never would be worth cataloguing, even in "n.c." volumes. I was unwilling to discard a considerable remainder which was packed in wooden boxes instead of brown paper bundles and returned to the basement.

Nearly twenty-five years later, in the late 1940's, Edward G. Freehafer, then serving as executive assistant in the library and later to become director, went through the collection again and found a great many that were placed in "p.v." or "n.c." volumes and quite a few that went to the reserve book room. He again placed the remainder in storage. Both of us hope that the time will come (more than 75 years after the Ford collection came to the library) when another "brash" young man will examine the collection and find more material worth cataloguing, some of it valuable enough to go to the rare book room. In another part of this volume I will give other incidents that indicate how far book selection comes from being an exact science.

2) The Ford gift did not complete the accumulation of pamphlets and other material that had been stored away in various parts of the library. The largest of the other collections waiting for a decision on its final disposal was made up of trade catalogues of all kinds. The library had hesitated to discard them but had not found a means by which it could afford to make them available. Dr. Williamson's "n.c." volumes proved to be an ideal solution. There were several groups which were of special interest to me. One was a collection of catalogues of bicycle manufacturers which dated back to the 1870's and 1880's, when high-wheel bicycles (high

wheels in front and small ones in the rear) were the custom. The larger group was for bicycles similar to but heavier and harder to use than those of today. All were bound and arranged by date or by manufacturer. I remember with interest and pleasure a reference letter that came to me in the 1930's regarding bicycles. The inquirer asked if they ever had been made with the small wheel in front and the high wheel at the rear. I looked in the "n.c." bicycle volumes, thinking that it was an absurd question, but to my delight I found that there was one year in the 1870's when a bicycle company experimented with and advertised a bicycle with a small wheel in front and the large wheel behind. This apparently did not work out satisfactorily because it was not listed the following year. The bicycle catalogues, all together, occupied perhaps one three-foot-long shelf in the bookstack.

The automobile catalogues were much more numerous and included those from the many large and small companies in existence during the first third of this century. I suppose, though I do not know, that the Ford Dearborn collection in this field may be larger than the one at the N.Y.P.L. But I doubt that it has as many catalogues of the minor and now extinct companies. I was particularly interested in these because a cousin of mine bought stock in one of these companies when it first came on the market; it was very successful for a while but in the end was unable to compete with the larger companies.

Another sizable lot was made up of catalogues of mail-order companies such as Sears Roebuck, Montgomery Ward, etc. Up to that time, I doubt if they had been available in any library. Today the Sears Roebuck file has been reproduced and is available elsewhere.

3) The final large group was much more miscellaneous in character. It consisted of material that had been received in earlier years for which no decision had been made in regard to its use. Most of this backlog had been acquired after the new library was opened in May 1911, although some of it dated from before the consolidation in 1895. To this older material

many of the current receipts, which amounted in the 1920's to roughly 125,000 pieces a year, were being added. I worked through the backlog gradually and kept up with the new gifts, which included many bound volumes as well as pamphlets, and by 1927 I finally was up to date with the old and current accumulations. The new gifts included some of the individual items that we had asked for. Many of them were small groups of material that the donors decided to send to the library to relieve pressure on their shelves at home or in the office. But they also included a considerable number of rather extensive collections and from those that particularly interested me I record a few to give an idea of the various types of material that the library received both by gift or by bulk purchases.

The J. P. Morgans, father and son, began to collect long before the Morgan Library was built and, as was to be expected, Morgan Senior gathered a great bulk of material which was expensive and showy but did not meet the standards of the Morgan Library after Belle daCosta Greene became librarian. These volumes, no longer wanted, were passed on to the New York Public Library, where the son was a trustee. They included a large number of elaborate "extra-illustrated" works and subscription volumes with illustrations. They came to me and were added to the library's art division, where they have been useful.

Mrs. Frank Sprague, a collector of Walt Whitman's work, asked me late in 1934 to clear out her husband's office (he had died in October). Its printed and manuscript material made a very welcome addition to the library's collections. Sprague was known as the "father of electric traction" and his electric motors made our high-speed elevators, our street cars (now almost a thing of the past), our electric trains and subways possible and have been the foundation of much of the development of Manhattan Island and our large cities.

An interesting though minor collection was the remainder of the material which Charles Eliot Norton, who might be called the founder of art studies in our universities, left to Harvard University. Mr. Lydenberg arranged to have the ephemeral material which Harvard did not want come to the New York Public Library. I had the pleasure of going through it and finding well-printed ephemera, a few letters of interest, and a mass of material with which we were unable to do anything.

Carrie Chapman Catt, who was prominent in the Woman Suffrage movement, arranged to have the files of the National American Woman's Suffrage Organization sent to the library. Her own papers ultimately went to the Schlesinger Library at Radcliffe College and I shall have more to say later about the undesirability of dividing important subject collections between institutions. The library received a large collection of material from Samuel P. Gompers on the labor movement.

In the 1930's the library acquired two great collections by purchase from second-hand book dealers through Richard Wormser and with the help of Robert Lingel, then chief of the acquisition division. One came from Thomas Taylor, a dealer in Taunton, Massachusetts. For 45 years he had been more interested in collecting than selling material. He had specialized in American imprints and acquired a great mass of pamphlets and paper-bound books, music, almanacs, broadsides, etc. His house, which was his office and store, became so full that in despair he had to give up. He had filled the attic and the stairs leading to the attic so full that he had been unable to get up and look at the material there for many years, and a similar situation was developing all through the house. For a few thousand dollars we acquired thirty-nine tons of material of great value, and it took me many months of my spare time to go through and decide on its disposition.

There was a similar situation with the collection from a second-hand dealer, Albert A. Bieber, who occupied an eight-room apartment over a saloon in downtown Jersey City. The apartment had been filled so full with books that his wife finally said that she or the books would have to leave. The poor man at last decided that he preferred his wife to the books, much as he loved the latter. He had specialized in American literature and books by and about women and, as was the case with the Taunton dealer, the collection filled to capacity several five-ton trucks.

The H. W. Wilson Company acquired back files of periodicals, many of them full volumes and some incomplete, which it used in connection with its indexing and then sold. The New York Public Library sometimes added to its collections from this material. One of the men connected with the work, Frank Peterson, was a collector himself who specialized in Seventh Day Adventist publications. He gave these to the library, thereby providing it with a remarkable collection of periodicals and pamphlets numbering several thousands, including material on the expected end of the world in the 1840's and the teachings of William Miller.

Immediately after the start of World War I in August 1914, the library began to collect everything that could be obtained relating to it and continued to do so. The catalogue for the collection grew to such an extent that the library despaired of finding space for it around the walls of the public catalogue room. Because of the War, catalogue cases were hard to find and very expensive and the library therefor built its own and placed them in the gallery around the public catalogue room. Although the library had good cabinet makers on its staff, we found to our chagrin that the wood used had not been properly seasoned and it shrank. The cases rattled around and the dust came in. We learned that it was not worthwhile to try to save money by making our own cases, a lesson that proved useful to me after my retirement when I was consulting on library building planning.

I remember with pleasure when we were able to obtain a very large collection of publications—some 5,000 volumes—printed by the American Board of Commissioners for Foreign Missions in the native languages of the board's mission stations in Africa, Asia and Polynesia. Many of them were the first printings in those countries and in the native languages. The library specialized in these languages because they were rarely collected in other libraries. After I went to Harvard we obtained a similar collection by gift directly from the American Board, as will be noted in the Harvard section of these recollections.

We bought what was considered the finest collection of Friesian history and literature in the country just before I went to Harvard. The New York Public Library was interested in it because of its policy of acquiring research material dealing with subjects on which academic institutions did not give instruction, and this type of language material seemed an ideal field. I was shocked when I reached Harvard to find that they had just purchased a similar collection. A few years later the University of Pennsylvania bought a third collection. It would have been more suitable if the three libraries had got together on Friesian. A Union Catalogue of the three is the only possible solution now.

A similar situation occurred also in connection with Icelandic material. For many years Cornell had specialized in that field. A Harvard professor named Schofield was an Icelandic specialist and left his personal library to Harvard. I foolishly arranged to have the resulting duplicates at Harvard brought to the New York Public Library on exchange while I was still in New York. In my Harvard years, when I realized the mistake and found that Harvard was buying intensively in the Icelandic field, I wrote to Stephen McCarthy at Cornell and asked him if they were in a position to continue to buy Icelandic publications in a comprehensive and inclusive manner, as I knew that his collection was superior to both Harvard's and the NYPL's. On receiving word that he was, Harvard became selective in its Icelandic purchases.

Both Harvard and the New York Public Library purchased important collections of French Revolutionary material and the New York Public Library and the University of Minnesota did the same with Mazarinades.

I could add to this list of unnecessary duplication of expensive collections so specialized that few scholars would use them, and it gradually came to me that these represented expenditures that should have been avoided. I resolved that I would try to find a way to prevent this as far as I could in the future.

This section could go on almost indefinitely. I will close it by recording the gift of a single volume that came to me personally when I was in the director's office as executive assistant. An elderly gentleman who was connected with one of the missionary organizations came in and handed me the somewhat battered Bible that the Bounty mutineers brought with them to Pitcairn Island and with which John Adams, the successor to Fletcher Christian, taught the children to read and, he hoped, to be better members of that isolated group.

Charles E. Dornbusch

Charles Dornbusch, when a senior in high school, came to visit the library with other members of his class, led by the librarian of the New Rochelle Public Library, who had previously worked at the N.Y.P.L. Miss Lawson, the librarian, told me that Charles had lost his father and felt that he could not go to college but must work to help his mother as soon as he graduated and thought he would like to go into library work. We employed him and soon found that he was very much interested in cataloguing and collecting. Without special encouragement he went to night school at City College and I remember with regret how he was mugged and robbed twice going between City College and the 125th Street Station of the New York, New Haven and Hartford Railroad as he went home after classes in the late evening. But he persisted. He became interested, among other things, in the collection of New England town reports, something which our documents division wanted. We arranged to have him go in his own car, without extra pay except for his travel expenses and gasoline, to small towns all through the New England states. There he gathered up tremendous quantities of their annual reports, going back in time as far as they were available.

Before Dornbusch started out on one of these trips, a young man from Boston came into my office and said that he was a great admirer of Jacob Riis, who had died some twenty years earlier, following his retirement to a country farmhouse near Barre, Massachusetts. Because of his interest in Riis, he had gone out to this house and found that it was occupied by a farmer of Polish origin who had rented it from Mr. Riis's widow. The farmer told the young man from Boston that he had a hard time keeping warm in the winter and that the house had scattered through it, in the attic and elsewhere, quite a collection of manuscript material that had been left there by Mr. Riis. He had complained to Mrs. Riis that he was having difficulty keeping warm and threatened to burn the "mess" in the stove or fireplace on some cold night. I confess that, while I was a bit suspicious of the young man from Boston, I was worried about the papers. On investigation I found that the Boston Public Library knew the young man and did not trust him. I decided that when Dornbusch made his next trip to New England, I would ask him to go to the house and look into the situation. He talked to the farmer, and was convinced that the papers would be destroyed. He gathered them together and put them into his automobile, drove all night to New York and was waiting for me when I arrived from White Plains at a quarter of nine in the morning and turned the collection over to me. I, of course, sent it to the manuscript division.

Two days later Mr. Riis's widow, who was his second wife, appeared at my desk, very angry, and said that we had stolen her husband's papers. I tried to reason with her and explain the situation but with little success. There had been no way to get in touch with her earlier. We were afraid that we would have to return the papers to Mrs. Riis and had no idea what she would do with them. Fortunately her stepson, a child of Mr. Riis's first wife, who was then one of the senior editors of *Reader's Digest,* came in and the situation was settled amicably and the papers were preserved. I thought nothing more about it until nearly thirty years later when I was doing consulting work at the University of Miami in Florida, and found that one of the senior professors was a grandson of Jacob Riis and had been trying to find out what had become of his grandfather's papers. I was able to help him and to refer him also to the Library of Congress, which had Riis material.

Dornbusch stayed with the library for many years. He became interested in military service newspapers and regimental histories, collected them on a large scale for the library and obtained funds to pay his expenses to travel to other countries to collect in this field. When I visited the great Australian War Memorial with its superb military history library in 1958, I found that Dornbusch had been there, and had collected Australian military histories and that he was *the* American librarian who was best known throughout Australia. Bibliographies of his military history material, including regimental publications and newspapers, have been published and are *the* source in that field. I think back with great pleasure on my being involved in bringing him, as a high school graduate, into library work. After he reached retirement age he set up a mail order bookshop at Cornwallville in the Catskills specializing in Catskill publications, and I hear from him regularly.

I am reminded of the Rear Admiral Hanford Collection, another adventure in connection with acquisitions. R. W. G. Vail, who had worked for six years at the information desk following library school in 1914, had come back to the library in 1928 and for something over a year had helped us acquire research material from other than the usual sources. He was a natural-born collector and worked in various libraries at different times, including the Theodore Roosevelt Memorial Association, where he organized the library which ultimately came to Harvard, the American Antiquarian Society and the New York Historical Society, with each of which I have been at least indirectly associated, as well as collecting for himself. He had a special interest in upstate New York, from which he had come. During this period he persuaded Miss Ruth Hanford, daughter of the late Rear Admiral Franklin Hanford, who had retired to a small town in upstate New York south of Lake

Ontario and had spent his time collecting local history material, to turn over her father's collection to the New York Public Library. Mr. Lydenberg and I were pleased. But some time after the arrival of the material, Mr. Lydenberg called me into his office where Miss Hanford was in tears, distressed by the fact that she thought that the library was not keeping the collection together as she had understood Mr. Vail to say it would do. Mr. Lydenberg asked me to take care of the situation. Miss Hanford came to my office and we went over the problem in detail and straightened it out to her satisfaction. Vail already had left for the American Antiquarian Society.

After I went to Harvard I found that James B. Munn, the head of the English department, was the same man whom I had known in the early 20's as dean of the Washington Square College at New York University. There he had helped me again and again by sending young college students to work in the library, and actually had paid for at least part of their tuition so that they could go to school at the same time. I naturally renewed my acquaintance with him, met his wife, and discovered that she had been Ruth Hanford, with whom I had dealt in connection with her father's collection. We became good friends. But I also learned to my sorrow that Professor Munn, during his New York University days, had asked Clarence Walton, then the head of acquisitions of the New York University Washington Square Library, to spend tremendous sums from Munn's personal fortune to collect French local history periodicals at the same time that we were building up the greatest collection in that field in the United States.

A Special Problem

It would be easy to record in detail many other experiences during this period in which I was involved with book acquisitions. I will content myself with one.

In the early 1920's a New York dentist, Frank P. O'Brien,

came to the outer office of the director and told me that he
had always been interested in the Beadle Dime Novels, which
he had read as a boy. He said he had been fortunate enough to
find a large collection of some 1,400 pieces that were in mint
condition, never used, and which he would be glad to give to
the library if we would place them on temporary display in our
large exhibition room on the main floor of the building. I took
Dr. O'Brien in to Mr. Lydenberg, and it was agreed that we
would accept the gift and arrange for the exhibition. We
examined the collection with great interest. The exibition
was arranged and a list of the books, which were paperback,
was printed in the *Bulletin* the same year—1922. Then, to our
surprise and chagrin, we found that the 1,400 volumes that
had come from Dr. O'Brien had been selected from a tremendous stock which represented the publisher's remainders for
all the Beadle novels and a copy of each was put on sale by one
of the New York auction houses. Our exhibition drew more
viewers than any exhibition the library had put on up to that
time and gave the sale the broadest possible publicity, so that it
came off with unbelievably high prices. From then on the
library tried to avoid gifts to be used for advertising purposes.
Dr. O'Brien remained a good friend of the library and later
gave us a collection of Japanese prints and some colonial
money.

Periodical Indexing

Soon after Dr. John Shaw Billings came to the New York
Public Library as its first director following the consolidation
of the Astor and Lenox Libraries and the Tilden Trust,
he followed his practice in the Surgeon General's library,
where he had indexed practically every medical periodical
article of any importance for the library's book catalogue and
the *Index Medicus*. He decided that the New York Public
Library should follow this example, not as inclusively as at the
medical library but for selected periodicals that were not

indexed in a standard American index such as those published by the H. W. Wilson Company. He selected only articles
dealing with specific subjects—similar, you might say, to the
subjects later chosen for the "n.c." volumes but on a larger
scale. In due course, Mr. Lydenberg took over this indexing
and carried it on for several thousand periodical titles and
arranged to have as many more sent to the special subject
division chiefs so they could provide coverage in their fields.
H.M.L.'s work was chiefly with material that was shelved in the
main bookstack and with titles that I had become acquainted
with there. He kept a pile of slips on his desk which he would
insert in the periodical at the beginning of each article that he
thought should receive a card in the catalogue. If there was a
table of contents on the cover or inside the front cover, he
would check the items there.

To make newly received issues of periodicals available to
readers as quickly as possible, we made it a rule never to keep
any periodical in the office for more than 24 hours. The
cataloguers then tried to do their part in the next 24 hours. In
the late 20's Mr. Lydenberg became busier with policy matters
and with American Library Association work and gradually
let me take over the checking. I did almost all of it between
1928 and 1934 and then all of it from 1934 to 1937 except for
what was done by the specialist. As far as I know, this work was
carried on at the New York Public Library on a larger scale
than anywhere else except for the National Medical Library.
One result has been that the New York Public Library's public
catalogue is of unusual value to its readers and to its staff who
are trying to help the readers. I cannot estimate the number of
these analytical cards in the catalogue but they must run well
over a million for important items that are otherwise difficult
to find.

The Slavic Collection

Chapter 6 reported the expedition to Russia made by Harry

Lydenberg and Dr. Yarmolinsky in the winter of 1923-24. It was not long after their return that Israel Perlstein came into my office. I had never seen him before. He said that he had come from Warsaw and now lived in New York. He had been able to get in touch with the Soviet Government in Moscow and they were sending him books which the Soviets had confiscated from the royal, grand ducal and other libraries and stored in warehouses in tremendous numbers. They were in need of funds and had sold to him large quantities of books. I went down to his eight-room flat on the lower East Side and found the walls of all the rooms had bookcases, this being the only place that the floors would hold them. The cases were full of books, many of them in fine leather bindings, and most of them in good condition. He admitted that he knew comparatively little about the value of books and that he had acquired them at so much a yard for folios, a smaller amount for quartos, another figure for octavos, and still less, of course, for duodecimos. He had done some research and had set prices on them which appeared reasonable to me as they did to Dr. Yarmolinsky and Mr. Lydenberg. We bought them on a large scale. I found later, after I came to Harvard, that Professor Coolidge, then director of the Harvard University Library, was purchasing similar material from Perlstein and this was also true for the Harvard Law School Library.

During my remaining years in New York, Perlstein continued to acquire additional Slavic material and we and Harvard continued to buy whatever we needed and could afford.

The above is far from the end of my experience with Israel Perlstein but as my remaining contacts with him came after my shift to Harvard, they will be reported in Part III of these recollections.

Chapter 13
My Assignment Record

Positions I Was Not Offered

I suspect that comparatively few librarians who have spent a long lifetime in library work can say that they were considered for but were not offered or did not accept as few positions as I did. I have been very fortunate in my work assignments although I have been through some difficult periods. I tend to be an optimist to such an extent that I have to be careful or I might be called a "Pollyanna"—if any of my readers are old enough to remember the novel with that name.

Since I decided definitely in August 1905 to become a librarian, I never have been without a library position. I have applied for a position only once in the more than 70 years that I have been in the field, and that application fortunately came to naught. I never have been unhappy about my work and so have not applied for a change. I have turned down only four positions, each of which would have brought me a large increase in salary, and I worked—if consultation and library association assignments are omitted—in only three different libraries in my 50 years of regular library service, before retirement in 1955. But during the years since 1905 I have had between 500 and 600 assignments in other libraries and thus it has been difficult to find the time to write this book. I have not accepted more than 1,000 other consultation assignments which have been offered to me.

The *only* position that I applied for was a mistake on my part. It was when I was in library school and I was wondering what to do next. I had two brothers living in Lawrence, Kansas, another who had graduated from the university there, a fourth who had worked there between college and medical school, and two others who had worked in Kansas and liked it. I had heard that Miss Watson (after whom the present library at the University of Kansas was named) was about to retire after many years of service. My handwritten application, which I am sure was not a good one (I do not have a copy of it), reached its destination and an acknowledgment came saying that Miss Watson had decided not to retire at the beginning of the next school year. This turned out to be fortunate for me because the University of Kansas did not have much of a library at that time. With my conservative nature, if I had gone there I probably would have stayed and the position would not have provided the variety of experiences and inspiration that I had during the years that followed at the New York Public Library. Miss Watson ultimately retired seven years later and was succeeded by Earl Manchester, a good librarian, who, after seven years there, went on to be the librarian at Ohio State University for 24 years. The Kansas library did not become a distinguished one until Bob Vosper, one of the finest in our profession, became librarian and, with the aid of Chancellor Murphy, built it up very rapidly.

There were three assignments for which I know I was considered but which, probably for good reasons, I was not offered. In 1911 William Dawson Johnston, the librarian of Columbia University, asked Miss Plummer if she had any young men in the school whom he might consider for a position which he expected to have to fill. She suggested me and an appointment was made for an interview. I went to the Low Library for the first time and had a long, friendly talk with Mr. Johnston. I never heard anything more from him, presumably meaning he was not impressed by my qualifications.

In the early 1920's, when I was in the New York Public Library director's office as assistant to Mr. Anderson and Mr. Lydenberg, President Lotus Delta Coffman, who recently had become president of the University of Minnesota, had lost his librarian, James Thayer Gerould, to Princeton and needed a replacement. He came to New York to look me over. At that time he had had comparatively little experience as president in looking for a senior officer. I was inclined to think after our futile interview that with the experience I had already had in selecting librarians I could have done better. Perhaps that only goes to show that at 32 I was giving myself too much credit. He started out by asking, "If you stay at the NYPL, what position can you look forward to?" As I was satisfied with what I was doing and the only possible promotion for me at the NYPL that would have interested me would have been to succeed Mr. Lydenberg, who was still in his 40's (14½ years older than I), I was unwilling to say that I looked forward to taking H.M.L.'s place. I replied that I was pleased with my present position and expected to continue in that assignment. President Coffman— quite naturally, I suppose— took this as a sign that I had no ambition or initiative and abruptly broke off the interview and left.

I did not see Mr. Coffman again for some 15 years. I was then chairman of the American Library Association's Board of Education for Librarianship and went to the University of Minnesota to accredit its comparatively new library school. Coffman still was there and he told me, "The University of Minnesota is so good that it does not feel that its graduate schools need accreditation." I was not ready to argue with him but simply replied that I thought I knew enough about libraries, librarians and recruiting to say that if a library school was not accredited, its graduates would have a much more difficult time in obtaining good positions than would otherwise be the case. This was during the Depression, there was a large surplus of library school graduates at the time, and I did not have to stretch the truth in making this statement. I confess that I left with a comfortable feeling when Mr. Coffman agreed that we should check on the school and said he hoped that we would accredit it, which we did.

The next time I know that I was looked over was some six years later. At the 1928 West Baden Conference of the American Library Association, Harry Lydenberg had expected to attend and had made reservations to share a suite with Franklin Hopper, chief of the NYPL's circulation department, and Andrew Keogh, the capable and respected librarian of Yale. H.M.L. found that he could not go and sent me in his place. As a result I came to know Dr. Keogh more than casually and, perhaps as a result, when he was looking for an associate librarian a little later he asked me to come to Yale and go over plans for his new building, which were well along at that time. He knew from H.M.L. that I was interested in building planning. I had had no real experience in that area, except that Columbia also was planning a new building and, through my friendship with Charles C. Williamson, its director, I had spent a good deal of time talking with him about the plans for what became the Butler Library. These plans had been drawn up by the same distinguished architect who was working on the Sterling building at Yale. The two libraries were completely different in style in practically every way, except that they were monumental in character, with ceilings which today seem unnecessarily high and monumental reading rooms which are difficult to light. Although they had about the same capacity for books and readers and gross square footage, the Columbia building cost approximately half as much as Yale's Gothic structure. As a result, Yale had to reduce its hours of opening temporarily in order to keep within the funds available for the building and its operation.

But to go back to my visit to Yale: ever since my boyhood, and especially in my high school and college days, I had preferred Yale to Harvard because I thought of the latter as being "snooty" (the only word I can think of for it). I suppose, being involved in athletics, I had been affected by my admiration for Walter Camp and his writings and exploits. I talked with Dr. Keogh and he then asked me to go over the new library plans with his senior assistants. Wisely or not, I criticized these plans severely for the stack tower, for the ornate main reading room, for what I later have heard called the "confession booths" used for public telephones, and for the high altar used as a charging desk, to say nothing of the book conveyor. On the basis of talks I had had years earlier with the Snead Company's conveyor expert, who had planned a satisfactory conveyor in the New York Public Library, I was convinced that the Yale conveyor was much too complicated and was bound to be troublesome, as it proved to be. I expressed my opinions freely and honestly. While Dr. Keogh was kindness personified and gave me an exciting new experience by taking me to Morey's (of "Whiffenpoof" fame) for lunch, I never heard from him in connection with the associate librarianship. The position was filled by Charles Rush, whom I knew, liked and respected but who never was happy at Yale. He ran into New England offishness and never felt accepted, perhaps because he was not a Yale graduate. I remember his telling me that in his seven years there he never was invited into the house of a Yale professor. He served later, as had Dr. Keogh before him, as a library advisor to the Carnegie Corporation and was very helpful to the American Library Association in that connection.

Lest you feel that the above report is sour grapes because I was not offered the job, I should add several points to my Yale connections and impressions. Yale was good enough to give me an honorary doctor's degree, the first that I had except for one from Oberlin. Dr. Keogh was one of the committee of three (with H.M.L. and Charles Williamson) that arranged for my first American Library Association appointment by asking me to make a study of cooperative cataloguing financed by the Rockefeller Foundation. This started me in outside work and undoubtedly was responsible for my further experience and advancement in library work.

This completes the list of positions for which I was considered but not accepted. I have to confess that I was not upset by any of the three and am sure that it was better for me to remain where I was at the New York Public Library.

Positions I Did Not Take

The first library position offered to me that I did not take was withdrawn before I had decided whether or not to accept it. Early in the spring of 1917, before we entered World War I, Dean Charles Nelson Cole talked to me about remaining at Oberlin after Professor Root returned in September of that year instead of going back to library school at the New York Public Library, from which I was on leave of absence while Professor Root was principal of its library school. This was recorded in Chapter 3 and will not be repeated here. I had looked forward to becoming Oberlin's librarian following Professor Root's retirement (he was 27 years my senior). I had been prepared to work in places where I could get the best and most varied experience until I was 40. I thought that I could support my family on the salary that I would receive in New York. I wanted additional and broader experience away from

Oberlin and so I hesitated and suggested that we talk about it later. Not long after, Professor Cole came to me again. The war had started. Many Oberlin men were enlisting and it was evident that this was no time to expand the staff. I confess I was a bit relieved that I did not have to make the decision and, of course, I was anxious to talk the whole thing over with A.S.R. before making it and there had been no opportunity to do so.

The next offer came completely out of the blue in the early 1920's, when the librarian at Ohio University in Athens was about to retire. I was asked to succeed her. This position failed to tempt me and I turned it down without hesitation. My work at the New York Public Library did not pay as much as I was offered but it was giving me the experience that I wanted and I felt that it would be more useful to me later if I remained in New York. I had the pleasure some 28 years later, however, of suggesting Frank N. Jones for the position at Ohio University, and when he left for the Peabody Institute Library after eight years, Walter Wright, his successor; both had worked with me at Harvard.

Next came a more tempting offer from Linda Eastman, who had become librarian of the Cleveland Public Library on the death a few years earlier of its great librarian, William Howard Brett, who did so much toward opening up bookstacks in public libraries and had brought the Cleveland library to the top rank of public libraries in the country. In the spring of 1922 Cleveland was about to build a new and fine library on a site which Joe Wheeler would have called a nearly perfect location, near the city's transportation center. Miss Eastman felt the need for a man to help her during the construction.

There had been two first-class men on the staff, either of whom might have been expected to take over when the time came. But Herbert S. Hirshberg, who had been reference librarian, had left Cleveland in 1914 to go to Toledo (he later became State Librarian in Ohio before going to the Akron Public Library and then came back to Cleveland as director of

the Western Reserve University Library and dean of its library
school in 1929). Carl Vitz, who had been vice librarian, had
just left to succeed Hirshberg at Toledo (later he went on to
Minneapolis and in 1946 to the Cincinnati Public Library,
became president of the American Library Association in
1944-45 and was chairman of the committee of which I was a
member to advise President Truman in regard to the appointment of a successor to Archibald MacLeish as Librarian
of Congress). I never could understand why one of these men
was not chosen by Miss Eastman at the time when she offered
me the position of vice librarian with the understanding that
she would retire within two years when the new building was
finished. I might add that she did not retire in 1924 but
continued in the post successfully until her retirement many
years later and then lived on for another 25 years before she
died at 96.

Miss Eastman came to see me at the NYPL and asked me to
come to Cleveland as soon as possible and meet with the
trustees. If I am not mistaken, she already had offered the
position to Ernest Reece, principal of the NYPL's library
school. I believe it would have been a mistake for him to take
it; he was not interested in that type of administration and not
particularly fitted for it. He said "no." I was very fond of him
and relied on his judgment as much as that of any of my other
friends.

The offer interested me very much. The salary proposed
was 50% greater than I was receiving, and when Miss Eastman
retired, if I took over it would be double my New York Public
Library salary and I would be head of what was generally
considered at the time the choicest public library in the United
States, with the possible exception of the New York library.
Since that time the Cleveland library, in the opinion of many,
has come upon evil days and more than one of the librarians
since Miss Eastman's retirement in 1938 has had unhappy
experiences there.

There were pulls for me in the direction of Cleveland. It was
only 25 miles from my home town of Elyria and 35 miles from

Oberlin, the two towns where I had spent 24 of my 33 years. My sister Marion, who brought me up after my parents' deaths in the 1890's, still was living in Oberlin in her 60's. My wife had been employed for most of the three years before we were married in charity work in Cleveland and her parents lived in Oberlin. My next older brother, "Ike" (Isaac Stevens Metcalf, named after my father), had worked for the *Cleveland Plain Dealer* for 10 years and, having no place to go for promotion except New York, to which he did not care to go, had become a partner in one of the country's leading bank advertising companies a few years earlier. He knew the political situation in Cleveland. He lived in Lakewood, a Cleveland suburb, and served on the board of the library there for many years, and was very much interested in the Cleveland Public Library situation.

I went out to Cleveland. Miss Eastman arranged for me to meet with the board of trustees and its president, John G. White, a great collector of folklore (he later gave his collection to the library). They confirmed Miss Eastman's offer. I also talked with Clarence Metcalf, a sixth cousin, who was a member of the library staff and for a time its secretary and treasurer and later its librarian. I talked with Miss Eastman before leaving, promised to make my decision the next day, and took the night train back to New York.

The decision gave me a rather restless night. I realized that I did not like the plans of the new building that I was to supervise. I feared that, when the time came, Miss Eastman would hesitate to leave as she expected to and I certainly would not be willing to try to push her out. My brother Ike was not sure how long the fine "silk stocking" library board of trustees would continue in office (it was appointed by the school board). Most important, while the library had a good reference department, its great reputation had come from being a leader in developing its branch library system. The position was one that should be filled by a man or woman who was a missionary at heart. While I had had a proper religious bringing up, I felt my real interest in librarianship was in the collections and in research library work and not in the best of the public libraries, however good it might be. So in the morning, after telephoning to Mart and making sure she would not be too unhappy about my decision, I sent a wire to say that I was not ready to leave our new home in White Plains, where we had been for only six months, or the New York Public Library's reference department. I suppose that this decision was not the one that would have been made by at least 90% of my contemporaries.

In the summer of 1927 Charles Williamson, then director of the Columbia University library and dean of its school, persuaded Professor Root to teach a course in administration at the Columbia School of Library Service summer session, and I saw something of him during the summer. My family was spending the summer in Oberlin without me and I took A.S.R. out to my home in White Plains from time to time for dinner and the night. I was far from a skillful cook but I could scramble eggs and we could have a fine time talking over the library world. He told me one evening that he was having prostate trouble and would face an operation on his return to Oberlin. Such operations took place in two stages in those days, particularly with a man who had a weak heart. Azariah stood the first operation well and preparations were being made for the second when he died suddenly on October 2, 1927, as the result of a blood clot reaching his heart. His death came at a serious time for Oberlin. Its president, Henry Churchill King, had retired at the end of the previous college year. Ten days later the dean of the Theological School, who had been acting president in 1918-19 during the absence of President King in connection with the peace conference following the First World War, died suddenly.

The new president, Ernest Hatch Wilkins, had come to Oberlin on September 1, partly, he told me later, because of its fine library and librarian. When Professor Root died, all three of the college's best known men had disappeared from the scene in the course of a few months. President Wilkins felt Professor Root's loss greatly and wrote to me that he was

coming to New York on October 12 to talk with me. I tele-
graphed back that I would be there. He did not realize that
Columbus Day would be a holiday in New York and, while the
library was open, the administrative offices were closed. As a
result, we had the office to ourselves. He talked very freely
about the Oberlin situation. I liked him and we became well
acquainted. I naturally wondered if he had planned to offer
me the librarianship, something that I had looked forward to,
and I confess that I was somewhat disappointed when he did
not. But a week later a letter came from him offering me a
salary double that which I was receiving and asking me to
come to Oberlin to look over the assignment and talk to
members of the faculty. I spent several days at Oberlin and
learned a great deal that I had not known about the situation.
The income from the Charles Martin Hall bequest (aluminum
money) had begun to come in, and a considerable amount was
available for increases in salaries. As I have indicated earlier,
the budget at Oberlin always had been tight. All salaries were
low and, since the budget had been made by a faculty committee, for years under the chairmanship of Professor Root and
later Dean Charles N. Cole, all full professors received the
same salary, except for the two men just mentioned, who
received several hundred dollars more for their special duties.

At one of the first faculty meetings after President Wilkins
arrived on September 1, he made two requests of the faculty.
The first was to divide the full professors into three approximately equal groups, one-third to be advanced from the
present $4,000 to $5,000; one-third to go up $1,500 to $5,500,
and the final third up $2,000 to $6,000. The president's
second proposal was to appoint, when he found a suitable
person, a distinguished professor, and to pay him a salary next
to his own and at least equal to that of the dean of the faculty.
After some discussion, the faculty agreed to both proposals.
President Wilkins then tried to appoint a committee to divide
the faculty into the three proposed groups. He was surprised
when no one was willing to accept appointment to the committee. President Wilkins had been dean of the University of

Chicago faculty of arts and sciences, he was a delightful man personally and a great scholar. But he knew little about Oberlin and its traditions, including the fact that for nearly a century it had been controlled by the faculty and not by the president and trustees.

When Mr. Wilkins found that no one would serve on the committee, there was nothing left for him to do but make the faculty division himself, whereby he made enemies of two-thirds of its members. In theory all this had nothing to do with me. But I became worried when I realized that I was to be put $1,500 ahead of the top-salaried faculty members, while most of the senior members of the faculty remembered me primarily as a boy who throughout high school and college had put away books in the library and later had in some way managed to make its wheels go around on two occasions while Professor Root was on leave. I spent two days visiting and talking with faculty members and the library staff. There had been many changes in the 10 years since I had left. I talked with the head of the chemistry department, who was new but who had made a great reputation for isolating Vitamin B-12 for the first time and who was sending more students on to graduate school than any other professor. I talked with Professor C. H. A. Wager, the English professor who always had been unusually good to me because of his close friendship with my brother Ike. I also saw Professor Ward, who in the preceding 10 years had brought the fine arts department up to a place where it was considered to be one of the best in the country.

I knew how Mart would be pleased to live in the town where her father and mother (both in their 60's and not strong) were living. The move also would please my sister Marion. It would be inexpensive for us if our children decided to go to Oberlin, because faculty children did not pay tuition, and I did not forget that this was the assignment that I had looked forward to ever since I had decided on library work 22 years earlier. As was the case with Cleveland in 1922, I slept on the situation on the Pullman that night. I realized that I was 39 years old, and I had determined that, until I was 40, I would choose the assignment where I would get the best and most varied experience that I could. Now was the time to move if I ever were going to. Then I realized that I belonged at the New York Public Library, not my beloved and looked-forward-to Oberlin.

I discussed the problem with Mart the next morning and she said it was up to me. So I sent word to President Wilkins and told Mr. Anderson and Mr. Lydenberg that I had decided to stay in New York. E.H.A. heaved a sigh of relief and said, "If you had gone, I would have given up forever bringing a young man into the office and giving him the experience you have had in the last nine years." I might properly add at this point that I did not mention that the Oberlin salary offer was double my New York one.

My refusal of the Oberlin position did not keep me from being on friendly terms with President Wilkins, whose scholarship and accomplishments in improving the quality of an Oberlin education I greatly admired. He had a first-class foundation on which to build. We became good friends. I appreciated the fact that when I did not send in a bill for my expenses for the trip to Oberlin, as he asked me to do, he gave me credit for my expenses against the long-term obligation in which I had involved myself when Oberlin was engaged in raising a large sum of money for endowment before the Hall gift became available. After Mr. Wilkins retired from Oberlin 20 years later, he moved back to Newton, Massachusetts, where he was born and brought up, and where the Harvard Library would be available to him. Since I had come to Harvard by that time and he had had his undergraduate and graduate years there and was still a productive scholar in Italian literary history, I was able to provide him with a study in Widener where he produced his great work on Italian literature. During the period when we were inclined to worry about suffering from bomb explosions from submarines during the Cold War, he placed one copy of his still unpublished manuscript in one of our vaults where it would be safe from fire. I also kept in touch with his three successors at Oberlin, of whom I shall have more to say later.

My next refusal is described in some detail in the chapter

entitled *Decision to Come to Harvard*. My one refusal
to leave Harvard during my 18 years there came as an indirect result of my acquaintance with Austin Evans, who for
a reason I could never understand came to Oberlin and joined
my senior class in Oberlin High School in 1906-07 without his
family. He was a very serious but likable young man of 24.
Our classmates averaged 17 or 18. We all liked him but never
had become well acquainted with him. After high-school
graduation, he disappeared as far as most of his Oberlin
acquaintances knew, until three of my Oberlin College
friends, two of whom were in high school with me, found him
at Cornell, where he had graduated and they all began
graduate school together and received their PhD's. Austin
later became a French history faculty member at Columbia
and subsequently a full professor and the head of his department. In 1941, when Dr. C. C. Williamson reached retirement
age, Austin became a senior member of the committee to find
a replacement. I think I had seen him only twice after our
senior year in high school in 1907. The first time was while I
was in college and he found that three of his high school
classmates had come to Cornell to play on the Oberlin College
football team against Cornell. The second was at the New
York Public Library when I took him into our closed
bookstacks to show him our French collection (somewhat to
my dismay, he felt it was not the equal of Columbia's). I saw
him again when he came to Harvard to tell me that if I would
come to Columbia to take Dr. Williamson's place as library
director and dean of the library school, he would arrange for
the call. I asked him to wait until I could talk to President
Conant about it. I saw Mr. Conant and said, "Here is your last
chance to get me off your hands without embarrassment." As
an administrative officer, I had no tenure. He replied
promptly, "Please do not take the position. We want to keep
you here." I did not leave. I already had talked with Elinor and
she said simply, "I'll be glad to go wherever you go." So I was
committed to Harvard until I reached the academic year
following my 66th birthday, when retirement became com-

pulsory for administrative officers. This was a Harvard Corporation rule requested by President Conant, who was afraid that, when he reached retirement time, he would be tempted to stay on as his two predecessors had done. I am glad I stayed at Harvard instead of going to Columbia at a higher salary, partly, I confess, because I realized that in spite of or perhaps because of my five-year term with the Board of Education for Librarianship of the American Library Association, I might not make a good library school dean. I will write later, however, of definite ideas I had about library school instruction and curriculums.

Chapter 14
Space and Equipment Problems
and
Attempts at Research

Space Problems

The NYPL's annual report for 1921 spoke for the first time of the approaching need for additional space for the reference department, and during the 20's the library came under more and more pressure for space. Some wooden shelving was placed in the basement under stack 1 to store little-used material. Early in the decade the Staff Association of the library had started what might be called a cooperative store under the large exhibition room on the first floor and when the library school moved to Columbia in 1926 the photographic work was shifted to its former classroom area. It was becoming more and more difficult for the staff to find inexpensive places nearby where one could have lunch; the cooperative store provided one for a time at very reasonable cost, with coffee and sandwiches which were consumed while one stood in the south court, from which there was an entrance to this area. But pressure for a regular cafeteria became great and one finally was provided by taking the small rooms on the east side of the south court. The serving counter was placed on the west side of the broad aisle, with chairs and tables along the walls not occupied by the service counter. A "lean-to", as we called it, was built into the court, projecting out far enough to provide additional seating. This was a cafeteria for the staff only. I had the task of arranging for the service and was able to find a first-class woman with experience in the field. At one end of the "lean-to" a large table was provided where the young men on the staff whom we had been fortunate enough to employ could sit and talk shop together. I had lunch with them practically every day and tried to persuade Mr. Lydenberg to join us, but he said he didn't eat lunch. We had very interesting discussions on technical library problems, how to deal with reference and circulation problems, classification, cataloguing, etc. It was a very useful part of my education.

But our great need for space was for shelving (I have already reported on the move of materials from the document and science and technology divisions in 1920 which filled most of the available space on stack 2). The first floor was occupied completely by newspapers, central circulation, and the central collection for the circulation department, which included the last copies of books that were no longer in great demand in the circulation department. The time finally came when something had to be done, and in the early 30's H.M.L.—with help, I suppose, from the trustees—looked for inexpensive space outside the library in which to store our less-used material. A loft building was found on West 24th Street; it had elevators and was built sturdily enough to hold concentrated book storage. Because of the Depression it was only partly rented and the cost at that time was comparatively low. There was enough unoccupied space so that the remaining renters could be left there throughout their contracts and possibly for even longer if they wished, and there still would be all the space the library would need for some time to come, with the possibility of increasing it as the renters' contracts ran out.

Inexpensive storage stack was installed for volumes of different sizes, including oversize shelving for bound newspapers and for the considerable collection of Braille volumes for the blind. The arrangements for moving then fell into my hands. The only suitable loading platform for outgoing and incoming material was in the shipping room next to the 42nd Street entrance, and its steady use during the day made it undesirable for our purposes. We decided to cut out a section of the marble wall below one of the stack windows near the center of the 80-foot-long west wall of the south court. We then could run "dolly" trucks, loaded or empty, between the stack and the moving trucks on a plank ramp that had a very slight slope down from the stack to the truck when the latter was full and up to the truck when it was unloaded. We had 20 "dollies" built with both ends high enough to hold six book boxes, each with a full shelf of books. Though much sturdier, these boxes were quite similar to those I had used in the Oberlin move 25 years earlier when I had charge of the transfer to the new Oberlin Library. We found we could rent a truck into which we could fit ten "dollies" in three rows of three, with the tenth at right angles to the others next to the rear door, thus preventing the others from crashing through.

The truck and driver were on duty from 9 to 5, with an hour off for lunch. In the library two boys were assigned to fill the 60 boxes of books that could be placed on the 10 dollies and pushed onto the truck after removing the 10 dollies with empty boxes returning from West 24th Street. At the storage building we had other members of the stack staff. The shipping room entrance there was somewhat below the level of the truck's platform, and it took three men to run the loaded dollies off the truck and down the ramp without crashing them, and then to reload the truck with the empty boxes.

We soon found that we could make seven round trips almost every day, with those involved kept busy all the time. Traffic delays were the major problem, not so much on 40th and 24th Streets as on 5th and 6th Avenues. The month of February, during which we undertook the move, turned out to have the heaviest snowfall within memory. At first we were appalled. But we soon learned that the city's snow clearance plans, at least in that area, resulted in a great reduction 'of traffic and thus our speed was increased rather than decreased. Seven round trips a day, each carrying 60 shelves of books, with a staff of only six persons including the driver, meant some 12,000 volumes a day if they were typical library volumes. Since a considerable percentage of them were oversize books we did not move 240,000 volumes but we took material which occupied the space of 240,000 standard volumes.

The moving job took about one month, with smaller transfers later, and altogether it helped to relieve the space problem until after I went to Harvard. But it did become necessary in the meantime to place shelving in the wide corridors on the first and second floors of the 42nd Street side of the library, to give up some of the exhibition space for paintings, and to install more desks and catalogue cases in the 40th Street corridors, in addition to using the south end of the 5th Avenue ground floor for the cafeteria that has been mentioned and installing more shelving in the basement.

By 1937 the West 24th Street building had become inadequate even as the renters disappeared. Some relief came with the construction of the Donnell branch at Rockefeller Center and later still with Lincoln Center for the Music and Theatre collections. But after I went to Harvard it became obvious that a much larger warehouse on West 43rd Street should be purchased on the same basis as the West 24th Street one, which then was given up. At that time compact shelving had been introduced and a considerable amount of it was installed in the new warehouse because it doubled storage capacity. I have been told that the additional cost of the shelving was greater than the rental cost of the space saved but I can not confirm this. I will report, however, in the fourth part of my Recollections, on the use of compact shelving, with which I have had a good deal of experience in recent years.

During the 1930's and my last years at the New York Public Library, Mr. Anderson and Mr. Lydenberg, with the help of the trustees, did everything they could to persuade the city to provide the library with additional space under its own roof. At one time a bequest made by Thomas Hastings, the architect who had prepared the plans for the building, provided money to help construct wings going out to Fifth Avenue, which he thought would improve the library's appearance. But approval for the plan was not obtained.

Later a prominent consulting engineer and architect, Gilmore Clarke, was asked to suggest plans to add to the library building without changing its outside appearance. He proposed that the courts be filled in and used to store up to a million volumes. This also would permit the installation of air conditioning throughout the building, thus solving the library's serious ventilation problem. Nothing came of this plan.

The Carrier Air Conditioning Company—this was in the early days of air conditioning installations—was asked about the cost of air conditioning, temperature and relative humidity control, and pollution controls. H.M.L., from his long struggle with the preservation of paper, was particularly interested in the idea. The report came in with an estimate of $500,000, which seemed a tremendous sum at that time, and it came with the reservation that success of the installation could not be guaranteed. The plan was given up. The air-conditioning problem will be discussed in more detail later.

Because of my interest in space problems, which went back nearly 30 years by this time, I felt that the library must have more book storage space even if it restricted use by readers who could be better served elsewhere. I thought that it should be under the same roof, and not accomplished by following Mr. Clarke's proposal for filling in the courts and, in my ignorance, I went to work on plans of my own. I checked the library's state charter, which said that its building could be placed anywhere on the block between Fifth and Sixth Avenues and 40th and 42nd Streets. It seemed to me obvious that an addition could be constructed immediately behind the present building, extending as far back as the end of the Plaza to where the present Bryant Park area began. This would make possible construction immediately behind the present building of about 120 feet overall with two new courts, each half the size of the present 80′ × 80′ ones, or 80′ from north to south and 40′ east and west, with a new unit the same size as the present rear 80′ deep bookstack and with areas matching the present ones on both ends. This would double the size of the present stack, providing space for between 2½ and 3 million books. The other new areas would amount to some 35,000 square feet on each floor.

On the top floor the plan would make it possible to double the area for the Main Reading Room as well as to provide for adequate growth for the public catalogue and the reference collection. The staff of the preparation division, which should be on the same floor as both the public and the official catalogue, also could be housed in the new areas on the 40th Street end. On the other floors and the 42nd Street end of the top floor, more space could be found for the subject reading rooms and their collections, carrels (which were not then available for advanced scholars) and additional staff areas, which were in short supply.

The distinguished west facade of the addition would repeat the present one and the ones on 40th and 42nd Streets would continue with the same general design as before. But it became evident to me that Robert Moses would not permit intruding on the park for the proposed addition even if it were agreed that it would be a proper solution to the library's space problem for both the city and the library. Since then the establishment of the collections primarily for younger students, whom I kept out of the library (very much to my regret) during the 1930's, has been taken care of by the acquisition of the old Arnold Constable building at the southeast corner of 40th Street and Fifth Avenue. Nothing came of the proposal for an addition to the 42nd Street building, and my work on space problems at the New York Public Library ended with little to show for it. I did not realize what the future held for me in building planning.

Equipment Problems

In Chapter 6 of this part, I wrote of becoming interested in book-truck construction. Earlier in this chapter, I dealt with alterations and new uses of space in the library, and earlier there had been my experience in supervising the move of the Oberlin College Library from Spear to the Carnegie building in 1908. At any rate, I seem to have been interested in building planning, equipment layouts, and handling books all of my library career. One of the first dreams I remember was when I was 10 years old. I had been reading one of the popular children's books about a private secondary school for boys and in my dream I tried to design a dormitory and fit in the stairs, the corridors, the toilets and so forth in as small a space as possible.

At any rate, as soon as I was well settled in the library office in 1920 and had struggled with the major rearrangement of the collections in the main stack, Economics and Documents Division, and the Science and Technology Division, I decided that something should be done to provide better vertical transport of books and staff between the main reading room and the seven-level stack beneath it. There were no connections except the stairs and four book lifts—dummies as we called them—at the desk at the center of the 330-foot-long rooms, plus another stairway and an elevator at each end of the area.

After I had talked over the problem with Mr. Anderson and Mr. Lydenberg, they asked me to make suggestions. I got in touch with the Snead Stack Company, whose headquarters then were in Jersey City. It had installed the multi-tier bookstacks in the areas the architects had provided in each of our three largest library installations, the Library of Congress, the New York Public Library, and Harvard's Widener building.

We told the Snead representatives that we needed an elevator inside the reading room desk going down through the bookstack to the basement, available only to the staff and for the return of books after use. Up to this time returned books were too often literally "thrown" into the book lifts; I must confess I had done this with armfuls at a time, which did the books and their bindings no good, to put it mildly. If they could go down to the stacks in the book trucks on which they already had been placed, it would save two rough handlings. A place to install the elevator was found in the one quiet corner of the desk, and the space required in the stack would entail the loss of only a comparatively few volumes in book capacity. The order for it was placed.

Then came the problem of book-lifts. There were four of these, two on each side of a tower that went up in the center of the desk area. The Snead Company suggested that two endless-belt conveyors replace two of the book-lifts, one on each side. The company's conveyor expert, Mr. Waite, told us that the simpler the design the more successful the conveyors would be. If they went up and down without any turn except at the top and bottom, and could be loaded at any of the stack levels and unloaded only in the reading room, instead of being capable of dropping off books on their return to the stacks, they would be less prone to get out of order. If they ran horizontally for a time and then up and down in two different places (as was done later at Yale and elsewhere) they would be more likely to break down. If one or both of the conveyors that we wanted broke down, the two remaining booklifts would keep us going.

Then came the problem of the horizontal fins hung on the endless belts at intervals to carry the books to the reading room from the stack. They had to be in fork form so that other forks at the reading room level could go through and slide the books off the fins. We decided it would not be safe to put the books directly on the fins because, if placed on them carelessly, one or more might slide off and fall down the shaft. So we designed a canvas tray with a steel frame and sides about six inches high. This protected the books and in the reading room the trays were dumped off onto a slanting shelf equipped with rollers that ran the trays down a slope that would hold a half dozen or so trays, giving the boys in the reading room time to remove them and take the books to the desk attendants.

To everyone's pleasure, the elevator, which was large enough to hold two of our four-foot-long book trucks, and the two conveyors worked out very well and have given good service for nearly 60 years. They were an important part of my education that has been useful to me ever since.

Attempts at Research

When I chose librarianship for my life work in 1905, it was because I wanted to be a reference librarian and help people find answers to their questions. I am not sure that this should be considered a sign of benevolence on my part and I think that it may have been based on the insatiable curiosity with which I always have been afflicted. I wanted to face and solve problems that would not require dealing with groups of people as teaching would do. I was shy enough so that groups tended to frighten me. But as I have already stated, I have always been thwarted in my wish to become a reference librarian because, to my regret at the time, I was shunted into administrative work. In spite of this I looked for problems that I could help to solve which would involve research in the broad sense of the term.

In 1920, the year in which I had other exciting experiences,

as reported in Chapter 6, Mr. Lydenberg asked me to go down
to the Mercantile Library on a mission which resulted in what
might be called research. I was to make arrangements for
bringing up to the 42nd Street building the large collection of
volumes that the Mercantile was giving to the New York Public
Library because its shelves were overflowing and it could not
afford to rent more space in the Alexander Hamilton Institute
building in which it then was housed.

The Mercantile Library was founded in 1820 and by 1850
had accumulated some 30,000 volumes and become one of
our larger libraries. It had continued to grow at a relatively
slower pace but much of the collection was no longer used.
Some 45,000 volumes had been stored like cord-wood on the
tops of bookcases going up eight feet or more. These books, I
found, were stored in no particular order and were covered
with up to an inch of dust. I went back to 42nd Street and the
next day, after buying a pair of overalls, something that I had
not owned since coming to New York City, arranged with our
building staff to send with me to the Mercantile a library truck,
book boxes that had been used in moving into a new building
nine years before, and two of the stack boys. The 45,000 pieces
that we brought included some 6,000 pamphlets, 22,000
volumes of bound periodicals, and many government documents.

I was particularly interested in the periodicals and soon
discovered that many of them were Poole sets—that is, had
been indexed in the William F. Poole indexes that had been
the most important index of general American periodicals up
to the end of the last century. It was evident from my experience in the stack that we lacked quite a few of them. I found to
my surprise by checking the Poole's index list that there were
more than 1,100 volumes that the library did not own. Many
of them had been published in small editions before the Astor
Library was established 70 years earlier but evidently had
been in the Yale Society Libraries over which Mr. Poole
presided when his first edition came out in the early 1850's. I
had the Poole volumes brought into the only open area of

bookstack and then checked through them myself when I
could get away from the director's office. I found more than
400 volumes indexed in Poole which were not in the library.
These, of course, were particularly important. There were
some 2,500 other periodical volumes that were not in the
library. In addition, 2,000 volumes were used immediately as
replacements or stored for future use to replace copies of ours
that were badly worn. The remainder were kept for exchange,
as I remembered how useful a somewhat similar collection
from the Oberlin Society Libraries had been in 1912.

On finding that there still were some 700 volumes indexed
in Poole that the library did not own, I decided to take on the
task of trying to complete our holdings. This might be called
an attempt at research work. I continued to watch second-
hand book stores and second-hand catalogues for the missing
700 volumes. A good many of them were obtained in this way
and many more were found in a collection held by the New
York Society Library. This was in the same crowded situation
as the Mercantile Library; they had a larger building of their
own but they also had a larger number of volumes in their
collection. By the time I left New York in 1937, the number of
volumes indexed in Poole which the library had not acquired
had been reduced to about 50.

My work in connection with the A.L.A. Cooperative
Cataloguing Committee and Board of Education for Librarianship gave me an opportunity to do more research which is
covered in Chapter 15. If you stretch the definition of the
term, you might decide that trying to plan for an addition to
the library, as recorded in Chapter 14, falls in this category.
But I am sure all of these were primarily administrative in
character, as was my attempt to devise a method to decide the
size of our public service staff required for Sundays and
holidays. I did not get any farther in that connection than
asking the New York Central Railroad how they decided on
the number of cars they put on their commuter trains on these
days (their answer, by the way, was that they had no method
except what might be called educated guesses).

But while still at the NYPL I did finally make two attempts to do what I considered research. The first was the preparation of an article published in the New York Public Library's *Bulletin,* pages 905 to 925, in 1936, entitled "Notes on Variation of Use of the Reference Department of the NYPL." I always had been interested in the way the use of our libraries for both reference and circulation changed from month to month and from year to year, and I thought it was worthwhile to try to explain it. Having been closely connected with the reference department from the time I took charge of the bookstack in the summer of 1913 until 1936, when I undertook this study, I knew something about all the changes in our methods of keeping records. I also was familiar with the effect of the restriction in use by undergraduates beginning in 1931, when we were overwhelmed by young people who did not need to use the great research library but who were looking for quiet seats and books which should have been found in their own academic libraries.

I had a record of weather conditions and could study their influence, which was comparatively minor on a monthly basis. I realized that the war must have had an effect, and I understood the effects of the different times of year. But beyond the things just mentioned and the regular increase in use from 1913 until the 1931 restriction, which was reasonably steady and which a library giving good service might expect, it was evident that there was another and very important factor, the influence of economic conditions. I prepared a chart showing the changes in use from month to month and year to year and then compared it with a similar chart for business activities which I found in the *New York Times.* Putting the two together, I found that if the one for business activity were turned upside down and moved along for a short period, it almost matched the chart of library use. This gave me satisfaction but I also understood that it was no more useful for predicting future demands on library use than Dow Jones or Standard & Poor Wall Street stock reports were for predicting the value of stocks in the coming months.

After completing the article, I went to work in such time as I could find on a similar study for the circulation department but was unable to complete it before leaving New York for Cambridge. I took the references with which I might have completed the study to Harvard but my work there prevented me from going farther with it. I do know that for many years we had found that, with a change of $100,000 in the city's appropriation for books, we could expect an increase or decrease of a million volumes in the circulation. Mr. Anderson had worked this out in the 1920's, and I was sorry not to have been able to see if business conditions had an effect similar to that in the reference department, where the available funds for new books did not vary much from year to year and the use of the older material was much greater than in the circulation department.

An earlier and more ambitious attempt to carry out a study that I had hoped would be useful for the library's reference assistants and for libraries elsewhere was a guide to the library's collections. I worked on this for at least four years and prepared hundreds of pages of manuscript dealing with the collections, many of which I had known something about first-hand or had heard of, and I had hoped to complete the task. But again my shift to Harvard made it all an idle dream and I turned over what I had done to Karl Brown. The NYPL published the result of his work in 1941 in a much more valuable and important volume than I, as a busy administrator and not an experienced bibliographer, could have compiled.

Brown's masterpiece has been brought up to date and to some extent replaced by Sam P. Williams' similar volume published by the American Library Association in 1975, with a change from "reference" collections to "research" collections in the title. I have made use of both of these volumes in these recollections.

Chapter 15
Library Association Assignments

Between 1905 and 1930 I kept my nose pretty close to the grindstone at Oberlin and the New York Public Library except for my student extra-curricular activities, working vacations during my Oberlin years, and refereeing football games and track meets, as already reported. It was not until 1929, when I was 40 years old and we finally owned our house in White Plains free and clear, that I felt we could buy a car. We acquired a second-hand Graham Paige for $400. I took very few vacations away from home in the Bronx or after we moved to White Plains until we had the car, although during a

few summers we all went to Oberlin by train and in several
other summers Mart went there with the children to give them
outdoor experiences not available in the New York area.
While in White Plains I spent my spare time working in the
garden and hiking around the countryside. We were in Oberlin at commencement time in 1921 and again in 1926 for
Metcalf family reunions. Two group pictures are shown in this
volume, one showing all of my father's descendants who were
able to come in 1926 and the other showing my nine brothers
who then were alive (four had died) and myself are at an
earlier gathering. My branch of the family was driven out to
Oberlin on that occasion by one of my college classmates, our
first long trip by automobile. But after we moved to White
Plains in 1921 I spent most of the summer vacations in my
fairly large garden and often I canned by the hot-pack
method in Mason jars (we still have some empty ones) as many
as 50 quarts of beans, an equal quantity of tomatoes, and all
the currants, strawberries, raspberries, and citron we could
produce in the form of jelly, jam, or sauce. We also made grape
juice from four kinds of grapes. Corn and lima beans were
staples. Winter squash was kept in the cellar most of the
winter. I even grew peanuts and popcorn to show the children
how it was done. Flowers were not neglected. I would go back
to work at the end of the month refreshed and as interested as
ever in the library, where my assignments gradually
broadened in scope and widened my experience and background.

   At the request, or at least with the consent, of Mr. Lydenberg and Mr. Anderson I took over an increasing number of
library assignments during these years until they included a
large part of the routine administration for the reference
department. Mr. Lydenberg never gave me a new assignment
but when I took over his work during his October vacation, he
would refrain from taking some of it back on his return. I
often suggested changes of practice that generally were approved. Other chapters tell of those that seem particularly
important.

I joined the American Library Association in the spring of 1913 while I was in library school. The dues were very modest at that time. Each new member received a number which showed him how many, going back to 1876, had preceded him, and my number was 5430. I could not afford to attend the annual conferences or mid-winter meetings, except for those in 1916 and 1919 which were held at Asbury Park, N. J., and the 50th anniversary conference at Atlantic City in 1926. To each of these I was able to go for a day or two, commuting from my home and thus avoiding the cost of meals and lodging. It was not until the conference at West Baden, Indiana, in May 1929 that I first attended one for a full week at the expense of the library.

At the three earlier conferences that I attended, I met many of the well-known librarians of those earlier years, including these former ALA presidents: John Cotton Dana, Herbert Putnam, Henry James Carr, Ernest C. Richardson, Frank P. Hill, Clement Andrews, Arthur E. Bostwick, Nathaniel D. Hodges, James I. Wyer (whose daughter married a nephew of mine in 1925), Hiller Wellman, Walter L. Brown, Thomas L. Montgomery, Chalmers Hadley, Alice S. Tyler, George B. Utley, Judson T. Jennings, Herman H. B. Meyer, Charles F. D. Belden, George H. Locke, Carl B. Roden, Adam Strohm and Josephine Adams Rathbone. Most of them I heard speak during the conferences and met when they were sitting on the hotel porches. Some of them came to the New York Public Library to see Mr. Anderson and Mr. Lydenberg and I also saw them there. I was interested particularly in the session at which Mr. Dana defended himself (I did not agree with him) for encouraging the Special Libraries Association when it broke off from the American Library Association. At the Atlantic City meeting I met the Vatican librarian who later became Cardinal Tisserant. I had the pleasure of taking him around the New York library later and met him again in Rome at the Vatican and at Notre Dame University in Indiana. In 1926 I met Dr. Guppy of the John Rylands Library and took him around the library's central building. On this same visit to the United States Dr. Guppy went to the Boston Athenaeum. There he met Elinor Gregory, who became my second wife 15 years later, three years after Mart's death. Elinor then was the reference librarian, and on her desk there was a fishbowl with guppies. He asked her what kind of fish they were. She, without thinking, replied "Guppies." He saw her embarrassment and said, "Don't worry, guppies were named after a close relative of mine."

Virtually all of the 40 ALA presidents after Josephine Rathbone I came to know fairly well in connection with the ALA, although there have been two or three since I retired in 1955 whom I have known only to speak to.

But back to my story: One day in the early 1920's I was asked by Mr. Lydenberg and Mr. Anderson, both of whom were members of the Century Association of New York (which might be called the city's intellectual professional club in the fields of art, administration, architecture, education, music, libraries, sciences, etc.) to make a study of the association's library, which apparently had not been running smoothly, partly at least because there was no suitable person in charge. I confess I have no memory of my report and I do not know if there is a copy of it at the Century, of which I have been a member since 1953. It was my first assignment outside of the library in which I was employed.

My First A. L. A. Assignment

In 1930, two years after I became chief of the reference department, H.M.L. told me that he had conferred with Charles C. Williamson and Andrew Keogh on a proposal for cooperative cataloguing. In a sense it was to follow Charles C. Jewett's attempt in the early 1850's, which failed because the stereotype plates, used for the cooperatively prepared copy from which cards were to be printed, warped and were unusable. Later attempts at cooperative cataloguing were made on a small scale by the American Library Association. Mr. Lydenberg was interested in the new proposal. I had felt

strongly since my study of the NYPL's cataloguing problems
in 1920 and during my time as head of the reference department's cataloguing division that there was unnecessary duplication among the research libraries in cataloguing books not
owned by the Library of Congress. I told Mr. Lydenberg of my
great interest in the project, said I hoped that funds could be
found for it, and suggested a method of organizing the study.

A few days later Mr. Lydenberg called me to say that the
Rockefeller Foundation had offered to finance a study of the
situation and that his committee wanted me to take charge. I
was somewhat taken aback, as it had not occurred to me that
this would happen. I then remembered that 11 years earlier I
had suggested the position that I was appointed to in the New
York Public Library office as executive assistant. In spite of
this, I accepted the cooperative cataloguing assignment with
the reservation that, while I would supervise the preliminary
study, I could call on someone else to do the field work which I
knew would be required and have a committee to determine
policies. I suggested Paul North Rice, who had spent six years
as chief of the preparation division, for the preliminary study.

Paul accepted the assignment and visited research libraries
throughout the country, though he was troubled by a bad case
of sciatica while on the road. Each library was asked to send to
me from its catalogue, following a definite method of selection
that Paul and I had worked out, 1,000 cards for books published and acquired during the preceding years. We thought
that this would provide a good cross-section. We gathered
some 30,000 cards in this way and arranged them alphabetically. We then searched the Library of Congress catalogue to
see how many were listed there, and we checked the Union
Catalogue to see how many of those without Library of
Congress cards had been acquired by more than one library.

The results were reported in detail in the *Cataloguers' and
Classifiers' Year Book,* No. III, 1932 and the *Library Journal,*
Volume LVIII (1932). Among other things it was found that,
if it were willing to wait a reasonable length of time, a library
such as that of the Massachusetts Institute of Technology,

which at that time was buying comparatively little foreign material, could obtain some 85% of its cards from the Library of Congress. The New York Public Library and Harvard could obtain somewhere between 20 and 30% of their cards. The other libraries came in between these extremes.

At this point it should be added that, in addition to the very fine field work done by Paul North Rice, we had an unusually good committee consisting of Margaret Mann of the University of Michigan Library School, Franklin Currier of Harvard, J. C. M. Hanson of the University of Chicago (former chief cataloguer of the Library of Congress) and Rudolph Gjelsness, who had left the New York Public Library and was at the University of Arizona. We were fortunate enough to be able to employ Winifred Gregory to take charge of the work at the Library of Congress. Herbert Putnam agreed to have the card division of the Library of Congress under Charles Hastings include the cooperatively prepared cards with those to be printed by the Library of Congress. The titles for which we believed cooperative cataloguing would be most useful were chiefly individual volumes in foreign monograph series which the Library of Congress had not analyzed even if it had acquired the titles. Each of the series was assigned to a cooperating library that was ready to follow Library of Congress rules. I discussed the matter with Mr. Hastings and he used such influence as he could to have the cooperative copy accepted by the Library of Congress cataloguers. He and Miss Gregory talked with the Library of Congress cataloguer who was in charge of the work and she talked with the cataloguers who checked the cooperatively prepared cataloguing. They were perfectionists and refused to accept copy without a complete revision, which, of course, cost the Library of Congress money and delayed the printing of the cards.

I made a practice of going down to Washington at least once a month by night train. I arrived at the Capital city at 7:00 a.m., had breakfast with my brother John (25 years my senior), who lived on 16th Street, N.W., then would walk with him to his office, near which I caught a streetcar to the Library of Congress, arriving there when the building opened. I would go directly to Herbert Putnam's office, as I felt it improper to talk with his staff without his knowing I was there. He usually was in his office an hour before the library opened. He would greet me cordially and often invited me to have lunch with him in the cafeteria in the library tower, which later was given up because of fire danger (it could be reached only by elevator). At other times he would suggest that I walk through the building with him as he told me of his library problems, most of which stemmed from his inadequate and poorly paid staff. I would tell him about the problems affecting cooperative cataloguing caused by the perfectionist cataloguers, and he would agree that something should be done about it. But nothing happened.

I saw a good deal of Mr. Hastings, who seemed to me to be the real backbone of the library staff. We could talk freely together. Frequently he would ask me why the New York Public Library ordered so many of what seemed to him to be unimportant European books. At the same time he admitted that he did most of the foreign book selection for the Library of Congress from the cards that the New York Public Library sent down for the National Union Catalogue.

I also became better acquainted with Winifred Gregory, whom I had known fairly well when she had a desk at the New York library while she was in charge of editing the first edition of the *Union List of Serials*. I saw a great deal of her later after I went to Harvard, when she was working as editor of the second edition of the *Union List of Serials* with headquarters at the Library of Congress. There she worked with James Thayer Gerould, who had retired from the position of librarian of Princeton University and whom she married some time after the death of his first wife.

I cannot resist telling this story about Winifred Gregory and Elinor Gregory, my second wife, and Fremont Rider. It was at the October 1933 Chicago ALA Conference, where Elinor (whom I did not know at that time) was attending her first ALA conference only nine months after she had been appointed librarian of the Boston Athenaeum. Fremont Rider, librarian at Wesleyan in Middletown, Connecticut, rushed up to Elinor at the close of a meeting and invited her to lunch. She was just about to take a train home to Boston but he was very persuasive and said he had something important to discuss with her. She was surprised, as she had not known him before, but finally consented. After they had ordered their lunches, Mr. Rider began to explain what it was that he wanted to talk about—and Elinor discovered that he thought she was Winifred Gregory, whom she had met for the first time only a few hours earlier. Both were naturally very much embarrassed.

The unsatisfactory situation with regard to cooperatively prepared catalogue copy continued for several years. Finally I took my courage in hand and spoke very strongly to Dr. Putnam about the situation. I told him that we had a wonderful opportunity to make progress in inter-library cooperation and could expand it as time went on but were failing because of the stubbornness of some of his perfectionist cataloguers. This was costing the Library of Congress money, handicapping the whole enterprise, and irritating the cooperating libraries. Finally, he told me that he recognized the problem and promised to act promptly and decisively. He did act the very next day—but unfortunately selected as new head of the Library of Congress catalogue department a very capable cataloguer about whom Charles Hastings was enthusiastic. Indeed, Hastings had sent this man to me in New York when the NYPL was looking for a head for our preparation division before Quincy Mumford took it over. I had talked long and carefully with him. He promised that if we would take him on he would double our catalogue department's production within a year. His proposal was that professional members of the department no longer would be divided into three sections—cataloguing, subject heading and classification. Instead, each cataloguer would receive his books when they left the acquisition division and take them all the way through the various processes—descriptive cataloguing, classification and subject heading—until they were ready for revision, labelling and preparation for the shelves. I was not convinced that his theory would work with our fine group of specialists. We had in the New York library at that time what I believed to be the finest group of cataloguers in the country, and we had been able to prevent unnecessary perfectionism without seriously affecting the quality of the work. We had doubled production since the 1920 study I discussed in Chapter 3. This had been brought about by the able work of Paul North Rice between July 1920 and July 1927 and I believe had been continued later by myself and then by Rudolph Gjelsness and Quincy Mumford.

The new appointment at the Library of Congress proved to be unfortunate. Julian Leavitt was unable to carry his staff with him. We almost gave up hope of enlarging the scope of the cooperative cataloguing work and decided simply to keep the enterprise going until Dr. Putnam retired. My term as chairman of the Cooperative Cataloguing Committee came to an end and John Russell, whom I knew well and who then was chief cataloguer at the National Archives, took my place.

In reviewing my work with the Cooperative Cataloguing Committee, I should not fail to emphasize the importance of the help given me by Franklin Currier, which impressed me so much that it was one of the considerations that persuaded me to accept Harvard's librarianship in 1937 after turning it down the previous year. One of the high points of my 75 years of library work came after my first report to the ALA Council on the cooperative cataloguing enterprise, when I received a letter from Margaret Mann, saying that she was proud to be a librarian because a member of the profession had made the study and prepared the report on which the committee's project was based.

Board of Education for Librarianship

I still was actively engaged in the work of the Cooperative Cataloguing Committee when I was appointed to the Board of Education for Librarianship of the American Library Associa-

tion, an appointment that continued until after I went to
Harvard. I was pleased because I had been inclined to be
critical of library schools and had been interested in them
since my Oberlin days when Azariah Root had been chairman
of a committee on library education, one of the first ALA
committees in that field.

In the 1920's Sarah C. N. Bogle, whom I fear too many of us
have forgotten but who was one of the most influential librarians of her time, became assistant general secretary of the
American Library Association. If I am not mistaken she was
largely responsible for the appointment of the first ALA
Board of Education for Librarianship with authority to study,
advise and accredit (when desirable) the growing number of
library schools. I shall not attempt to deal in detail with the
work of this committee, the members of which, like those of
other ALA committees, were appointed for long terms. For its
first few years, the board, largely under the influence of Miss
Bogle, accredited schools on a quantitative basis, which probably was the only way to start out. The criteria were primarily
the number of instructors and courses, financial support, etc.

Miss Bogle died early in 1932. She had been born in White
Plains and was buried there. I learned that Dr. Fred Keppel,
the president of the Carnegie Corporation, was to attend the
funeral service. I knew that he lived in Croton on Hudson,
some 30 miles up the Hudson River, and commuted on the
main line of the New York Central Railroad. To get home
from White Plains he would have to go back to the city and
change trains. I sent word through Harry Lydenberg that if
he would come to the White Plains station after the service, I
would meet him with my car and drive him to Croton. It was
an unusually warm day, with high humidity and a drizzling
rain. We met as agreed but when I tried to start the car, it
would not although a few minutes earlier I had had no
difficulty when I had driven from home on Battle Hill. I
finally gave up and Dr. Keppel had to go back to the city on the
next train. I called the garage, a repair man came and wiped
off the carburetor—and the car started without trouble. I
drove home chagrined and felt that I had better avoid Dr.

Keppel from then on. Fortunately for me I was wrong. We became good friends and I had satisfactory dealings with him, except on one occasion, until his death in 1943.

By 1934, when I was appointed to the Board of Education for Librarianship, it became evident that the time had come for a re-accreditation of library schools based on quality. I talked over the appointment with Mr. Lydenberg and accepted it with his approval and with the knowledge that it would involve considerable travelling and time away from my office. Mr. Lydenberg believed strongly that librarians should be of service to their country and profession in any way they could.

It was fortunate for me that William Warner Bishop was chairman of the board that year. I did my first accreditation visit, at Rosary College in a western suburb of Chicago, with him. That evening he patiently went over with me what he had seen. Perhaps realizing my handicap when it came to writing, after we agreed on the details he wrote the final report (much to my relief), giving me an opportunity to put in comments whenever I cared to. This was the first of the qualitative accreditations. We were fortunate enough to have Anita Hostetter as secretary of the board, with headquarters at the office on North Michigan Avenue, and most of my share of visiting in the following years was with her. Later, when I was chairman of the board, I visited the Simmons College Library School with Joe Wheeler. We thought well of it but Joe, one of our influential and stimulating librarians in more than one field, had a prejudice against teaching library handwriting in library school. When I recommended accreditation to the ALA Council, Joe spoke up so strongly against including library handwriting in the curriculum that poor June Donnelly, then dean of the school, broke into tears, much to my embarrassment.

In some ways the most potentially embarrassing task the board had to undertake during my term was the accrediting of the University of Chicago Graduate Library School under Louis Round Wilson, who was rapidly bringing it to the first rank of schools, and the University of Michigan Library

School, where Dr. Bishop, whose term on the board had
ended, was director and dean. Fortunately, both schools were
excellent. Another school that I dealt with, which gave me an
especially good experience, was the University of North
Carolina at Chapel Hill under Susan Akers. A trip to several
Pennsylvania state colleges which were giving courses for
school librarians gave me an opportunity to become acquainted with school libraries, of which I had seen practically
nothing since my days in Elyria High School, where there was
one of the finest early high school libraries in the country. I
had been fortunate enough to visit Brooklyn Girls' High
School library under Mary Hall while I was in library school.
Miss Hall had been trained by Miss Plummer and was reference librarian at Pratt Institute when my sister was her assistant. High school libraries were just beginning to come into
their own. School librarians still were comparatively few and
far between. This has been one of the great changes in library
work in the last 50 years.

But as far as I was concerned, during my term with the
Board of Education for Librarianship the almost month-long
trip that I made in January 1937 was the most interesting. I
went with Miss Hostetter to California, primarily to check on
the five schools that already were established in that state. This
was far enough along in the Depression so that nearly 100
colleges and universities which were having difficulty finding
positions for their graduates were thinking of establishing
library schools. The Board of Education felt it had a duty to
stop them because there was a surplus of librarians at that time
and salaries were falling rather than going up. Berkeley,
under Sydney Mitchell, was going well and undoubtedly
should be continued. San Jose, under Joyce Backus, seemed to
fill a need with its undergraduate school. The Los Angeles
Public Library was about to drop its school and the one at
Riverside was weak. But the University of Southern California
just had organized a school (which I did not approve of) and
the University of California at Los Angeles was planning to
establish one. Miss Hostetter and I both felt that we should try

to persuade them to give up the idea. We visited the Los Angeles public library, U.C.L.A., the University of Southern California, the public libraries at Long Beach, San Bernardino and Santa Barbara and the Claremont colleges. We were fortunate to visit Pomona College, one of the Claremont group, on the day Rachmaninoff was giving a concert. William S. Ament, the acting president, whose substitute I had been on the football team at Oberlin in 1908, had us seated beside Mrs. Rachmaninoff and we had a delightful evening. But the long, long trip back to Los Angeles by streetcar late that evening was not so pleasant.

At the University of Southern California we talked with President Kleinsmid. He had insisted a year earlier that he was going to start a library school whether one was needed or not because it would give his university one more graduate department than any other institution in the country.

During our Los Angeles stay President Sproul came down from Berkeley to talk over the U.C.L.A. situation. As a result, the library school there was not started until nearly 25 years later, when Larry Powell did it successfully at a time when it was badly needed. After having discouraged so many library schools from starting, I wondered later whether I had been responsible for the shortage of library school graduates in the 1960's. But my conscience has stopped troubling me in recent years. As a result of our trip a report on the California schools was prepared and published by the ALA.

On our way back from California we stopped at Denison, Texas, where there were two library schools, one for men at the university and one at the women's college, then the largest women's college in the world. We decided not to stop over in San Antonio, where the Catholic college was hoping for accreditation for its library school. Our train stopped in El Paso long enough so that I hoped I could walk across the Rio Grande River bridge into Mexico. But I found that the bridge was so long there was not enough time to do it. My interest in travel and new countries is perhaps indicated by this attempt and will be made clearer in Part IV of these Recollections.

Several other related matters should be noted before closing this section. I might say that, with my strict Puritan Congregationalist bringing up, I was slightly embarrassed to start off on a long trip with an attractive young lady and no chaperone. While we were waiting for the train in the Chicago depot at the beginning of the trip I was relieved when Anita's father and mother appeared, perhaps to look me over and decide whether it was safe or not. We found that my oldest brother, Wilder, who was 34 years older than I, was well known to them and they felt that I was safe. Miss Hostetter proved to be a very pleasant companion and we enjoyed the trip, one high point of which was seeing the famous clog dancer, Bo Jackson, who was on the train. At the stops he would get out onto the platform and exercise by running backward at what seemed to be tremendous speed for that kind of locomotion. He was met at Los Angeles by a large, noisy crowd of admirers.

My last library-school accreditation trip was with Eleanor Witmer, then librarian of Teachers College at Columbia, with whom I drove down to Trenton, New Jersey, to see the Trenton State Teachers College, which had a library school. She reminded me that she was on the ALA's nominating committee and asked if I would be willing to run for president, which would mean that I would serve for the year 1942-43. I asked her to give me time to talk to President Conant about it, since I knew that it might require considerable time away from my position at Harvard, to which I had gone only three years earlier. Mr. Conant was doubtful about my taking the time, he said he thought that undoubtedly I would be nominated again if I refused it this time and suggested that I wait. My answer was that the war was coming on and that there might not be an ALA meeting in 1943, so this would be the best time to accept as far as Harvard was concerned.

I might add that this was one of the last times that only one person was proposed for president-elect to become president automatically the following year. In 1938 two men were nominated, Charles C. Williamson and Ralph Munn. Williamson was much the older of the two; he was director of the Columbia University Library, dean of what was considered one of the best library schools in the country, and author of the Carnegie report on library schools, so it was taken for granted by many persons that he would be elected. He was defeated and as an indirect result, the election procedure was changed to a single nominee. This again was given up a few years later, perhaps because I did not make a good president. While defeated candidates naturally have felt badly, it has not been considered a disgrace to lose, although I think it not unfair to say that when Henry Van Hoesen ws defeated, much to his surprise, by a younger man in the late 1940's, it came as a bitter disappointment, since his friends had convinced him he would be the winner. I speak of this simply to illustrate a bit of the history of American Library Association politics.

In this connection, I can add that in the mid-1930's I was nominated for the ALA Council and was defeated. I was not surprised and my feelings were not injured. A few years later when I was nominated for the executive board I won unexpectedly, almost surely because by that time my work as chairman of the Committee on Cooperative Cataloguing and on the Board of Education for Librarianship had called my name to the attention of the ALA membership. I always have believed that members generally vote for a person whom they have heard most about, whether they know him or not, rather than because he represents the best choice. The present custom of asking nominees to state their attitude toward ALA problems that must be faced should help but I doubt that it makes much difference in the final decision. In more recent years candidates for president nominated by petition rather than by the nominating committee have been elected on three occasions.

During my term on the Board of Education for Librarianship the board became interested in library internships for library school graduates and, while not ready to propose this, I arranged to have Francis St. John suggest it and an article about it was published under his name. It was some 10 years before a similar plan was adopted by the Library of Congress and several other large libraries, and later still by the Council on Library Resources.

During that term it also was found that, because there was a surplus of librarians, some fairly large academic libraries were bragging that all members of their staffs were library school graduates. I considered this a great mistake financially for the institutions involved while at the same time it tended to lower professional library salaries. As a result of this and of articles inspired by the board, the number of graduates on library staffs declined from an average of well over 50 percent to one-third and even to the one-quarter which is common today in the United States and Canada. At this time I became very much interested in the possibility of training paraprofessional librarians, either in library schools or junior colleges, to do work that, it seemed to me, did not require college graduation or full library training. Though Dr. Williamson at Columbia was interested in the proposal, he was unable to persuade his faculty to act on it. But when I found at Harvard that Franklin Currier was having most of the cataloguing done by high school graduates who could type and that his cataloguers were simply revisers, I became convinced that this was not an impossible dream. At the other end of the line, I was equally convinced that library schools were not doing what they might do in training administrators. This subject will be dealt with later.

American Library Institute

Early in the century a group of librarians decided that men who had achieved distinction in the profession deserved special recognition. Under the leadership of Melville Dewey, Ernest C. Richardson and others they organized what they called the American Library Institute. In order to prevent themselves from ultimately becoming "a group of retired old men," they arranged to limit the group to 100; each member was to serve for 10 years, and could be elected for a second term if still active. The 100 were divided by lot into 10 groups, each with 10 fellows. One group was to be retired each year. The other members would select their successors. It was possible and often desirable, of course, to re-elect any or all of the 10 who had completed their terms. But any one of them could be replaced with a new fellow. Those who were not re-elected were considered "retired", not "gone to seed." It was to be a self-perpetuating group but it was not expected to be a deteriorating one.

The Institute considered that it consisted of those who might properly be called the "cream" of the library profession. The fact that no woman was invited was apparently not considered. The members thought of themselves as primarily a discussion group. They did not try to emphasize programs although they met regularly and Dr. Richardson did his best to persuade them to take some action. He prepared numerous papers, some of them important, that were printed. I had a set of the reports that I inherited from Azariah Root after his death in 1927 and gave to the Harvard Library years ago. The Institute had a secretary, who unfortunately was not as active as he might have been, at least while I was a member. His chief duty was to arrange for meetings and a program.

I had heard about the group even before going to library school but it never occurred to me that I might some time become a member. The most important things that I can recall about the publications were reports by Dr. Richardson advocating what he called "title a line cataloguing." He wrote that too often cataloguing cost almost as much as the books themselves. He insisted that, if we were content with one line for each main entry, giving the name of the author and his initials, an abbreviated title and perhaps the date of publication, it would provide us with a list with which we could find more than 95% of the books. The money saved would make it possible to increase book purchases. He apparently was not worried about the cost of the space occupied by the books

which could not be found and the complications which would
ensue.

Sometime around 1930, after I became chief of the reference department of the New York Public Library, I found
myself elected to membership in the Institute about the same
time that Paul North Rice was elected. We wondered whether
we wanted to belong to an organization in which we did not
believe. But we decided that it was better to belong and
criticize from within than to stay out, because if we were not
members anything that we had to say would be considered
"sour grapes." At the 1932 ALA conference I became involved in a discussion in which Dr. Richardson gave me a good
calling down for not pushing his theory of title-a-line cataloguing in connection with the cooperative cataloguing with which
the committee of which I was chairman was struggling.

A few years later Dr. Williamson tried to revivify the Institute and get some action out of it. He obtained funds from one
of the foundations and arranged for a meeting in Atlantic City
with talks by several younger men, one of whom I remember
was Charles Gosnell (later librarian of New York State and
then New York University), who spoke on his specialty of
Latin American acquisitions. As in the past, the leading members of the organization were too busy to take time for
something that they did not have to do and in which they were
not involved directly, and nothing more happened.

About this time Charles David was elected to the Institute.
He was not a trained librarian but had been a professor at
Bryn Mawr and the University of Pennsylvania and librarian
of the University of Pennsylvania, where he revived that
institution's library, which had been sliding downhill badly (he
was responsible for the successful Philadelphia Union
Catalogue). Paul and I found that Charles felt very much as we
did about the American Library Institute. Eventually he was
elected secretary, and the three of us finally got a vote through
the organization by which it was disbanded and its few remaining funds were turned over to the American Library Association.

"The Large Librarians"

The "Large Librarians" group was a completely informal one made up of librarians of the large public libraries. It had no organization or name as far as I remember but we used to speak of the members simply as the "Large Librarians," more in jest than anything else. The group met at the annual ALA conferences and midwinter meetings. I never was a "large librarian" but Mr. Anderson did not go to meetings in his later years and Mr. Lydenberg was so active in other ALA matters that he often asked me to take his place at the meetings. It was simply a discussion group and I remember little of the discussions except that the sessions gave me an opportunity to become better acquainted with the senior public library librarians, such as Carl Roden, Chalmers Hadley, Linda Eastman, Gratia Countryman, Frank Hill and Arthur Bostwick. My chief memory of these meetings was listening to words of wisdom pouring out of the mouth of Arthur Bostwick who, as I already have said, spoke more easily and to the point than anyone I have known. After I went to Harvard and became a university librarian, I fell out of this group, of course, and I do not know what became of it.

Local Library Groups

Librarians have a tendency to be "joiners" and in most large American cities there are one or more organizations of librarians in addition to the American Library Association and the Special Libraries Association. I naturally belonged to the New York State Library Association, although I did not begin to attend their meetings until my later years in New York because travel funds were scarce. But I finally did get to a number of meetings at Lake Placid, which through Melville Dewey's invitation often was the meeting place of October. I even became first vice president of the New York Library Association and escaped being president by shifting to Har-

vard at just the right time. There also was a New York City
Library Club, and the New York Public Library Staff Association, just as there were staff associations for the Brooklyn
Public Library and the Queensboro Public Library. I already
have written of the New York Public Library Staff Association
in which I had a part.

Other organizations sprang up, prominent among them the
Special Libraries Association, which was backed by John Cotton Dana, much to the disgust of many of us. But it has become
a very active and worthwhile group, both nationally and
locally. When I came to Harvard I found that its Boston
branch was *the* organization that librarians belonged to even if
they were not special librarians. There was a male organization in New York called the Archons of Colophon, with
William W. Rockwell, librarian at the Union Theological
Seminary, as the leading spirit who kept it on its feet for many
years. I remember attending meetings of this group after
moving to the Cambridge area. The Grolier Club in New
York, the Rowfant Club in Cleveland, and the Club of Odd
Volumes in Boston, to each of which I belonged at one time or
another, were collectors' clubs, with many members who were
librarians. The Bibliographical Society of America should be
added to this list, to say nothing of friends of the library
groups that have sprung up throughout this country and
England. There also are the subject groups, such as the Music
Library Association, the Medical Library Association, the Law
Library Association, the State Librarians group, the Library
Trustees and many others, some as divisions of the American
Library Association and others which are independent.

But the American Library Association, which has included
subject and functional divisions and probably is too complicated for its own good, is the one I feel all professional
librarians should join. I will not attempt to go further here
except to repeat that I have always felt that the main emphasis
should be on the American Library Association so that it can
bring united pressure to bear on governmental bodies to help

libraries financially, something that always is needed. I shall write or already have written about this in more detail elsewhere.

In the 50's I was made an honorary member of the ALA. Since that time I have been comparatively inactive with the exception of work with the building planning committee, which at first was an independent group and then became an ALA committee.

I have reserved for another chapter an account of the Association of Research Libraries. It was organized in the early 1930's and I have attended more meetings of ARL than of any other group.

Chapter 16
Some Odds and Ends

German Patents

Sometime in the middle 1930's (I do not remember the exact date) Mr. Lydenberg told me that he had learned that the Deutsches Museum in Munich had a complete set of the German Patent Office drawings and specifications, which they would send to us in exchange for a similar set of United States patents. We knew that we had a nearly complete duplicate set of United States patents and we decided to complete it so that the exchange could be arranged. We found that there was no full set of the German patents in this country and we thought it advisable to make every effort to correct the situation. The United States patents for which we lacked duplicates numbered only a few hundred, were scattered over the years and were out of stock in the Patent Office. The total cost of reproducing them would be comparatively small. Armed with a list of the ones we needed, I went to Washington and called on the Patent Commissioner, who said he thought it could be arranged to have those we needed reprinted. We were ready to pay for the work. The commissioner then turned me over to his chief clerk, who told me that because of the Depression he had been told they could do no reprinting. Unfortunately, the commissioner then agreed with him.

Our next step was to go to the Patent Commissioner's predecessor, whom Mr. Anderson knew and who was on good terms with the present commissioner. Though he said he thought he could make the needed arrangements, again the answer came back, "No," with a letter that obviously had been written by the chief clerk. Mr. Lydenberg took the problem to our board of trustees and one of its members, a Wall Street broker and a book collector, volunteered to write about our problem to Franklin D. Roosevelt, an old friend of his. H.M.L. and I prepared a letter, I took it down to Wall Street and the trustee signed it. After some delay a letter signed by the President came back; from the wording, it was obvious this also had been written by the patent office's chief clerk. It explained that the President was sorry but, in view of the government's financial situation, nothing could be done.

H.M.L. then decided that the senior U. S. Senator from New York, Robert Wagner, might get a private bill through Congress providing for the reprinting. I called on Senator Wagner in the Capitol and he sent me, by way of the underground tunnel, to his office in the Senate Office Building to talk with his legislative secretary, who later became a judge in the Federal District Court of New York and held other important positions. The secretary was very cordial and helpful and arranged that a desk and typewriter be placed at my disposal. I might add that any typewriter that I can find today does not know how to spell but his did very well for me. He then suggested that I go to Senator McAdoo of California, who, he said, would be the best Senator to join with Senator Wagner in arranging to place a private bill on the Senate agenda which would enable us to obtain the needed reproductions.

All of this took a good many trips to Washington. I went nearly every Sunday evening for several months, taking the last train from White Plains to Grand Central Station, then walking across town to the ferry to Hoboken, from which the Baltimore and Ohio Railroad train left after midnight for Washington. I would find the same porter on the train week after week (on one occasion, after I had missed a week, he seemed to rebuke me for my non-appearance). On reaching Washington, long before office hours, I would go to my brother John's apartment for breakfast, walk with him on the way to his office and then catch a trolley that stopped near the Senate Office Building. Despite all the efforts of Senators Wagner and McAdoo, they were unable to get the private bill through. I am convinced, perhaps mistakenly, that they did all they could. This was my first realization that much of the power in Washington rests in the hands of the chief clerks. It also left me with the feeling that I was not cut out for the task of political lobbying. Mr. Lydenberg and I were convinced that my failure was a serious matter. It was not too much later that the Second World War began and the United States was left with no way of being sure what the Germans had developed in the way of new weapons. At that time our patents had not included anything about which the Germans did not know.

Pensions

During most of my time in New York the library suffered from lower salaries than those provided in many of the other large libraries in the United States. The same situation held for staff pensions. In fact, no provision for pensions was made until shortly before I went to Harvard. The city claimed that circulation department employees, although paid by the city,

were not city employees because they were under the direction of a private corporation, the New York Public Library.
The reference department, except for repairs to the main
building, was supported by gifts and the income from private
endowment funds which were increased gradually but not
enough to support it as the trustees and the director wished.
While use increased steadily until 1930, the library always was
under financial pressure and succeeded only with difficulty in
keeping its fine staff together. Senior employees were loyal
and it was possible to persuade a great many of the new library
school graduates to come because of the fine experience they
could obtain. There also was the knowledge that it would be
easy for them to find positions elsewhere thanks to that
experience and to the fact that the library would help them
find other positions when it was unable to promote them.

The large Payne Whitney bequests, amounting to some
$14,000,000 just before the beginning of the great Depression
in 1929, made it possible for the reference department to ride
through the next decade better than many other libraries.
The circulation department finally was able to arrange with
New York State authorities to include the staff in the state's
contributory scheme, which was a generous one. The reference department was admitted into that state scheme in 1936.
I remember well that Harry Grumpelt, the library's financial
officer, and I met with state authorities in Albany that year
and were able to conclude arrangements for a contributory
pension scheme with half (if I remember correctly) of the
contributions coming from the employees and the other half
from the library. It was understood that persons already on
the staff would receive one percent of their final salary for
each year they had been employed before the installation of
the pension scheme and 1½% from then on. All of the funds
not provided by the staff members were to be paid by the
library, not the state or the city. Each staff member who left
the library before retirement age would receive when leaving
a lump sum representing his own contributions and interest.
As you can imagine, this was a tremendous relief to those of us

who had been at the library for a good many years. I remember that when I left a year later, I received something like
$400, which had been my contribution to the scheme from the
time it was put into effect until I left.

But this was not the first help that the library was able to
provide for its older employees. A few years earlier two
women in late middle age or more came into my office one day
and introduced themselves as "Miss Smith" and "Miss Jones",
then the one who called herself "Miss Jones" said, "These are
not our real names." She went on to say that her mother, who
had lived to a good old age, had had a very difficult time in her
later years because of lack of funds and she wanted to do what
she could to make life easier for older people who had retired
or had reached the age when they should retire but felt unable
to do so. She asked if we had such persons on the staff. I was
able to say immediately that we had an elderly gentleman in
the Music Division who was in his middle 80's, another in the
reading room of a similar age.

(I should add that this reading-room attendant, who put
reference books back on the shelves after they had been used
by the readers and helped readers find them, had told me
when I took him on some years earlier that he was 66 years old,
but that he was well and active. I had not hesitated to employ
him. I later learned that he had been much interested in
Robert Burns, the Scottish poet, and had written quite a
number of books about him. I looked him up in *Who's Who in
America,* found him listed there, and discovered that he had
been 76 when we had taken him on and now was in his early
80's.)

There was another reading-room attendant known to be in
his early 80's and others who had reached the time when
obviously they should have retired but had felt unable to do
so. I told the two women about our problem. They were
shocked and Miss Jones said there was something that she
could do about it and she would. Within the week she brought
in a cashier's check for $40,000 which, of course, did not give
her name and which she said we could use to take care of the

persons just mentioned. She added that there was a "home"
near 110th Street which would provide suitable quarters and
care for several of those who were not housed satisfactorily.
We made the arrangements promptly. One of the men who
already was in his 80's felt that with the help we now could give
him he would not need to go into an old folks' home. He came
to see me some time later to say his doctor had told him,
"While you're 85 now, there's no reason why you shouldn't
live to be 100."

Miss Jones later told me that her name was Miss Smith and
invited Mart and me to a party on a Sunday afternoon near the
cathedral. Later, after I had gone to Harvard, she asked us to
stop off at her summer home near Monterey, Massachusetts,
on our return from a holiday trip but we were unable to do so.

In connection with pensions, I should go on to state that
before arrangements with the State of New York were made, I
had been on an American Library Association committee
trying to arrange for pensions for librarians. We were able to
obtain help from the actuary who was in charge of the Carnegie Corporation (T.I.A.A.) scheme which academic libraries throughout the country had been using for some 20
years.

The 1928 Election Campaign

Older readers will remember the Hoover-Smith campaign in
1928. Al Smith had been a successful governor of New York
State and Hoover had made a reputation through his success
in feeding the starving Belgians during and after the First
World War. The campaign naturally waxed hot. One day a
Mr. O'Brien came in to the NYPL to complain because he
could not find a file of a British mining annual. He said that it
told of the scandalous behavior of Herbert Hoover in Australia around the turn of the century, when he was a young
mining engineer. Obviously, said our visitor, Hoover had had
enough influence to keep the volumes out of the country or, if

they had reached the United States, his agents had managed in some way to destroy them. I hadn't heard of this mining yearbook and it was not listed in our catalogue and never had been. I immediately ordered a complete file from our British agent, Stevens and Brown. When it arrived, we could find nothing in it that discredited Mr. Hoover, and I reported this to Mr. O'Brien.

Mr. O'Brien dropped in again a few days later and said that he had been shocked to find that we did not have a complete file of the reports of the Commission for Relief in Belgium, 1915 to 1919, which indicated that Mr. Hoover, who was reported to have saved the lives of many starving persons, had taken advantage of his position to make himself a rich man with the funds placed at his disposal and that his agents had been able to prevent these reports from reaching the United States. If this were not true, he said, how does it happen that you do not have a file? Again I must confess that I was shocked when I found that we did not, although I knew that Mr. Lydenberg had done his best to acquire everything connected with the war. I immediately got in touch with the Hoover Library at Stanford University and asked if they knew how we could obtain a copy. They sent us a complete file and again we found nothing that would discredit Hoover. We learned that Hoover was being attacked in at least one of our city newspapers for his misdeeds in Australia and Belgium.

You might say that this represents my only entry into politics. I am inclined to agree with the statement that Sir Charles Hagberg-Wright, librarian of the London Library, made to Elinor Gregory (Metcalf) when she called on him soon after her appointment as librarian of the Boston Athenaeum. He said that a librarian in the performance of his book selection duties should have "no religion, no morals and no politics."

Jury Duty

Soon after becoming executive assistant at the NYPL, I found that Mr. Lydenberg was accustomed to serve a turn on the

Grand Jury in White Plains every two or three years. He said
that it was his duty as a citizen to do so and he felt that all
members of the library staff should serve if called. It was not
much later that I was called for petty jury duty by the Southern District Court and H.M.L. told me that I should serve. My
salary would not be cut for time away from the library if I
would work at any time during the month when I was not
actually serving on a case or waiting in the jury room to be
called. I found that this new experience was an important part
of my education; I learned a great deal about human nature
and something about lawyers' tactics. It seemed to me that
altogether too large a percentage of the men called for jury
duty found excuses for not serving and that a considerable
number of those who did serve were men (not women at that
time) out of work who were looking for the $5 a day compen-
sation and were interested more in helping unfortunate persons on both civil and criminal cases than enforcing the law.

Most of the cases on which I served were minor civil suits
that, it seemed to me, should have been settled out of court, or
cases in which the pre-1933 prohibition law had been violated.
I found that the judges were inclined to be indifferent and the
majority of jury members were determined to declare the
accused "Not Guilty" even if it was evident to me that they
were.

There were only three cases of special interest during the
time when I was on call for a month every other year. The first
involved as U. S. Assistant Attorney in charge of the prosecu-
tion a young man named Thomas Dewey, who made a very
competent presentation of the government's case but impressed me as a very disagreeable young man. It was not very
many years later that he became governor of New York State.
In 1948 he lost his campaign for the Presidency to Harry
Truman, perhaps because of the unpleasant impression he
made on people even when they recognized him as one of the
most capable administrators we have had in government in
this century.

The most important case on which I served involved a retail

merchant and a wholesale sugar company; very large sums of money were at stake and the lawyers on both sides were eloquent and knew all the tricks of the trade.

The third case that I remember was a minor civil damage suit—a charge of negligence in connection with an accident. The plaintiff was asking for what seemed to me to be an unnecessarily high sum. I found that the impecunious members of the jury wanted to delay the decision until the next day in order to draw another day's pay from the government. This was at the end of my jury duty, and I had a commitment to speak at a library dinner in Atlantic City that evening. I didn't want to break the appointment so I undertook to persuade the jury that the amount of damages they had in mind was altogether too high. I was able to arrange a compromise at a much lower figure, one I felt still was unreasonably high. I would have held out for a smaller settlement but for my desire to get off to Atlantic City on time. How wicked was I?

This story has been told primarily as background for what followed. I reached the conference on time and at the dinner was seated beside another speaker who just had become president of Drexel Institute in Philadelphia, coming there from the presidency of the University of Akron, against whose football team I remember playing in my college days. When this man, whose name I do not remember (and I am not now a good enough reference librarian to find out), found that my name was Metcalf, he said that was interesting because it was a name he had not been familiar with until the previous year, when during a meeting of Ohio college presidents the Oberlin president told him of an application received from a girl named Metcalf. She was asked to give some biographical information on her application blank and had written, "I was born of mid-Victorian parents." I then realized that this was written by my daughter without her parents' knowledge. My new friend, I confess, was a bit embarrassed when I told him that I must have been the girl's father. But, as I stated in the introduction, I am now an anachronism and it is easy to understand that 45 years ago I might have seemed to a teenager to be a mid-Victorian parent.

Columbia University Graduate School of Library Service

As I have written earlier, I had listened to Mr. Anderson talk with Albany about the transfer of their library school to Columbia, where it would be joined with the New York Public Library School. As a member of a joint committee of the alumni of the New York State Library School and the New York Public Library, I suggested that both groups become members of the Alumni Association of the Columbia University School of Library Service and that the association should add to its title "and its predecessors." Perhaps as a result, I became the president of the Columbia School Alumni Association the same year the American Library Association had its conference in New Haven.

In the meantime I attended the dedication of the new school at Columbia in the autumn of 1926. Dr. Williamson very properly invited Melville Dewey to speak and introduced him by saying that Mr. Dewey had started the first library school at Columbia just 40 years earlier, when this was difficult because it was before the days of self-starters. I was amazed when apparently only Dr. Williamson, Melville Dewey and I seemed to recall what was used to start an automobile before the days of self-starters.

Dr. Williamson was chosen to develop the school and the library because of his report on library schools for the Carnegie Corporation a few years earlier. This report, it was hoped, would have the same effect on library schools as the Abraham Flexner report had had on medical schools somewhat earlier. It brought about the transfer of several schools from public libraries to academic institutions, and has influenced library-school curriculums and organization ever since.

I had known Dr. Williamson during his three New York Public Library assignments between 1911 and 1921 and had become well acquainted with him through our Catskill Mountain Columbus Day weekend hikes, which began in 1920. He knew of my interest in library building planning and kept me in touch with his plans from the time he began work on what is now the Butler Library. This proved to be very useful to me later.

Two years after Dr. Williamson went to Columbia he asked me to teach a course on the history of libraries for the school's second-year students. I knew that I was unprepared to teach the history of libraries outside the United States and suggested that Mr. Lydenberg might be willing to undertake that part of the course, which he agreed to do. While I had known for many years from my experience in Oberlin and the New York Public Library that I was not cut out for teaching, I was interested in the subject and wanted to learn more about it. I taught one half of the one-semester course for four or five years and spent a tremendous amount of time preparing for it. I know I did not do it well and have been embarrassed ever since when I think of what my students, Constance Winchell and Bob Downs among them, must have thought of me and the course. But I learned a good deal and developed a theory about the causes of the development of our libraries, beginning with the work of Joseph Green Cogswell at Harvard in the 1820's, the Jewett years at the Smithsonian, and the tremendous changes after 1876 following the organization of the ALA with Justin Winsor, Melville Dewey, William F. Poole, C. A. Cutter, R. R. Bowker and others of our founding fathers. Mr. Lydenberg's appointment and mine came to an end in 1933 when the Depression forced the school to cut its budget.

My direct connection with Columbia was not renewed until some time in the 1960's when I taught a summer-school course on library administration and library building planning, which was after my three years' teaching experience at Rutgers University, 1955-58, and when I felt far more comfortable in teaching than I had 35 years earlier.

Lucky Chances and Coincidences

When someone complained about "bad luck," Elinor's grandmother used to say that there are also "lucky chances." I don't know whether you will regard the events that follow during my New York Public Library years as "lucky chances" but they seem worth recording.

An amazing incident occurred while I was chief of stacks. I already have told something of my work there. It was a very busy place and we sent up to the reading room as many as 7,000 volumes a day on orders that came down from the public catalogue room in the form of what we called "call slips." I was kept so busy taking care of snags and complaints of all kinds, which were bound to result with a staff largely made up of teenagers, that I rarely "ran" a call slip myself. But one day when I happened to be on the stack level where the school textbooks were shelved, a slip came down asking for a copy of McGuffey's First Reader. In my school days, from the first to the eighth grade (there were no junior high schools in those days), I had used all eight of McGuffey's Readers between 1894 and 1901. For one of the few times in five years as chief of stacks, I "ran" the slip myself, found the volume, and, as I returned down the center stack aisle to send the book up to the reading room on one of the book lifts, I opened it for old times' sake. It seemed familiar and, believe it or not, on the title page I found written quite legibly and carefully, in the boyish, left-handed writing that I used during my first four years in school, the name "Keyes Metcalf."

For a moment I could not believe my eyes but I finally realized that it must be true and figured out a likely sequence of events. When we moved from Elyria to Oberlin in 1904 to occupy much smaller quarters, the family's library was weeded extensively and the "weeds" were given to the Oberlin College Library, which did a large exchange business with the duplicates that Azariah Root had collected assiduously. In due course, this volume must have gone to the New York Public

Library's collection on exchange before I went to New York
and had fallen into my hands with the odds ten million to one
against it. McGuffey's Readers by that time had become
collectors' items and you may be sure that my copy never went
back to the bookstack. If I am not mistaken, it has been in New
York Public Library Reserve "Rare Book Collection" for more
than 60 years. I might add that if the call had been put in for
any of the other Readers from the second to the eighth it
would not have been for my copy, because I have to confess
that after my mother's death, during my first year in school I
had acquired the bad habit of eating the margins of the pages
of my textbooks.

Another coincidence comes to mind. In 1912, when I was
making the wheels go around at Oberlin as executive assistant
during the absence of Professor Root on sabbatical leave, the
New York State Library building in Albany was burned and
most of its large collection, which had been brought together
by Melville Dewey between 1888 and 1907 after he was "fired"
from Columbia for including women in his library school, was
destroyed.

Dewey had been succeeded in Albany by Edwin Hatfield
Anderson. When the latter went to the New York Public
Library, his successor, James Ingersoll Wyer, sent out an
appeal for replacements for the burned volumes, with emphasis on periodical sets. I remembered that in 1908 when I
had done the physical work of combining the students' Union
Library Association collection in Oberlin with the college
library, there were many duplicate copies of "Poole Sets" and
these still were in the Oberlin duplicate collection. I wrote to
Mr. Wyer and in due course some 2,000 volumes, which now
would be worth a considerable sum, were shipped to Albany.
Fortunately, Azariah Root did not object to this on his return
later in the year. But my story is not yet over. In 1947 I was
asked by Charles Gosnell, then the New York State Librarian,
to study his library and make suggestions. I accepted the offer
and, with the help of Andrew Osborn, studied the library and
published a report. I found and recognized the 2,000 volumes
on the shelves there.

I might finish this story by saying that in between two of the events just described my nephew, the brother of my niece ("Molly" Curtis' wife), was married to James I. Wyer's only daughter. In the summer of 1928 I was in Oberlin helping another niece, Marion Root (Azariah's daughter), clear out her father's house after his death. Marion, who had been head cataloguer of rare books in the New York Public Library for many years until her retirement in 1956, had joined the New York Public Library staff before I became personnel officer and no nepotism was involved. Azariah Root was an accumulator rather than a collector, as I fear my wife and I are, to say nothing of my two children and their spouses. I have travelled widely throughout the world for more than 20 years encouraging all librarians (except those in charge of the great ones with unusual collections such as the New York Public Library, the Library of Congress, Harvard, Yale and the British Museum, which I call libraries of record) to dispose of their less-used books in some way, sending them to cooperative storage libraries such as the New England Deposit Library or the Center for Research Libraries in Chicago or giving them to a library which needs them more than they do.

But to get on the track again, while I was undertaking this clean-up job in the house that Azariah had been in for 40 years, J. I. Wyer appeared. He, like Azariah, had taken advantage of his position to acquire inexpensively a large postage stamp collection. Azariah had found this hobby to be a great relaxation. With his daughter's consent, we sold his collection at a nominal price to Mr. Wyer.

Chapter 17
I Decide To Go To Harvard

One day in March in 1936 Harry Lydenberg called me into his office and introduced me to a fairly slender visitor, James Bryant Conant, who had been president of Harvard University for nearly three years. Mr. Lydenberg said that Mr. Conant had come to him to ask about a candidate who had been recommended to him for the librarianship of Harvard College with the prospect of becoming director of the university library in a year or two because the incumbent, Robert P. Blake, wanted to return to full-time teaching and research.

H.M.L. said that he knew the man only slightly and that, as I knew him better, what I could say about him might be useful. I spoke my mind frankly and without any over-abundance of enthusiasm. I had become fairly well acquainted with the librarian under consideration, as I had with the librarians of most large libraries in the country, through ALA meetings and my committee work. I felt the candidate under discussion would not be satisfactory.

When I was about to leave the office, Mr. Conant asked Mr. Lydenberg what we were doing with micro-photography and H.M.L. again referred the question to me because I had been connected closely with the library's photographic work since 1913. He suggested that I show Mr. Conant our installations and discuss possible future developments in the field, which I did. After Mr. Conant left I thought nothing more about the matter, nor did it occur to me that I had been asked to the office so that I could be looked over (I do not know to this day whether or not that was the case). At any rate, I already had decided to spend the rest of my working days in the New York Public Library because I was in the position that I had looked forward to ever since I decided not to go to Oberlin nine years earlier. However, within a week word came from Mr. Conant offering me the position of librarian of Harvard College with a salary 25% larger than I was receiving as chief of the reference department of the New York Public Library.

In his letter Mr. Conant suggested I get in touch with Mr. Blake and make arrangements to look over the situation at Cambridge before making my decision. I followed his suggestion and for the third time in my life went out of New York to consider another position. Not knowing a hotel in Cambridge and having heard of the Somerset in Boston, I made a reservation there and agreed to have breakfast at the Faculty Club on Quincy Street in Cambridge with Dr. Blake the morning after my arrival. We were the only persons at the club for breakfast that day. I put in most of my time at Harvard's Widener Library, which had housed the main Harvard College collection for 21 years.

I saw Alfred C. Potter, then the librarian of Harvard College, who had succeeded William Coolidge Lane eight years earlier. Mr. Potter, who was 69 years old, had been in the library since 1889, the year I was born. His chief interest, as it had been for some 47 years, still was in the acquisition program, with an emphasis (chiefly by use of second-hand catalogues) on filling gaps in the great collections that had been acquired by his predecessors, particularly John Langdon Sibley, Justin Winsor, first president of the American Library Association, and that great book collector, Archibald Cary Coolidge, under whom Mr. Potter had worked between 1910 and 1928.

Next I talked with Franklin Currier, who, after a short time at the Boston Athenaeum, had joined the Harvard library staff in 1894, had been head of the catalogue department since 1902, and was to retire three years later. I had become acquainted with him through his membership on my Cooperative Cataloguing Committee in the preceding years. He had impressed me at that time with his common sense and the amount of work that he and his staff produced. He was spending such spare time as he could find on what was to become his great Whittier bibliography. In spite of my interest and some experience with cataloguing I knew that one of my great needs would be a good head cataloguer—and decided that if I came to Harvard I would not have to worry about that aspect of the work except for the problem of finding a successor to Currier in a few years.

I also talked with Walter Briggs who had started in the Harvard library as a page in 1886 and had been there ever since, except for five years as reference librarian in Brooklyn and six years as librarian of Trinity College in Connecticut. Harry Lydenberg had turned down the position of assistant librarian in charge of public service when Widener was opened at a salary that was less than he was receiving as chief reference librarian in the New York Public Library and Briggs had come back to Harvard to fill that position. I might add at this point that I believe Mr. Lydenberg was offered the position of director of the University of Chicago library in 1927 before Dr. Raney accepted it, and that Mr. Conant had come to see him in 1936 in the hope of persuading him to come to Harvard even though he was 61 years old at the time. I believe Mr. Conant turned to me after H.M.L. said "no".

My next conference was with Clarence Walton, who had succeeded Mr. Potter in the order department soon after the latter became librarian. Though he was much younger than the other department heads, all three assistant librarians were receiving the same salary while Mr. Potter, as librarian, received $1,000 a year more than the others and a great deal less than I was being offered. I should add that, owing to an unusual situation, the head of the rare book department, George Parker Winship, had not been in the library for 2½ years and was on terminal leave until August 31, 1937, his normal retirement date.

This salary situation surprised me and I was nonplussed at being offered considerably more than any of the others. I realized that Harvard had not yet caught up with the rest of the library world in its pay scale although faculty salaries were high for that time.

During my Cambridge visit I had dinner at Dr. Blake's home with his library committee, which had been almost unchanged in its membership during the preceding years. There I first met George Lyman Kittredge, the great Shakespearean scholar, the man most responsible for building Widener's folklore collection, and Chester Noyes Greenough, another of the well-known Harvard professors, who had been dean of Harvard College and was the master of Dunster House. I was greatly impressed by both of these men but was told that they were about to retire from the committee. While both retired before or during my early days at Harvard, I had dealings with both of them later. While I was welcomed by the group very cordially the atmosphere did remind me of what I had heard—namely, that Harvard was a snobbish place and that, with my unsophisticated background, I would not feel at home in it. Then there was the added fact that I knew the

Harvard Tercentenary was coming in September, the month I would come to Harvard if I accepted the position.

Finally I told Dr. Blake I would go home and think it over for a few days before giving my answer. This I did; I turned down the offer and went back to work at the New York Public Library, much relieved to have the problem off my mind and with the firm conviction that I would continue as chief of the reference department as long as the New York Public Library would have me. I should add that later I was relieved that I had not agreed to go to Harvard in September because in August Mart had to undergo an emergency major operation at just about the time we would have been moving if I had accepted the offer.

Soon after my decision to remain in New York I received a letter from Dr. Frederick (Fred) Keppel, president of the Carnegie Corporation, with whom I had had some earlier acquaintance. He asked if I would be willing to prepare a statement setting forth in some detail why I thought Harvard should have a trained librarian, something that it had not had up to that time in the strict sense of the word. I went to work on it, talking it over with H.M.L., who had kept in touch with Harvard since his graduation in 1896. After showing him the draft and making use of his criticism, I sent the report to Dr. Keppel and forgot all about it for the next ten years. Then one day in the mid-1940's it occurred to me that this letter might have had something to do with what happened in the spring of 1936. So I called Miss Bonn, Mr. Conant's secretary, and asked if it would be proper for her to check Mr. Conant's correspondence with Dr. Keppel and see if in the spring of 1936 she had received from Dr. Keppel an unsigned statement entitled "Why Harvard Should Have a Trained, Professional Librarian." She called back to say she had found it and would send it over to me. It was a nine-page, single-spaced document entitled, "Some Notes that Might be Called Writing Out Loud on the Question of why, All Things Being Equal, a large University should choose as a Director of its Library a Professional Librarian in preference to a Member of the

Teaching Staff." It never has been published. In this connection, I should state that if I had known as much about the Harvard library when I wrote the statement as I did later, I would have worded it differently as far as building up the library's collections was concerned. I had no idea of the wonderful work performed by Archibald Cary Coolidge and Alfred C. Potter in this regard. They had done so in spite of the fact that their relations with the departmental libraries had not been as satisfactory as they might have been. But what I had to say still applies to the general run of universities here and abroad with one exception which I should like to emphasize.

Most institutions, when a new director is needed, face problems which the retiring director has not succeeded in solving. It may be important to find a man who can solve those particular problems, whatever his background and training may be. This proved to be the case at the Library of Congress when Archibald MacLeish succeeded Herbert Putnam and at Harvard when Paul Buck succeeded me. By the time of MacLeish's appointment, I had learned that it had become the custom at Harvard, whenever an important administrative position became vacant, to look for a person who could cope with the things that needed to be done at that time.

To go back to my story: the next spring, in April 1937, Dr. Blake appeared at my desk in New York one day without advance notice to say that he was resigning as director of the Harvard University library as of the end of August, that he was authorized to offer me the position, and that he hoped very much that I would accept. The salary would be the same as that of a full professor at Harvard at the time. I agreed to visit Cambridge again and to look into the situation more thoroughly than I had the year before. Mart and I drove to Cambridge, had lunch with Mr. and Mrs. Conant in the president's house, and I talked with Dr. Blake again and found how relieved he would be to be able to go back to full-time teaching and research. He went over the library budget with me in detail. President Conant also emphasized

that Harvard was ready to come into the modern library world
and wanted a librarian with the background and training that
I had, and that I would be given a comparatively free hand to
make changes.

Mart and I then drove to Wellesley, where we talked with
my sister about the situation, and to Belmont, where Dr. Blake
had taken me the year before, to look over the area where new
homes were being built. Then we drove back to White Plains
to "sleep on the situation". I had a long talk with Ernest
Reece, who was then at Columbia and whose judgment I
respected greatly in such matters. He advised me to accept the
offer. I consulted Dr. Keppel at the Carnegie Corporation
with the same result. Next came the discussion with Harry
Lydenberg. It was evident that he was torn between his loyalty
to Harvard and his belief that Harvard needed me, and the
fact that he did not want me to leave the New York Public
Library. He knew very well how very much I relied on his
judgment and I again hesitated to leave the position in which I
had expected to remain indefinitely. Later I learned through
his family that he had hoped I would succeed him as director
but knew the place already had been promised by the trustees
to Franklin Hopper, chief of the circulation department. Mr.
Hopper, a good friend of mine, had been tempted by the
opportunity to succeed James Thayer Gerould at Princeton,
which was his college. Mr. Gerould was to retire in another
year. Mr. Hopper was a natural successor to Mr. Lydenberg
and I always had expected his appointment as director of the
New York Public Library if Mr. Lydenberg retired soon
enough.

Mr. Lydenberg suggested that I talk over the matter with
Frank Polk, president of the NYPL's Board of Trustees. Mr.
Polk, apparently knowing there was no promotion in view for
me in New York, indicated that he supposed I was considering
Harvard simply because of the large increase in salary. Actually, thanks to the New York State retirement scheme in which
the New York library had been included (partly with my help)
only a year earlier, and considering the fact that I would have

been in New York well over 40 years before retirement, I would have been better off financially by staying there instead of going to Harvard and having to start afresh with a pension scheme in which I would be included for only 18 years and which provided for only one-sixth of my salary when I retired.

I confess that I was provoked when Mr. Polk took the attitude that salary was my chief concern. So I told Mr. Lydenberg that, unless he urged me to stay, I was prepared to leave. He then said, "What can I do to replace you?" I suggested Paul North Rice, who had returned to New York a year earlier to become director of the New York University library after ten years in the Dayton, Ohio, public library. H.M.L. then said, "If you will go and put it up to Paul and persuade him to come, I will be willing to face your leaving." Paul already had found in his short time at NYU that the situation was discouraging and that the chances of making any real progress were poor but hesitated to leave so soon. However, he did agree that he would come to the New York Public Library as chief of the reference department, taking my place for the second time as I had taken his twice before. I went back to H.M.L. with this news and he said reluctantly that he hoped I would stay on at least until September 1, to which I agreed on condition that neither Harvard nor the New York Public Library would announce the change until after the American Library Association met in New York City late in June (publicity before that might have involved me in a lot of questioning). I then sent my acceptance to Mr. Conant and the appointment was approved by the Harvard Corporation and Board of Overseers at their next meetings.

After the ALA meeting in June I again went to Cambridge at Mr. Conant's request to consult with him and others involved in the plans for the Littauer Center, which was in the hands of Coolidge, Shepley, Bulfinch and Abbott, an architectural firm that at that time had planned more Harvard buildings than any other, including most of the seven houses—they are called colleges at Yale—that had been built in the early 1930's. I found this a fascinating as well as frustrating assign-

ment because no program had been written for the building
(programs, I admit, were not customary in those days). Professor Cole, librarian of the Harvard Graduate School of Business Administration, had been consulted about the situation
but there had been no consensus of opinion on the part of the
faculty members involved. I later found to my surprise that
two of my Oberlin classmates who had been good friends of
mine had been called in and had reported on what the Center
should attempt to accomplish. Their reports, which covered
the field that they had been asked to study, gave little help in
connection with the building plans and, since nearly half of
the building was to be for library use, I had to take responsibility for that part of the building planning. More of this later.

This trip gave me an opportunity to go house-hunting. We
soon found that the cost of a house in Cambridge was beyond
our means and I wanted land enough to have a good-sized
garden such as I had enjoyed during our 15 years in White
Plains and all through my boyhood. So we tried Belmont,
looked at a good many houses we could rent for a year while
we became acquainted with the area—and ultimately decided
to buy the new house we had seen the previous April. I am still
there more than 40 years later. It has one-third of an acre of
land. It is an American Colonial eight-room house with a large
secluded porch. Before buying it I called Harvard's maintenance building department and they sent out their senior
assistant, who checked the house thoroughly and reported
three criticisms: The irregularly shaped slate stones in the
front walk probably would break up within a few years (they
are still holding together); there was only one entrance to the
living room except for the door to the large secluded porch
(while this has caused occasional inconvenience, it has not
proved serious because we do not have large parties); between
the large cellar and the cold room was a cross-beam which
might provide tempting access to termites (this also has not
happened, I am glad to report).

We had enough money for a down payment (the total cost
was only $14,500 and the taxes $350 a year, a small fraction of

the present figures) so we decided to buy the house without delay. It suited us very well and the purchase never has been regretted.

I finished my work at the New York Public Library by August 20 and considered the last ten days as vacation or "terminal leave," giving time to pack up, move, and get settled in Belmont. We had no trouble in finding a satisfactory mover, who packed everything in one large van. The movers reported that, because of the heat, they would have to drive up in the night although they were packed up by noon, and the family with our two children and the cat (the children would be going back to Oberlin in the fall) drove up to Cambridge and stayed overnight at the Continental Hotel, where I later lived for one year. The van arrived on time and we moved in and were well settled by September 1, when I reported for work in the Widener Library building.

INDEX

400